Jundai Yamada

KOTSUJI'S GIFT

The Daring Rescue
of Japan's Jewish Refugees

Maggid Books

Kotsuji's Gift
The Daring Rescue of Japan's Jewish Refugees

First English Edition, 2025

Maggid Books
An imprint of Koren Publishers Jerusalem Ltd.
POB 8531, New Milford, CT 06776–8531, USA
& POB 2455, London W1A 5WY, England
www.korenpub.com

Library of Congress Catalog Card Number: 64008481

ISBN 978-4140815991

The publication of this book was made possible
through the generous support of *The Jewish Book Trust*.

ISBN 978-1-59264-710-1, *hardcover*

Printed and bound in the United States

"If Sugihara was the Pitcher for the Jewish refugees,
Kotsuji was their Catcher"

This volume honors the memory of

Abraham Setsuzo Kotsuji זצ"ל

and pays tribute to
Rabbi Meir Soloveichik,
Jundai Yamada, Andrew Saidel,
and to all those who are working to
recognize, and eternally remember,
the courage, heroism, and אהבת ישראל,
Kotsuji exemplified.

פייג'א רבקה בת אסתר הענטשא ומשה אריה
מנחם צבי בן מרדכי ולאה

רחל מירל בת חנה שרה וישראל צבי
מנחם מענדל ליפא בן אריה ובתיה מלכה

For the daughters of Kotsuji Setsuzo and Kotsuji Mineko,

Aiko, Teruko, and Yuriko

Contents

Author's Note

This volume includes both Kotsuji Setsuzo's memoir, *From Tokyo to Jerusalem*, first published in 1964 in the United States, and my own book, *Inochi no Biza wo Tsunaida Otoko* (The Man Who Extended the Visas for Life), released in Japanese in 2013. Since publishing the book, I have remained in awe of Professor Kotsuji's choices in life and have continued my research over the past 12 years. This English edition contains important new findings.

Born in 1899 to a Shinto household bound by tradition in Kyoto, Kotsuji converted to Judaism when he was 60 years old after many twists and turns in his life. He was an extraordinarily rare Japanese person, who made inspiring decisions in challenging times, and thus saved lives.

Six decades have passed since Kotsuji published his memoir. In his autobiography, he tells of a life which spanned a tumultuous period, including times of warmth, sadness, irony, and joy.

It is important to note he cultivated the core Bushido belief that one should "help those in need" from his childhood, and he never lost sight of the importance of basic human goodness in offering a helping hand in a world thrown into turmoil. This humanity caused him to come to the aid of the Jewish refugees who found their way to Japan. And it was this dedication to humanity which inspired me and drew me to his story.

After his courageous deeds on behalf of these refugees, he was forced to flee to Harbin, chased out of Japan, his own country, during the war. Japan subsequently surrendered in August 1945, but Kotsuji was persecuted in China, which had suffered greatly during the war.

The deeper I delved into Kotsuji's life, the more I learned of the tragedies of the war. Now, more than ever, I deeply feel the vital importance of peace for all of us. It is my hope that readers will be inspired by the extraordinary story of Kotsuji Setsuzo and the Jewish refugees that unfolded 85 years ago, and see it as a testament to spreading world peace and developing lasting friendship.

Finally, a word about names. Kotsuji wrote his book in English, and names are presented in the Western tradition, with first name followed by family name. My book first appeared in Japanese, so names are written in the Japanese tradition, with family name followed by first name. I retained this order in the English edition, with the exception of my own name.

Kotsuji refers to his two daughters by their given Western names, Mary and Julie. In my Japanese-language book, I use their original Japanese names, Teruko and Yuriko, and I continued doing so in the English edition.

Jundai Yamada
Tokyo, Japan

Acknowledgments

My journey of discovery with Kotsuji Setsuzo has been filled with fortuitous meetings and discoveries, a continuous series of surprises that were hard to imagine, let alone anticipate.

I would like to give my thanks here to the people whom I have met, and who have assisted me in countless ways throughout this exploration.

To Andy Saidel, my fellow traveler on the quest to discover Kotsuji Setsuzo, with whom I have shared so much time in Tokyo and Kyoto since we first met. With your deep understanding and friendship, precise ideas and speed, you guided me and became the driving force for this effort. You are without question the brains behind this book project, its leader. Thank you.

To Zvi Hauser, who was responsible for the first official recognition of Kotsuji's deeds by the Knesset in 2022. I am deeply grateful for your magnificent vision and the continuous support you have shown to me over the course of this project.

I would like to express my heartfelt gratitude to Dafna Kaplansky who first introduced Andy and me to each other.

And to Doreen Jackson, with your magnificent English translation of my Japanese book. I will always be thankful for the opportunity to work with you.

I would like to express my gratitude again to Yuuki Shimizu, Michio Shimizu, and Tokiko Inoue for their support in gathering information and writing.

To Rabbi Soloveichik whom I met for the first time in Kyoto and who authored the deeply personal foreword to the book. Our discussion together in Kamishichiken's legendary beer garden, just steps from where Kotsuji-san was born, is an experience forever etched into my heart and memory. I will also never forget your expression of warmth, gratitude, and love to Teruko-san when we visited together in her nursing home. I am so grateful to you for your friendship and guidance in helping me to make this book a reality.

I am very grateful, in order of your tenure, to Your Excellencies Ambassador to Japan Nissim Ben Shitrit, Ruth Kahanoff, Yaffa Ben-Ari, and Gilad Cohen, for your guidance and friendship.

I would like to express my deep appreciation to Susumu Harema of Kamishichiken for contributing such a wonderful jacket comment for the book, and also to Masashi Iwamoto, whose assistance with my research in Kyoto was indispensable.

And to my friend Arieh Rosen for your words of advice, please accept my deep gratitude. Thank you very much also to Randy Channell and Ken Tsujino for your support and fellowship always. It has meant so much to me.

To the very able team a Koren Publishers led by Matthew Miller, with special thanks to David Silverstein, Tani Bayer, and Nechama Unterman. Thank you so much for your guidance and friendship. Without you, this book would not have been possible.

Finally, to all of the many people who shared their precious insights and knowledge with me, and who supported me on this path with their generous hearts – and to Kotsuji Setsuzo himself, the fascinating, extraordinary man who made these connections possible, my heartfelt and endless gratitude.

Foreword

Rabbi Dr. Meir Soloveichik

A bestselling book by psychologist Robert Cialdini is titled *Pre-Suasion: A Revolutionary Way to Influence and Persuade.* In the midst of this very non-Jewish volume, which has been translated into forty languages, we are suddenly given a picture from 1941 of two rabbis from Eastern Europe who found themselves in front of the Japanese foreign ministry in Tokyo. They were two of the leaders from a group of thousands of yeshiva students, who had been given a transit visa by the Japanese Consul in Kovno (Kaunas), Chiune Sugihara, allowing them to flee across Europe and Asia, arriving in Kobe, Japan. Two of those Jews were my maternal grandparents, Rabbi Shmuel Dovid and Nachama Warshavchik.

Meanwhile, Germany was allied with Japan; and as Cialdini writes:

> The Nazis had sent Josef Meisinger, a colonel in the Gestapo known as the "Butcher of Warsaw" for ordering the execution of sixteen thousand Poles, to Tokyo. Upon his arrival in April 1941, Meisinger

> began pressing for a policy of brutality toward the Jews under Japan's rule – a policy he stated he would gladly help design and enact. Uncertain at first of how to respond and wanting to hear all sides, high-ranking members of Japan's military government called upon the Jewish refugee community to send two leaders to a meeting that would influence their future significantly.

Thus, two rabbis came down from Kobe to Tokyo, and in what must have seemed a surreal moment, met with the Japanese generals. The rabbis received an utterly unanswerable question: Tell us, why do the Nazis hate you so much? One of the rabbis was frozen, terrified, but the second, Rabbi Shimon Kalisch, known as the Amshinover Rebbe, remained calm. As Cialdini describes, he delivered a response to the Japanese generals:

> Rabbi Kalisch's knowledge of human nature had equipped him to deliver the most impressive persuasive communication I have encountered in over thirty years of studying the process: "Because," he said calmly, "we are Asian, like you."
>
> The older rabbi's response had a powerful effect on the Japanese officers. After a silence, they conferred among themselves and announced a recess. When they returned, the most senior military official rose and granted the reassurance the rabbis had hoped to bring home to their community: "Go back to your people. Tell them we will provide for their safety and peace. You have nothing to fear while in Japanese territory." And so it was.

"We are Asian, like you." The story is true, famous, striking, and amusing. But it also embodies a very serious point. The Land of Israel is poised between East and West, and in a certain sense its worldview of the human person can be seen as a balance between the two. The modern West has emphasized the individual, endowed with rights; the East, as anyone who has traveled there will see, has a greater focus on the collective, on duties. Judaism has always sought to synthesize these elements, to celebrate the human individual while reminding us of what each of us owes to others. Rabbi Jonathan Sacks recalled a fascinating conversation with the great historian Paul Johnson, writing that he asked him "what had struck him most about Judaism" during the long period he spent researching it for his masterly *A History of the Jews*:

> He replied in roughly these words: There have been, in the course of history, societies that emphasised the individual – like the secular West today. And there have been others that placed weight on the collective. Judaism, he continued, was the most successful example he knew of that managed the delicate balance between both – giving equal weight to individual and collective responsibility. This, he said, was very rare and difficult, and constituted one of our greatest achievements. It was a wise and subtle observation. Without knowing it, he had in effect paraphrased Hillel's aphorism, "If I am not for myself, who will be (individual responsibility)? But if I am only for myself, what am I (collective responsibility)?"

This is a wonderful point, and in truth, Hillel's most famous mantra is not only about responsibility, but also about identity. We each have the potential, and the obligation, to develop our unique gifts, to allow our individual "I" to emerge; but at the same time, if I see my "I," my very self, as atomistic, alone, unimpacted by others, there would be no "I" at all. For in truth, every one of us is who we are in part because of the sacrifices of others, in the past or present. To focus solely on one's own life in one's self-understanding is to only see part of the picture.

It is with this in mind that we may appreciate the fact that the photograph featured in Cialdini's book is incomplete, cut off; in the original photo, there is a Japanese gentleman standing to one side of Rabbi Kalisch. This is Setsuzo Kotsuji, whose tale is told in this extraordinary autobiography. As important as Sugihara's lifesaving visas were, they expressly permitted only transit through Japan, and it was through Kotsuji's efforts that the Jewish stay in Japan was extended, week after week, month after month. Those, such as Rabbi Chaim Shmulevitz, who had encountered Kotsuji in Japan, knew well what they owed to this man, which is why they so ardently embraced him decades later when this Japanese hero embraced Judaism.

But few remember this story today. Thus, in a striking way, this photographic lacuna captures the way in which, as the story of the Jews in Japan is told, he has been largely, inexplicably, inexcusably out of the picture. The fiftieth anniversary of Kotsuji's passing went largely unnoticed as well in the larger Jewish world, and his name would inspire recognition among a paltry few.

This would be profoundly regrettable even had he written nothing about his story; but in fact he has left us this book, *From Tokyo to Jerusalem,* that is so much more than a memoir; it is, in a certain sense a religious classic, the story of a man raised in the religion of his ancestors, who ultimately turned to the Jewish faith while still retaining a deep respect for his own Japanese past. All these aspects of a biography unlike any other made up the "I" that was Setsuzo Kostuji; all these elements merged together to form one of the great heroic personalities of the twentieth century. And now that his memoir has been republished, Kotsuji's tale can finally receive the recognition it deserves.

"We are Asian, like you"; Kotsuji was truly an Asian Jew, and the magic of the memoir is the way in which he embraced the faith, and the people, of Abraham, while his Japanese heritage continued to inspire his story. "I was raised," he tells us, "in that ancient religion of Shinto, a religion existing already at the dawn of the history of Japan." His family, it was said, dated "back to 678 AD, when the Kamo shrine in the Kamo section of Kyoto was dedicated." By his generation, the Kotsujis were no longer priests, but his father did dedicate himself, and then train his son Setsuzo, to perform for the family one of the major rites of Shinto, the "lighting of the sacred fire." His discovery of the Bible, and his informing his parents that he could no longer perform the rituals of his ancestors, inspired a striking reply, communicated by his mother:

> Your father admits that you are doing well these days. He thinks it may be due to the book you are so eagerly reading. He says that if this is so, it must be an excellent book and the religion in it is good. And if God is only One, he would have it only that way. You may go ahead with your new faith. Only remember your ancestors, and be proud of your great heritage.

"Remember your ancestors." This Kotsuji did, even as he became the only Hebrew scholar in Japan, a man who sought out Jews to share with them his love of their people's story, and who ultimately risked his own wellbeing to help Jews in crisis, and to defend Judaism from its detractors. He did this selflessly, motivated both by his own original heritage and the Hebrew Scripture that had changed his life. In perhaps the most important passage in the book, one which informs us profoundly as to who he was, Kotsuji tells us his two sources of inspiration in deciding to take action, the *Bushido*, the Samurai moral code his parents had taught him, and the Tanakh, as he writes:

> I was determined, however, that I would do what I could and use what influence I had to help. There is a *Bushido* saying which goes, "It is cowardice not to do, seeing one ought"; running away from trouble went against the grain of my youthful samurai-trained notions of honor and pride. Further supporting me were words of the Old Testament: "Grass dries up, and shoots will wither, but the word of our God stands firm; always."

We must pause to ponder the passage, to marvel at the merging of two different cultures and traditions in this one man, in this act of heroism; two codes commanded him, the Bible and *Bushido*, Scripture and samurai, the small boy merging with the profound moral man he was.

Here we have a man raised to honor his ancestral heritage but who cherished the Scripture of Israel; a man who knew Japanese and Hebrew; a man who loved Abraham's journey, and suddenly found Jews on a miraculous journey of their own; a man inspired to act by the combination of samurai sayings and Semitic Scripture; a man who paved his own unique path and suddenly was perfectly providentially positioned to help thousands of others in one precise moment. Do I not owe him gratitude as a descendant of those Jews, to include Kotsuji in the picture that is my own life, my own sense of self? If Kotsuji is cut out of the picture of Cialdini's book, if he is largely unknown, does that not make me all the more obligated to include him in the picture that is my own family history? And am I not obligated to do what I can to ensure that this tale, one so Japanese and so Jewish, is told in both Japan and the Jewish world?

Fortunately, there is already a moral beacon in Japan that has begun that task. The Jewish obligation of gratitude lies at the heart of the story of Kotsuji that is told by Jundai Yamada, whose own incredible examination of Kotsuji's legacy is also chronicled in this volume. Jundai has sold thousands of copies of his book, his Japanese account of Kotsuji's heroism, and here it is finally presented in English. In the book, he describes his striking visit to the daughter of Rabbi Chaim Shmulevitz, Rivka Ezrachi, who remembered the celebratory gathering in Jerusalem following Kotsuji's conversion:

> "My father talked about Kotsuji all the time," she said. "My father always felt *hakarat hatov* toward Kotsuji, and also to the many other Japanese people who helped them. He always said he would never forget what they did for us."
>
> ...When Rivka told this story, her husband began to speak in Hebrew, which Rivka interpreted for me. "*Hakarat hatov* means gratitude in English. This is a very precious word in our religion. When we wake up in the morning, we are thankful that we have been given another day to live. This is what gratitude means for us. It's very important."
>
> Waking up in the morning. This is something most of us take for granted. But he said to be thankful for each morning. I wonder how many people really feel gratitude for just waking up in the morning?

These remarkable reflections by Jundai Yamada were written before October 7, and they resonate even more at this moment. The past many months have been difficult ones for the Jewish people, but the courage, and resilience, reflected in Israel and the Jewish world have made manifest what even the enemies of the Jews have noted about us – that we love life, that we well understand its fragility, and that we therefore place gratitude at the heart of Jewish existence. That Kotsuji himself would devote his life to Judaism and the Jewish people, and help protect so many, is thus a great source of gratitude, one of the remarkable ways in which Providence has revealed itself in Jewish history. That a distinguished actor from Japan would be so moved by this story that he would travel the world to research it, and work to tell it to his countrymen, is a miracle all its own.

This past, unforgettable summer, I visited Japan with my family, and – thanks to Andrew Saidel, who has also devotedly dedicated himself to preserving Kotsuji's legacy – I had the very good fortune, and the very great blessing, of becoming friends with Jundai Yamada. At one point, as we discussed all things Kotsuji, Jundai reached into his bag and pulled out an object, holding it forth as he asked me what it was.

It was what Jews call a mezuza; a sacred scroll containing some of the most famous verses of Deuteronomy, contained in a case. I explained to Jundai the nature of a mezuza, and how Jews traditionally see it as a sign of God's protection. Jundai, in turn, told me that he had received this mezuza from Kotsuji's daughter – to whom Jundai had introduced me this summer – who had told him to affix it to his door.

This small moment is emblazoned in my mind, a brief episode embodying the tale told in tandem by the two Japanese men in this volume. Setsuzo Kotsuji was himself a mezuza to countless Jews, a providential protector of thousands, a man who came to lavish love on the Hebrew letters inscribed inside, and whose own life was defined by the central creed placed by Jews on their doors across millennia: *Listen, Israel: the Lord our God – the Lord is one.* Today, the tale of Abraham Kotsuji is being told thanks to Jundai Yamada, who had held Kotsuji's mezuza in his hand, and has affixed it to his door. And, as I close my preface to this remarkable book, my *hakarat hatov* to them both is overwhelming.

From Tokyo to Jerusalem

Abraham Setsuzo Kotsuji

To the memory of my parents

My Spiritual Journey

It was September 20, 1959. I lay on the operating table of the Shaare Zedek Hospital in Jerusalem. Dr. Nahum Cook stood at my side, a scalpel in his hand, prepared to perform the ritual of circumcision.

"What am I doing here?" I asked myself. "I am sixty years old, a Japanese, the descendant of a long line of Shinto lords, priests of the Imperial Household of Japan. What brought me to this place? Why did I come to this one spot in the world, surmounting such odds as few men have surmounted in a lifetime?"

This book was written to answer these questions for myself as well as for those who have wondered at how a Japanese found and took to his heart the God of the Old Testament.

It was Bernard Geis, my publisher [of the original edition, 1964], who urged me to write my story. To him I shall be forever grateful. I would like to express my deepest gratitude, too, to James Collier for his invaluable assistance in the preparation of this book. And to Mineko, my wife, and Mary and Julie, my children, who provided for my spiritual journey their patience, warmth, and understanding.

Abraham Kotsuji

Chapter One

The eight-year-old Japanese boy and his father stand before a shrine in Kyoto, an important town in central Japan, about 250 miles from Tokyo. It is one of the hundreds of top-ranking shrines in Kyoto. It is May 15, the festival of the Kamo Shrine. The boy is excited. He has seen the steady parade of relatives in and out of the house all day, eating and drinking lavishly. He has seen the fire-red carpets spread over the *tatami* sleeping mats, and the *manmaku* curtain with the family crest gracefully dyed on it stretched across the latticed front of the house. He has walked out with his father, partly to exercise their taut stomachs but mainly to visit the Kamo Shrine. They clap hands and bow reverentially before the shrine. The boy is moved by the solemnity of the occasion. The father takes advantage of the moment.

"Setschan," he says quietly, "it is time that you knew of our ancestors who served here for 1,400 years."

The boy is puzzled. "Served? Served how?"

"They were chief priests of this temple."

The boy is astonished. "Priests?"

"Yes."

"But why are we no longer priests, father?"

It is difficult to explain to an eight-year-old. "We did not give up our priesthood, precisely. Neither I, nor Grandfather. In ancient days we, the Kotsuji family, were a celebrated priest-clan. But then ... times changed."

The boy is serious, only half comprehending. "Where did the ancient days go, father?"

The father smiles. "The old days can never come back, except in the mind."

"How, father?"

"Look up and close your eyes," the father says.

And so, the father and son stand together in the ancient shrine, eyes closed, concentrating solely on the eternal silence and tranquility prevailing in the sanctuary. The noisy festival crowd, the present day is gone. They contemplate the glory of ancient days. Then, together, they open their eyes, and Setschan turns a shy face to his father. The father's face is dignified, but affectionate.

Then the moment was over. Yet it was never over, for it remained with the boy for almost sixty years. In one sense, the father was wrong. True, the ancient days cannot return; yet in a way the boy, after the pilgrimage of a lifetime, has gone back to the ancient days.

I was that boy. I was raised in the ancient religion of Shinto, a religion existing already at the dawn of the history of Japan. Over the fifty-odd years of my life from my early adolescence, as scholar, as teacher, but mostly as seeker, I groped my way through Shinto, searching, always searching, for a religious resting place. I found it on the twentieth of September, 1959, when I entered the covenant of Abraham through the solemn rite of circumcision in Jerusalem, to become, to my knowledge, the first Japanese convert to Judaism. This is the story of that search.

I was born on February 3, 1899. By the old calendar of feudal Japan, February 3 was New Year's Eve. It is called Setsu-bun, a word meaning "the season," the opening of spring. Accordingly, I was named Setsuzo – the third day of the season. Affectionately, my parents called me Setschan. To some who are close to me I have been Setschan ever since.

My mother, whom I resemble, stood five feet five inches, tall for a Japanese woman. Her name was Fukuko. Her eyes were deep set, which annoyed her vanity, for most Japanese women have relatively flat eye sockets. Like Japanese women of her time, she was not highly educated. She made up for her poor education with a stubborn intelligence. She would argue her points against anyone. Once she even did battle with a Doctor of Law, who finally had to confess he was wrong.

My father, Kisabro, was stout, of medium height, and both strong and healthy. He never once visited a doctor throughout his entire life. His nose was large for a Japanese, and his lips had a Caucasian thickness. A reserved man, he felt that it was the mother's business to distribute affection, the father's to demonstrate dignity and present an example for the children to emulate. I was close to him only on a few occasions in my life, and as a child I regretted his reserve, what seemed to me then a lack of love.

I should not have complained, perhaps. My brothers insisted that I was my mother's pet, and in truth she was always proud of me, always boasting of me.

My father did not have to earn a living. We were upperclass people. In the Japan of that time class was established by family lineage, not by property, or money. As members of an old family descending 1,400 years through a line of Shinto priests, we stood high in the social hierarchy. My father lived from his inheritance. He spent his time in horticulture, practicing the traditional and difficult Japanese art of growing dwarf plants.[1] He was, moreover, a scholar of Classic Chinese, and of course he worshipped often at the Shinto shrines which dotted the city of Kyoto.

I was the baby of the family. There were, besides me, my eldest brother, Genjiro, ten years older than me, who became a brilliant mathematics student; my second brother, Kiknoske, who survived a series of misfortunes to become a self-taught genius at the classic art of the Japanese Noh-play; my older sister, Mitsu, who died in a street-car accident; and a second sister, Hisako, who married into a wealthy Tokyo family.

I recall the dawn of my life not as a consecutive sequence of events, but as a series of isolated pictures or images, like magic lantern slides projected onto the wall of a darkened room. I can hardly call them memories.

---

1. In Japan horticulture of this sort is not mere gardening but is virtually considered on a level with music and painting.

At my age it seems as if the events they picture happened not to me, but to somebody else. Thus, it is more fitting for me to tell the early part of my story in the third person.

The first of these images is symbolic and prophetic. The baby Setschan is perhaps four. He sees two flickering lights – whether they are oil lamps or candles he cannot tell. He hears a voice reciting words unintelligible to his small mind, but recognizable as the voice of his father. The image is of a pair of oil lamps, wavering on the Shinto altar, and the voice is the short prayer of evening. The image will haunt Setschan for the rest of his life. He need merely recall it to invoke a mood of solemnity, of awe, a deep religious feeling which neither teacher nor preacher could ever have taught him.

The lantern projects another image. The custom then was for the mother to carry the child on her back, his legs spread as if he were riding a horse. Setschan remembers one woman whose back meant something special to him. Once he found himself being carried on a different back. He grew enormously unhappy and wept. No matter what divertisement the poor, harassed woman offered him, he wept for many hours. Finally, she grew angry and demanded, "What is making you so unhappy?" He simply cried harder, for Setschan was a stubborn and moody boy. At last, the woman whose back he loved and so yearned for ran to rescue the wretched child. The woman could only have been his mother. The compassion she poured on the forlorn little soul made up for his distress. The emotions born from this incident have had an unfathomable influence on the man Setschan grew to be. The longing for a religious home and the inexorable search for it which shaped the whole of Setschan's life is paralleled by the passionate yearning for the comfort of the familiar back.

It also reveals the stubborn set of Setschan's mind. His mother held to the notion that the child should not be corrected away from home, especially when he was on an outing. Scolding could wait; during the expedition the chance for a moment of pleasure should not be denied the child. Even for rude behavior she admonished softly and moderately.

One day, when Setschan was three or four, she took him downtown. They were happily walking along, hand in hand, when Setschan was suddenly attracted by a window full of display ornaments. The centerpiece was a mammoth model steamship, perhaps three feet long, and perfect in all details. Setschan stopped dead on the sidewalk, absorbed and enchanted by the wondrous object.

"Mama, I want that ship."

She tugged his hand to make him move along. "This ship is not to be sold. It is only for display."

"I want it."

"Perhaps we can find another ship to buy sometime." She tugged at his hand again. "Come with me now."

"No. No, this ship, this ship, only this ship."

She gave in, beaten by his implacable will. They entered the shop, and she asked the price. The salesman explained that the ship was not for sale but meant only for display. However, he said he would be glad to let it go for fifty yen.

The mother was astonished and dismayed by the price. Fifty yen was equal to several hundred American dollars. It was impossible for her to buy the ship, and she told the boy so. The boy stood firm. "See the dancing doll," she said. "Look, over here, Setschan." But he would not be diverted. Crying and howling, he was dragged from the store. He clutched at an iron rail running along the window where the beautiful ship was displayed, continuing to scream as his mother attempted to drag him away. A crowd collected; the mother was embarrassed and abashed. Finally, she broke his grip on the pipe and, half in tears herself, carried him still struggling down the street to a toy shop, where numberless small boats lay on their sides on the shelves. None of them would do. His mother despaired. Then all at once, the boy's eye lit upon a monkey doll. "I want that," he said.

Weak with relief, the mother bought it for him immediately. The price – roughly equivalent to fifteen dollars – was not insignificant. The doll was cheaper than the ship, however, and it taught the mother a lesson which she later repeated to the child: "To be a captain or a monkey-keeper is all the same to a child."

At the age of five Setschan was prepared for kindergarten. This posed a problem, for, incredibly, the boy had not yet been weaned from his mother's breast. Japanese children at that time were usually suckled for two years – a system that still exists in many parts of the world. Long breast feeding has the advantage of nurturing a natural affection between mother and child; at the same time, it hinders the growth of an independent child. In any case, Setschan's mother had nursed him far too long. He had to be weaned before he could enter kindergarten. Even today he remembers this. Although he cannot recall the precise taste of the milk, he remembers the sweet pleasure of the suckling and his assumption that somehow life would go on this way forever.

It did not. One day, as his mother sat on her folded knees, as Japanese do, Setschan climbed up to ride her legs as a horse, and then, as was his habit, he opened her kimono to suck. A hard, bitter taste flooded his mouth. Shocked, surprised, and hurt, he burst into tears.

He was tasting dried carp's liver, an old-fashioned medicine used in Japan at the time, which his mother had made into a paste and smeared on her nipples. As he stared up at her, his small face contorted with unhappiness, she said gently, "From now on Mamma's milk will be bitter, Setschan. Instead, you will get cow's milk, and I shall give you candies. It is time to go to kindergarten. The other children will laugh at you if you are still sucking at your mother's breast."

There is a saying, "A good medicine tastes bitter." Perhaps in this case it was true. Nonetheless, the shock of the experience, and the consequent lesson that happiness does not last forever, remained with Setschan for the rest of his life.

But Setschan was not finished with pre-kindergarten surprises. He needed various things for his first trip out into the world: new kimonos, woolen European-style shorts, sandals, shoes, and a small leather bag for his books and paper.

His father took him to a large leather shop to purchase the bag. The brutish smell of leather assailed his nostrils, and he knew for the first time the primitive raising of the hackles, the instinctive signal to beware. Setschan had never played with other children; the rude smell of leather – which even today he can remember – raised his fear of facing for the first time a band of other children.

But he went to kindergarten, and not only survived, but grew to enjoy it. He sang, studied, and during lunch hour he played games. The favorite game among the kindergarten children was "Genji and Heike," Japanese "Cowboys and Indians." The Genji were the "good ones." This game tells us something about the meaning of shame among the Japanese. The power struggle between the Genji and Heike families, both descended from emperors, which erupted into war for control of Japan in the twelfth century provides the historical background of the game. It was a period when warriors wore highly colored armor, swords, and sheaths of splendid workmanship inlaid with gold and silver, and bows made by great artists. The war has always captured the imagination of the Japanese, much as the battles of King Arthur have fascinated the West, and it particularly enticed the boys in Setschan's kindergarten, for Kyoto had been the country's capital at the time of the struggle.

At the beginning of the game several white Genji flags and several red Heike flags were placed in a basket. The white flags of the Genji were of course most desirable, since by the rules of the game the Genji must win. Thus when the boys were released for lunch, there was a wild scramble for the white flags. Psychologically, the red flag holders were beaten before they started. As play continued from day to day it began to take on a realistic tone, as if the emotions of the original struggle had come to life again. The whites grew unruly and began to oppress the losers. They began to punish the reds, to badger them physically, to make them cry. It was, however, not so much the physical damage as the shame of defeat that made the losers weep. Ultimately, when the schoolteachers realized what was happening, the game was stopped, and the flag basket was taken away. But this did not happen before Setschan took his turn with the red flags. The bitterness of this experience impressed his malleable mind with the conviction that sympathy must be extended to the less favored. His later learning made this ideal a permanent part of his view of life.

Setschan was beginning to know life: victory and defeat, happiness and despair. He was now to learn the harder lessons of love and death.

There lived, in his neighborhood, an unforgettably beautiful girl with soft hair and an exquisite voice. Her name was Ren, and Setschan called her O-Renchan. It became O-Renchan's custom to visit Setschan at his house every Sunday, arriving early in the morning and staying until noon, when someone came to take her home for lunch. One Sunday, when she had come as usual, nobody came for her at noontime. The two children, overjoyed, ate lunch together, and played nearly until dusk before O-Renchan had to go. She promised to come again the following Sunday. She failed to appear – not that Sunday, nor any Sunday after. Then Setschan overheard his father and mother whispering in their bedroom. They were saying that O-Renchan was dead; they were saying that Setschan should not be told, for he was a sensitive child.

Setschan did not quite understand death. He knew, though, that it was a very serious matter, for it had prevented O-Renchan from visiting him. Feeling as though he had been put under a taboo, he slipped away to another room, where he collapsed, curiously exhausted, on a *tatami* mat. After a while he heard his mother, aware of his sudden silence, looking for him. When she came upon him, she ran to him crying, "What is the matter, my son?"

He said nothing. She took him up on her knees and gave him a compassionate embrace. Slowly, the love flowing from her warmed the coldness in his soul and brought him back from his anguish. But the pain long remained, for he had poured all his love and affection onto the beautiful O-Renchan.

Life for the small boy was not, however, all sorrow and tragedy. Japan is a nation given to festive and traditional holidays. Kyoto, with its enormous number of Buddhist and Shinto shrines, is particularly rich in traditional gaiety. In the Japan of the time, a religious holiday was usually the signal for a joyous, happy occasion. The solemnity which accompanies Christian holidays, such as Good Friday or even Easter, is largely absent from Shinto ceremony. Parishioners of a Shinto shrine usually live nearby. On a festival day, long curtains or cloths bearing the family crest were stretched across the front of the home. Sometimes the latticework face of the house was removed, opening the rooms directly onto the street. The children dressed up. The parents tried to keep from scolding them, at least for that day; usually the children got a bit of pocket money – the boys for tops, the girls for paper balloons. Vast quantities of festival foods, usually various kinds of dried fish and special vegetables, were prepared and served to the friends and relatives who dropped in, with unlimited quantities of the beery rice wine, sake.

Then, when all were thoroughly full, they dressed in costumes of ancient tradition and paraded through the streets carrying the gilded and decorated portable shrine which had been removed from the main shrine altar. Before them went the musicians dressed in the costumes of old-time noblemen, playing ancient music on reed pipes, small drums, and cymbals. Ultimately the long, colorful procession arrived at the shrine just as the sun dropped behind its ancient roof, and the music rose to a crescendo.

Such a festival could hardly avoid leaving a mark on the young boy's mind. Setschan was fascinated by the color, the noise, the ancient grace, caught up with a feeling that somehow, he was reliving an experience out of the great past.

Another traditional event which Setschan experienced for the first time in the autumn of his fifth year was what the Japanese called the mushroom hunt. The town of Kyoto is surrounded by low hills. In October a kind of mushroom called *matsutake,* or pine mushroom, can be gathered on certain of the hills which are thickly covered with red pine trees. Customarily a group rents one of the hills and hunts mushrooms for an entire festival day. The person who collects the most mushrooms is awarded a mock prize. He is allowed to sit next to the prettiest girl, or perhaps choose the prettiest of the group. Amid laughter and merriment, volunteers slip down the hillside and scoop up the water which flows under the layer of decayed pine needles blanketing the slope. Boiled in this water, rice and the meat of chicken they have brought along has a heart-soothing, exotic taste. Then, as the sun goes down, the whole group troops in a single file slowly down the narrow hillside path heading for home. Setschan's first mushroom hunt took place in beautiful autumn weather; Setschan remembers with happiness the softness of the air and the bright blue of the sky.

Another pleasant memory of that autumn was the annual athletic meet of Setschan's school – a kind of kindergarten Olympics. The boys race fifteen or twenty feet only, and all get a paper flag of the rising sun as a prize, regardless of how fast they run. What Setschan remembers is that he did a great deal of running.

These events in the life of one small child were being played out against a far larger event – one of tremendous importance to Japan. Forty years later, it was to have considerable effect on Setschan's life. Russia had been moving into Korea and Manchuria, territory the Japanese considered under their sphere of influence. The Japanese offered to negotiate, but Russia, already a major world power, was confident that she could defeat so small a country as Japan and therefore refused to negotiate. On February 6, 1904, the Japanese broke off diplomatic relations with Russia. Two days later, without prior declaration of war, Russia attacked the Chinese fortress Port Arthur, the terminus of the Manchurian railroad. It was an ancient town strategically located at the tip of the Liaotung Peninsula, a finger which sticks down between Korea and the north coast of China.

Belated declarations of war appeared on February 10. The whole country boiled with anger. Caught up in the excitement, children ceased their normal play and turned to games of war. On hillsides, in and out of bushes, they charged across their battlefields. Casting lots by the old Japanese method of scissors, paper, and stone, the children picked one lucky boy to be a gallant and isolated Japanese soldier. The rest were "Roskies." Over the long afternoon the Roskies would fall on the slopes one by one, until the gallant, isolated, and finally victorious Japanese soldier was the only one left.

But the real war was not so simple. Bottling up the Russian fleet, the Japanese gained a few quick victories, broke into Port Arthur, and then settled down to a siege of the fortified high point, Height 203, named after the meter markings on the military maps. These battles brought the Japanese face to face with machine guns for the first time. They did not understand them; they thought that the Russians were using some kind of magic, for every time they heard the ferocious sound of rolling drums, soldiers died where they stood. Nonetheless, they did not panic, determined to die bravely. The fighting was bloody and exhausting. On July 6, 1904, a special suicide unit flung themselves three times against Height 203, suffering enormous losses in vain; among the dead were two sons of the Japanese General Nogi.

For the people of Japan, the month of November was very dark. The people gave up the luxury of pleasure, bending their whole spirit toward the fighting at Port Arthur. Finally, after great losses, the southwestern portion of the height was taken. Then boredom and exhaustion set in on both sides. Russian and Japanese soldiers were often separated only by the thin iron wall of the stronghold which the Russians were defending. One day some Russians pushed a bottle of transparent liquid through a gap in the iron of the stronghold. Startled Japanese soldiers handled it warily, fearful that it might be explosive. Veteran soldiers, however, realized that it was vodka. Thereafter men of both armies exchanged food and drink. It became clear to General Nogi that his troops had lost their fighting spirit, and he called for a new army, which arrived in December. The mood of the people was heavy, and even little Setschan, listening to the adults talk, became aware of an atmosphere of foreboding. Luxuries were curtailed, and daily another man from the neighborhood was conscripted.

The Japanese attack on Height 203 began on December 5, 1904. Early in the morning thousands of soldiers observed the last sake-drinking rite, a tradition dating back to knightly days. Then they rose, charging to the high wall which divided them from the Russians and leapt over it. The Russian machine guns began to explode, but from the Japanese who leapt over the wall there was an odd silence. As more and more men poured over the wall, the terrible machine guns roared, and the odd silence of the Japanese continued. It was the silence of death. On the other side of the wall the Russians had driven swords and spears into the ground. As the Japanese soldiers streamed over the wall, they were skewered like fish on the sharp spears, and machine-gunned where they fell. It was only when the mound of corpses reached a height of six feet that the remaining troops could tramp over the backs of their dead comrades and sweep the Russians out of the fortress.

With the fall of Height 203, Port Arthur was doomed, and on the third of February – little Setschan's birthday – the Russian commanding officer, Stessel, handed over to General Nogi the guns, warships, arms, ammunition, horses – the whole of the military force of Port Arthur. The Emperor, hearing from General Nogi how gallantly the Russians had fought, allowed Russian officers to keep their swords and soldier straps. This was a typical example of Japanese war etiquette, a remnant of the feudal code of samurai chivalry. In the traditional samurai code, no enemy leader would be beheaded; but he would be permitted to undergo the rite of *seppuku,* the self-immolation called *hara-kiri* in the West.

Important as the victory of Port Arthur was, it was taken soberly by the people at home, for it had cost the lives of ten thousand veteran troops. Conscription age was raised, and raised again, until it reached the age of forty-five. Setschan saw the father of a kindergarten playmate disappear into the army, and never return. He grew uneasy for his own father. He saw two of his uncles called to the battlefield. His uneasiness increased. One day he timidly approached his father.

"Father, will they make you a soldier?"

"Perhaps. Perhaps not. You see, I am the first son. The first-born son need not go, so that the family lineage can remain continuous.[2] Do you understand, Setschan?"

Setschan felt relieved.

"But if there is another big battle like Height 203, even first-born sons may have to be soldiers."

Setschan's face grew anxious.

"Setschan," the father said softly, touched by the boy's concern, "if I must go to war, you will offer the holy fire in my place. Will you be sure to remember, Setschan?"

The boy nodded.

"As long as you do it, God is with you."

"Father… "

"And God will be with me also and support me… in Manchuria."

Setschan began to weep silently, tears pouring from his eyes, as he struggled not to cry out. The father's eyes moistened. Then suddenly Setschan could stand it no longer. Crying "No, no, no, no," he burst into full tears, and charged into his father's belly, his face contorted with the expression of a raging beast, the sobs choking his breath away. Even when O-Renchan had died, he had not felt this anguish.

His father comforted him. Then he led him to the altar and showed him how to kindle the oil lamp.

This was a significant event in Setschan's religious life. The offering of the sacred fire is one of the major rites in Shinto. The lamp is a simple, shallow dish about three inches in diameter. It is made of unglazed pottery, which means that the tradition dates to the period before ceramic art was well developed. It is filled with oil, and the pith of a kind of rush, weighted to keep it upright, is floated on the oil. Several ritual methods

---

2. The Japanese of that time believed that lineage was transferred through the first-born son; for that reason, first-born sons were especially valued in the family and the community.

are used for lighting the lamp. The simplest and most common method is to place a bit of cattail or rush on a flint and strike it with steel. The sparks ignite the bit of rush, which is then used to light a sulfur stick, which in turn is used to light the sacred fire in the lamp. The method is not easy, but it is considered sacrilegious to use matches to light the sacred fire. The technique, of course, was too difficult for the six-year-old Setschan; it was years before he mastered it. Fortunately, his father was not conscripted, and there was no need for him to learn to light the fire in a hurry.

Setschan's father remained fearful that he would be called up, and for the next several months he made special efforts to indoctrinate Setschan in the Shinto heritage, helping him to learn the prayers by rote. He took the boy to various shrines after sunset to pray at the altar in the darkness. Setschan stood a few feet behind his father, watching two dim lights flicker from afar at the inner altar. Setschan was mature enough to realize that in the event of his father's death, he would be expected to carry on the ancestral tradition. Yet fear for his father's life cast a shadow over his understanding of the Shinto religion and planted the doubts that were to cause him so much distress in later years.

After the fall of Port Arthur, Japan moved rapidly from victory to victory. On March 10, 1905, General Oyama captured Mukden, the ancient capital city of Manchuria, along with five hundred cannon and two hundred thousand Russian troops. The people of Kyoto normally celebrate the blossoming of the plum trees with sake parties in March. Overjoyed by the coincidence of the coming of spring and the great victory, they paraded through the streets night after night shouting, singing, and carrying paper lanterns. On May 27 and 28, Admiral Togo destroyed the Russian Baltic fleet in the Tsushima Straits, which run between Japan and Korea. The tide of victory ran with the Japanese, but the country's forces were nearly exhausted, and when President Theodore Roosevelt offered to negotiate a peace settlement, the Japanese were glad to accept. Diplomats from Russia and Japan met at Portsmouth, New Hampshire. The Japanese demanded a huge indemnity for the losses they had suffered, together with the Russian island of Sakhalin. The Russians balked, and eventually Roosevelt persuaded the Japanese – who were not in a condition to continue the struggle in any case – to settle for half of Sakhalin, and no indemnity. But when the treaty was signed on September 5, the people, who had hoped for reparations to relieve them of the ponderous tax burden the war had imposed on them, grew violently angry. In Tokyo, mass meetings took place in front of Hibiya Park and Shintomi Theater. The mobs went on to burn some official buildings and a few street cars. Unappeased, they vented their hatred of President Roosevelt on Christians in general, destroying a number of Christian churches. Setschan's older brother, now sixteen, read this news to the young boy. He decided that the people of Tokyo must have lost their minds, since the people of Kyoto found the incident unbelievable.

In the long run, the reparations were of little import, for the effects of the Russo-Japanese war on Setschan, Japan, and indeed the world at large were enormous. Russia, its morale broken, moved directly from war to the 1905 revolution, a preview of the Communist revolution in 1917. Japan emerged from the war a world power. Unfortunately, the grasp of the militarist clique over the country had been very much strengthened.

A prophetic incident occurred to Setschan during the war. A household servant – a young girl of thirteen named O-Yoshi, whom he liked very much – had taken him out for a walk, when suddenly they came upon twenty red-bearded Russian prisoners of war in nondescript uniforms. The Russians were in the care of a young Japanese officer.

"Are they Roskies?" the boy called in a loud voice.

"Shush," hushed the girl, frightened that a Rosky might hear him and become angry. "It is not good manners to ask questions like that so loud," she whispered in his ear.

The Japanese officer began calling the prisoners' roll. One of the names called was "Kagan." It was Kagan who, a few moments later, when the roll call was completed, approached the pretty maidservant and the small boy with a smile and handed Setschan a bit of pound cake and patted him on his head. Then, as they marched away again, looking sad and disgraced, Setschan watched them, feeling sorry for the soldier named Kagan who had been kind to him.

Kagan is the Russian word for Cohen. Unknowing, Setschan had made his first, prophetic contact with the Jewish people.

Chapter Two

Until the end of World War II, Japan was a nation with a distinct class system, more defined than that of England, where the tradition of lords and ladies still lingers. At the time of Setschan's youth, despite the fact that Japan was rapidly modernizing, a man's lineage was almost the most important fact about him. The upper class which existed then was composed mainly of families descended from the nobility of the feudal days. The aristocracy at the top had descended from ruling families.

The author is not inclined to place much credence in the mystique of "family." Nonetheless, the science of eugenics has shown that a family which makes careful choices in its marriages will improve its stock, and that a family which does not choose carefully will rapidly lose its position in society. The Japanese aristocracy, which because of its wealth and privilege became self-indulgent, corrupted its bloodlines with consanguineous marriages, or marriages to inferior stock which produced physically weak offspring.

Old families develop a rich cultural life to hand down to succeeding generations. A sound physical heritage cannot be created in one generation, and it takes at least three generations to form a good cultural heritage. These theories have been borne out in practice. Despite the fact that the aristocracy was officially dissolved after World War II, families of good lineage continue to comprise the core of the social structure. An old family does not gain respect by right of birth; it gains it from its cultural record.

The Kotsuji family, according to tradition, dates back to 678 AD, when the Kamo Shrine in the Kamo section of Kyoto was dedicated. The Kotsujis were attached to it as priests and given a piece of land near it to hold in perpetuity. How the first Kotsuji came into this living is a little difficult to discover. At one time, however, a Kotsuji served at Ise, the Grand Imperial Shrine. It seems likely that he was a descendant of emperors: second or third princes were often appointed to the priesthood, partly to honor them and partly to keep them in a position where ambition could not drive them to foment rebellion.

It seems likely then, that when Emperor Kammu moved the imperial capital to Kyoto in 794 – about the time Charlemagne was being crowned in France – he brought a Kotsuji with him and established him at the Kamo Shrine. According to family tradition, the imperial household observed about seventy rituals at the Kamo Shrine every year. For eleven hundred years the Kotsuji family remained attached to that shrine. They were not rich people, but they were accorded enormous respect. They absorbed the music, ritual, and religious feeling of Shinto.

The fate of Setschan the man is curiously interwoven with foreigners – especially Americans and European Jews. In 1853 an American, Commodore Matthew Perry, sailed his frigates into the fortified harbor of Araga with the express intention of opening the country to world-wide trade. Impressed by his armaments, the Japanese permitted America to send an ambassador, Townsend Harris, to the country to negotiate a trade treaty. Treaties with Holland, Russia, England, and France were signed shortly afterward. In the people's eyes, this influx of foreigners was a disgrace. The stock of the militarist government fell, morale collapsed, confusion spread, and the government tried one desperate expedient after another to bring order to the country. The government failed, and in 1867, after seven hundred years of rule, the military turned the real power of the government back to the emperor, who had been for many centuries nothing more than a highly revered figurehead. The emperor's name was Meiji, and this crucial event in Japanese history is called the Meiji Restoration.

Emperor Meiji was a dynamic man. He moved the capital to Tokyo and set about breaking up the feudal system under which Japan had lived for over a thousand years. The rapidity with which Japan flung off the cloak of the past and entered the modern world has always been a historical wonder. Among other acts, Emperor Meiji tossed the two-thousand-year-old system of hereditary priesthood out on the tide of the age. Priests were henceforth to be appointed in rotation by the government. Thus, due to a turn of history, there is no longer a Kotsuji at the Kamo Shrine.

Traditions die hard, and a thousand-year-old tradition dies very hard indeed. Setschan's father had been born in the year 1864, during a period of confusion when great changes were sweeping the country. His grandparents had grown up under the old regime, when the country was closed to foreigners, and the Kotsujis were priests at Kamo Shrine. It will be understood, then, how powerful the influence of traditional Shinto must have been around the young boy Setschan, and what emotional struggle on his part, and pain on his father's part, a breaking away would occasion. This was no ordinary boy in rebellion against his father. This was a man flinging off a thousand-year tradition to take up the religion of the people who had brought his own family low.

Shinto is not a system of ancestor worship, as the shallow observations of some Western writers maintain. There does exist excessive reverence for ancestors in Shinto, but much more than mere ancestor worship is involved. What makes Shinto sometimes difficult for Westerners to understand is that, unlike many religions, especially Christianity, Shinto is not concerned with doctrine or ethics. Its ethics are very simple: obey the father. Shinto has almost no doctrine. The key to Shinto is *ritual.* Shinto is an animistic religion, which uses ritual and symbol to give life meaning and direction.

This becomes clearer when we see how Shinto must have been created. Life, not philosophy, creates religion. In the ancient days, when man first came to Japan, the threat of disaster existed everywhere. Typhoons produced enormous rains and jungle humidity. Mosquitoes, insects, and wild beasts preyed on the people from without; germs and viruses from within. The first concern of the early inhabitants was survival. First, to overcome the outbreak of disease, they turned to "purification." Japan is a country of running water, and so they learned to bathe constantly. The cleansing rituals and the exaggerated emphasis put on bathing and purification in Shinto may have sprung from just such a circumstance.[1]

There was also the need for salt, the most basic of foods. In man's primitive stage, salt must have been one of his major medicines. Even today, salt-prepared plum is used in many places in Japan as a medicine to prevent cholera, typhus, constipation, and various skin diseases. In Shinto, although the medical usages have been forgotten, salt occupies an important place in the purification rituals.

The third means of purification in ancient days must have been the waving of branches to drive off insects, noxious spirits, and perhaps smaller wild animals. In Shinto, twigs from a *sakaki* plant – a member of the camellia family – are used in purification rituals. Bells may have entered the ritual for the same reasons. And of course, fire, as in the sacred lamps lit each evening in good Shinto homes, is an important means of purification. If primitive women went out at night, they had to try to look like goblins by carrying a comb in their teeth. A woman was also expected to hold a torch with a mirror behind it to magnify the light.

All these things remain in the Shinto religion in symbolic form. Thus, Shinto is a symbolic recreation of the life-and-death struggle for survival of the ancestors of Japan. The ancestors have become gods. Shinto is therefore known as "the way of the gods." It is easy to see how ancestor worship could become part of this religion; yet it is equally easy to see that reverence for the ancient way, not the ancestor, is the key to it. When a Japanese comes to the shrine he is not thinking of a specific ancestor, but of something vaguer and more amorphous – the spirit of his ancestors. It must be remembered that the Japanese are not inclined to analyze. They regard analysis as shallow in the face of deep feelings. Most Japanese do not think of all these things when they worship; they

1. The public bathing house, where people of both sexes wash in the nude, is part of this same tradition.

simply partake solemnly in the religious feeling and the sense of deep peace the Shinto ritual creates.

This was the tradition in which Setschan grew. Every opportunity was taken to indoctrinate the boy with Shinto thought. Often, for example, his father told him stories at bedtime. These stories, which he told in simple language, were about the people and customs of ancient Japan.

Meanwhile, Setschan advanced from kindergarten to the primary grades. During these years he was a somewhat sickly child, and sometimes it was difficult for him to fall asleep at night. He was often kept home from school; his memories of those early primary school classes are vague. He remembers coming back to school after long absences. What he recalls most about the early years of school is the burgeoning of an interest in music and an aptitude for it. In his kindergarten year, for example, the class joined the other grades in a traditional song for the New Year's ceremony. It was a solemn song, ending with the cadence mi-so-fa-re-do, which the children almost always sang incorrectly. The error stung Setschan's ear. After the ceremony he innocently went to his female teacher, and announced that his school-fellows were singing the song incorrectly. Her face was warm and smiling as she patted him on the head. "You are right, dear boy. You are very nice." Then she turned aside to a neighbor and said, "Isn't it wonderful to see so small a child with so good an ear for music." For Setschan, it was like being approved by the Muse.

Here again the Shinto influence is felt. One of the most important elements in the Shinto rite is music. Shinto music is called *gagaku.* It was introduced, like much else of Japanese culture, from China, and is characterized by harps, reed pipes of various sorts, an elaborate harmony called *Sho,* small drums, and high-pitched gongs. It is based on a series of dissonances, usually five, which to Western ears sound queerly off-pitch, and it is usually played in legato fashion. It produces in the listener a feeling of pathos, an exquisite antique mood. As he awakened to life, the young Setschan came to enjoy the music of the shrine with deep feeling. Its influence in forming his artistic taste was enormous.

Perhaps even more important than school or music was the feeling he developed for horticulture. His father leased a patch of land on which he practiced horticulture for his own amusement. Besides general flower gardening, he kept about five hundred potted dwarf plants, a collection which included virtually every variety of plant which can be successfully dwarfed. As Setschan followed his father through the garden, the man continually murmured softly, almost as if to himself, a flow of explanations for everything he did. Only occasionally did the son raise a question, and the answer always came in the same low murmuring voice. It was a masterful method of teaching. The boy learned how to transplant, how to produce bigger flowers, why certain trees hate to grow under others, how to plant a cutting – in sum, most of the basic knowledge of Japanese gardening, except for stock-grafting, which requires a difficult technique. While giving his son pointers on nature, Setschan's father interspersed bits of Confucian wisdom, or commentary on life. On rare occasions, a plant revealed a sudden mutation. "See the ghost," the father would marvel.

Inevitably Setschan wanted plants of his own. Sympathizing with his son's obviously deep affection for natural life, the father set aside a tiny patch of land about two feet square for the ambitious boy. Setschan managed to grow a few cuttings in his patch. He was overjoyed. With visions of himself as a little landowner, he decided to enlarge the garden. Rushing to a nearby hill, he spent half a day pulling from the earth trees as large as he could manage. He planted them in his garden, watered them thoroughly; for three days he watched them with vast impatience. Then they began to wither away one by one. Painfully Setschan watched them die.

Stubborn and determined, after further instructions from his father, he set out again, this time heading for the hills which surround Kyoto like the edge of a basin. It was a fine, clear, mid-autumn day. As he got up into the hills, he had to pass through what in those days was called an "Eta" village.

Scattered across Japan, but mostly on the outskirts of the large towns, Eta villages have their roots a thousand years deep in Japanese history. Near the beginning of the Heian Period,[2] Koreans began immigrating to Japan in great masses. Their culture was derived from the Chinese and was further advanced than Japanese culture. They brought with them techniques for making hide and leather from animal skins, needed not

2. The time when the capital was first transferred to Kyoto.

only for implements of warfare, but for the instruments of the rapidly developing shrine *gagaku* music.

At the same time, however, the extreme compassion of the Buddhists for animals, which led them to abhor slaughtering them, was growing. The Buddhists also believed in the transmigration of souls or *samsara*. Since this meant a human soul might inhabit the body of an animal, slaughter was regarded as obnoxious. If a man killed a dog, he might be killing his grandfather or even his father. The Japanese, in order to find their way out of this dilemma, drove the leather makers out of the cities, into little villages of their own in the hills. Gradually the leather makers became untouchables, the meanest caste. They were not allowed to have social intercourse with normal people. They were not even allowed into the towns except to beg for alms on New Year's Eve.

After the Meiji Restoration, these laws were revoked. Yet legislation could not sweep away the feelings of inferiority of the people of the Eta villages, nor could it remedy their physical breakdown due to intermarriage, lack of sanitation, and decent medical care.[3]

Setschan went through such a village and on into the forests where he spent the day digging up a few trees according to the new lessons his father had taught him. On the way home, in the Eta village, he encountered the dirtiest boy he had ever seen. The boy had just come out of a house. His clothing was filthy, his face looked as if it had not been washed for a hundred days, and his eyes were bleared from trachoma. Setschan was shocked by the sight, and he stood staring at the filthy boy.

The urchin recognized Setschan immediately as a town boy. "Hey," he shouted, "what do you think's so funny?"

Setschan stared blankly back.

"What're you staring at, boy?"

Setschan could think of no answer.

"Come on, answer. I'm not going to let you pass until you do."

Setschan suddenly realized that he was in grave trouble. He was in the hills alone. There was nothing to prevent the Eta boy from beating him seriously and perhaps sending him home naked. He was frightened.

3. It wasn't until after World War II that the Eta people began to melt into the general population.

But then he remembered his samurai teaching. A true samurai will not be dismayed even when he is surrounded by a million devils. If he must die, he will die proudly and serenely. He saw in his mind his family crest, and he was strengthened. Pulling himself up straight, he stared directly into the eyes of the snarling Eta boy. The effect surprised even Setschan. The boy continued to shout at him, but he kept his distance.

For what seemed an eternity, Setschan held his ground. The Eta boy, vexed by his inability to overcome his sense of inferiority in the presence of the well-dressed town boy, suddenly raised a cry. "Hey, Kuma… Tora… Genko… come on out and help me give this town boy a licking."

At that point Setschan realized that only a miracle could save him. He remembered the story of Inokuma Nyudo. Inokuma Nyudo is a mystery man who serves a young master as vassal but remains invisible until needed – somewhat like the genie Aladdin rubbed from his lamp. What Setschan needed was Inokuma Nyudo, and he wanted to cry out for him.

Eta boys began to appear at the doors of the houses. And then Inokuma Nyudo appeared, in the form of a dozen men of Kyoto returning through the village from a picnic. Setschan knew some of them well. He raised his hand to wave to them. They returned the gesture, and the Eta boy fled, as did his cohorts who drew themselves back like leeches into the mud. Setschan made his way safely home.

Nothing is without its lessons, and in the end the incident proved valuable. Years later, when the grown Setschan had to face torture at the hands of the secret police, or the invading armies of the Russians, who threatened to shoot him down in the street, he was able to face them with a quiet, confident manner and even maintain a serene mind. This was, in part, the result of his samurai training. For Japanese boys of the day, *Bushido* – or the "way of the samurai" – was perhaps an even more profound influence than Shinto. Often regarded by Westerners, who associate it with the huge swords of the samurai, as a bellicose tradition, *Bushido* is actually an Eastern version of the chivalric code. Originally the code of the ancient Yamato tribe, whose descendants ultimately became emperors of Japan, the *Bushido* tradition gradually spread through the populace at large. Like knightly chivalry, *Bushido* is a code of behavior, stressing the virtues of courage in battle and serenity in the face of death. Like chivalry, it clung to exaggerated ideals of personal honor and prestige – so exaggerated in fact, that the proper response to dishonor was suicide.[4] In addition to these soldierly ideals, the true samurai possessed gentler qualities: courtesy, honor, and fidelity. The Western idea that the *Bushido* ideal was responsible for Japanese militarism is incorrect. It is true, of course, that the militarists capitalized on some of the *Bushido* notions. The belief that a man who died for the Emperor went immediately to heaven as a god helped to create the suicidal kamikaze pilots of World War II. But true *Bushido* is far more than a code of war. It is difficult not to love and respect the man who adheres to the genuine *Bushido* code.

The young Setschan was strongly influenced by the *Bushido* code, especially through the man who taught him in second and third grades. Yamamoto-*sensei*[5] was a teacher with a wonderful sense of narrative as well as a sense of humor. He illustrated the ideal of *Bushido* by announcing that he would cure a stomachache by hitting his belly with his fist. The personality and teaching of this good man had a powerful effect on Setschan, an effect which not only supported him during the incident in the Eta village, but many other times throughout his life.

The plants Setschan brought home through the Eta village were successfully transplanted. Setschan learned how to treat the roots and how to cut back the little branches; he learned how to expose the plants to sunlight only a little bit at a time. He was able to sense when a plant was feeling strong or weak – or even when it was happy or unhappy. His love for gardening was obvious, and he was eager to continue to penetrate deeper and deeper into the mysteries of the natural world.

His father recognized the strong pull horticulture had for the boy and one day said to him, "Setschan, how would you like to go to agricultural school when you are bigger?"

Setschan was curious. "What do you do there?"

---

4. Self-immolation – *seppuku* or *hara-kiri* as it is usually termed in the West – was traditionally done by making two straight slashes across the belly, so that the dying man disemboweled himself. Later, however, the slash was reduced to a small ritual cut, and a kind friend would end the pain by stabbing the neck.
5. The word *"sensei"* is a suffix of honor, something akin to the English "sir."

"Learn. Learn to grow all sorts of plants."

"Even fruit trees?"

"Of course. Apple trees, pear trees, peach trees – whatever you want."

"And can I eat the fruit?"

The father smiled. "Certainly you can."

The decision was not yet sealed, however. Setschan's oldest brother, Genjiro, was nineteen at the time. To the nine-year-old boy, Genjiro seemed to be an old, advanced, and inaccessible person. Because he was the first son, and therefore the bearer of the family bloodline, his opinion was respected by his parents, and often his word was final. Inevitably, the father asked Genjiro what he thought of the idea of raising Setschan for agriculture.

Said Genjiro, "Setschan is not strongly built. Botanical study will inevitably demand a good deal of physical labor, and Setschan won't be able to stand it. Better to prepare him for a more sedentary life."

Genjiro was a mathematician and had the mathematician's love of precision and accuracy. He did not like making mistakes, and as a result he was inclined to be cautious and sometimes negative in his thinking. But Genjiro's views sounded sensible, and they influenced his father. The idea of agricultural school for Setschan was dropped. Ironically, Genjiro, for all his caution, was grievously in error. It was the terrible grind of study and the speculative life which virtually destroyed Setschan's health later on. It is a curious thing that the life of study requires a considerable degree of physical health to sustain the intensity of concentration and the long hours the student's work requires. Perhaps if Setschan had gone into botanical work, the physical labor out of doors would have strengthened him.

It seems a sad and almost tragic thing that the offhand opinion of a nineteen-year-old boy should have so deeply affected the course of a man's life. If Genjiro had spoken one positive word, Setschan would have become a botanist. His life, in the ordinary sense, might have been far happier, for he might have avoided the zigzag path of theological doubts, the endless pilgrimage in search of religion, and the mental anguish which is the invariable lot of the doubter. For Genjiro, the incident was a trifle, easily forgotten. For Setschan the incident involved his entire life.

It seems, however, that God provides alternative paths in life. One need not earn his bread with his highest talent. It is often the case that a man can shine brightest, can enrich his life, and make a larger contribution to the world through a talent which he does not use in his daily work. One should not abuse Providence, for only the Almighty One can ultimately decide the worth of one's life.

It may seem a little curious to the modern reader that Setschan abandoned an ambition which meant so much to him simply because of a word from his father. In the Japan of Setschan's boyhood his reaction was perfectly normal. Japanese children were brought up under a system far more authoritarian than anything we can imagine today. Not only was the child constantly faced with figures of authority – parents, schoolteachers, priests, and government officials – but he was expected to conform to countless, extremely minor rules. His comings and goings were regulated, the forms his spare-time pleasures took were limited, his behavior in the home and at the dining table were forced into ritual patterns. There was, among Japanese boys, always the undercurrent of rebellion, but it rarely broke into the open. It would have been extraordinary if Setschan had taken sharp issue with the decision about his career made for him by his father. Rebellion was to come, but not yet.

In fact, Setschan's rebellious feelings took a rather curious form of expression, an expression which was to have a considerable effect on him later. At ten he began to study English. His textbook was illustrated with pictures of American life – of boys and girls playing together freely, of games, and good times. Setschan was struck by the contrast of what seemed like so lively and gay a childhood compared with the controlled one he was living. Immediately he thought that sometime, somehow, he must run away and go to America. He did not; but the result was an absorbing interest in the West. A few years later, he built a Western-style desk and chair for his study; and in time his absorption in Western culture was to lead him to much, much more.

Although Setschan did not show it, the loss of his horticultural career was painful to him; he was aware that his poor health had been exaggerated. His father, for example, thought that the boy probably had a cardiac weakness – a supposition which had no evidence to support it. By the time he was in fourth grade he had become a brisk and active boy, always eager to be out and doing something. He was a boy who desired to please, true enough, but that did not mean that he would be happy without expressing his own personality. Boy-like, he simply could not sit still for five minutes at a time. This need for activity led him, during the summer vacation at the end of the fourth grade, to his first real accomplishment. For the first time he learned a skill without adult help.

Kyoto sits in a basin, surrounded by high hills. It is about twenty miles from the Pacific Ocean at Osaka, too far for boys to go to the ocean beach. Behind the town lies the huge Lake Biwa. At the time, it was under the control of the Butoku-kai, or Martial Arts Association, which used it to teach the complexities of the art of classical Japanese swimming. The Kamo and other rivers near Kyoto are icy cold, sufficiently so to induce cyanotic symptoms within a few minutes in those foolish enough to swim there. For boys who want to swim, there are only a handful of small ponds – virtually marshes – spotted around the town at the base of the hills. The still water in these ponds is warm. Most of them are from three to six feet deep, shallow enough for safety, although occasionally boys who braved deeper areas drowned.

That summer Setschan decided he must learn to swim. He did not tell his parents, who would surely forbid him, but walked instead to a pond called Komatsu-ike along with a group of other boys. Once they stripped, it was simple to tell the veterans of the pond from the novices: the veterans were burned dark by the sun, while the skin of the others was pale and white.

Feeling somewhat ashamed of his pallid skin, Setschan stood on the bank of the pond, wondering exactly how to begin. He was musing thus, when suddenly he felt a thrust from behind, and then he was in the water, arched like a bow with the sudden shock. He could neither shout, nor cry for help, but began thrashing wildly, gulping water every time he opened his mouth. On the bank, the fifteen-year-old who had pushed him in stood watching nervously, and other spectators ran frantically up and down the bank shouting, “Help him out, somebody help him out.”

But while they were shouting, Setschan struggled the five feet to the bank by himself, and climbed up onto the bank, his chest heaving from the effort. He was vastly astonished to realize that he had become a swimmer.

So was the somewhat relieved boy who had pushed him in the water. "Bravo, very good," he shouted. Setschan, still struggling for breath, could not answer. He stared at the boy, caught between elation from his accomplishment and indignation for its cause.

"What's your name?" the dark-brown boy asked.

"He's the youngest brother of Kotsuji," somebody told him.

"Kotsuji's brother?" His attitude changed rapidly. Genjiro had a considerable reputation as a scholar among the boys of the neighborhood, for he had won a prize scholarship in a contest with hundreds of other boys. "I'm sorry," the boy said, somewhat alarmed. "I didn't know you were Kotsuji's brother. I... ah... was just trying to teach you how to swim."

"It's all right," Setschan said. "I swam all right."

"Yes, yes," the boy replied. "Someday you'll be a great swimmer."

Later, Setschan, feeling warm and glorious, walked home with the boy who had pushed him, stopping together in a rice field to skewer dozens of locusts on a wire. At home Setschan toasted the locusts over a fire in the charcoal brazier which always burned in Japanese homes of the day, and when the little creatures turned from green to dark brown, he ate them with soy sauce. He did not, however, tell his parents what he had done, for he was afraid they would forbid further swimming. Thereafter, every afternoon all through the long summer vacation, he went to the pond and practiced swimming. On the way home he would catch more locusts. He still lacked the courage to tell his parents the truth; they simply believed he went locust hunting every afternoon.

The summer gradually slipped away. Then one day Setschan accidentally overheard his parents talking. He heard his mother say, "Have you noticed how brown Setschan is getting? He's beginning to look like an Indian."

The father shrugged. "He's getting sunburned from hunting locusts in the fields."

"No," his mother said, "the color is a little different from an ordinary sunburn."

"Perhaps we'd better keep a watch on him."

Suddenly Setschan wanted to pull back the whole vacation to its beginning. His dishonesty made his mind uneasy. How was he going to cover it up? Sooner or later, they would discover the established fact that he could swim ten or twenty feet. He meditated: We can return stolen things; we can go back to the place we have come from; why can't we return to an early point in time? But the paradox in the reasoning was too deep for the boy, and he stopped pondering it.

Shortly thereafter he stopped swimming, too. He was sitting in the house when his father approached him, with a grave face.

"Setschan," he said solemnly, "I've discovered that some bad boys in the neighborhood have been going to the marsh every day to swim. One of them has finally drowned. I'm going to find out who they are."

Setschan sat straight and still, staring at his father like a mouse facing a cat. But his father said nothing more; he turned and walked away. Setschan stopped paying homage to the marsh from that moment on. His intense love for the sport remained, and until the clear sun signaling the approach of autumn began to shine in the old town, he continued to wish for his daily swim.

Hazardous as the adventure had been, the daily exercise, both swimming and locust catching, did wonders for his body. Setschan was no longer a weak, sickly boy.

This almost immediately had a happy result. On the third of November the school traditionally held an athletic contest, involving running, jumping, and other typical schoolboy games. During the preliminary practice sessions, Setschan discovered to his great delight and amazement that he was the fastest runner in his class. To his happy wonder, the discovery made him a small hero; the boys started to respect him, and the girls cheered him on in shrill voices. Setschan was at the age when the girls' opinion mattered very little. Holding honors among the boys, however, was an important thing. And when the athletic meet was finally held, Setschan took first prize in his class, and became the object of flattery and attention from his classmates. Finally, Setschan was rid of the feeling that he couldn't compete physically with the boys around him.

Important as his athletic successes were in the making of this Japanese boy, far more significant was the presence of a teacher named Tomosaburo Nakajima who took over his class that same autumn. Looking back on him from the age of sixty, the author is certain that Nakajima-*sensei* was a great teacher. He was unquestionably the man with the finest personal qualities Setschan met during his entire education. His effect on Setschan's development is incalculable. He maintained his dignity always. He neither scolded nor was mean; he was never harsh; nonetheless, his pupils always obeyed him. For example, if a boy was joking and chattering with his friends around him, Nakajima-*sensei* would simply stop talking, until the queer silence alarmed the noisy boy. When the startled student came to himself, Nakajima-*sensei* would cast a silent benevolent look over him for a few moments, before he continued his teaching. Within a few months the entire class was completely under the spell of his serene and virtuous teaching. Nakajima-*sensei* always tried to find the very best in his students. He found something to appreciate in even the worst pupil; gradually, he raised the level of the pride of the class in its work. Before, Setschan had never bothered to do any homework but had slipped by on natural talent. Under Nakajima-*senseii*, he began to do a little extra work from time to time, in order to get top grades consistently.

In the fifth and sixth grades, Nakajima concentrated on indoctrinating his pupils with the value of virtue. He was always careful to give his students detailed reasons for man's need for virtue. He explained that animals do not have virtue; only man has cultivated it. Virtue, he taught, will be counted virtuous even when hidden. Advertising it – if people fail to acknowledge it – will cause it to lose its value. Unacknowledged virtue will make your face shine, he taught; hypocrisy will not. The good act need not be deliberately hidden; to display it, however, is a step on the road to hypocrisy.

Before the year was out Setschan had a chance to put this teaching into practice. Nakajima made it a rule to take his class on a monthly picnic as a reward for diligence in their work. They usually went to Mount Hiei, which rose 2,800 feet from the northeast corner of the city, overlooking the beautiful Lake Biwa. Setschan was asked to bring up the rear, to see that there were no stragglers. As they came up to a steep place called Kirara Pass, the fastest boys pushed on a considerable way ahead, and the slower boys dropped further and further behind. Finally, one of these – a smaller boy – simply stopped and dropped to the ground.

"Hey, what's the matter?" Setschan asked.

"I'm hungry, and I'm too tired to walk anymore," he gasped.

"Where's your lunch?" Setschan asked.

"Tsutsumi's got it. He carried it for me. He's way up ahead."

Setschan had nothing to offer the boy. He had already eaten his lunch. Yet he had to do something.

"All right, you can make it," he said cheerfully, in an attempt to rouse the boy's flagging spirits.

"No, I can't. I'm dying," the boy moaned.

Suddenly Setschan decided to carry the boy the rest of the way up the mountain. Bending, he raised him up over his back and began to drag doggedly up the slope. His legs grew heavy, his pulse began to hammer, and despite frequent rest stops, his breath rasped in his throat. Grim and determined, he pushed on, staggering under the heavy burden. Finally, he came to the rest point where the others were waiting and let the boy down. As the boy hungrily gulped his lunch, Setschan felt like a soldier who had taken a stronghold; victorious, but exhausted. The beating of his heart slowed after a few moments, but his legs continued to feel odd. There were still six more miles of walking to do, and by the time the party broke up at dark, his leg muscles stung with needle pricks and jumped with mild spasms. Once home, he ate in utter silence and slept like the dead.

The next morning at school, the boy he had carried greeted him with "*Kino wa ohkini,*" which in Kyoto dialect means "Thank you for yesterday."

"Do you feel all right now?" Setschan asked.

"Yes, I'm all right. How strong you are, Setschan."

"No, not so strong...." He couldn't find the words; but the boy's thanks were reward enough, and he was happy. It wasn't for a month that the teacher discovered what he had done and added his praise to the reward.

Of all the influences on the boy Setschan the most subtle and perhaps the deepest was the city of Kyoto itself, which he took in with his every breath. Consider: The city has been breeding history for twelve hundred years and longer, since it first began as the capital of Japan. When London and Paris were only collections of rude houses, Kyoto was the seat of a court rich in literature, painting, and architecture, and it was the capital of a populous country. Everything the boy Setschan saw as he moved through his hometown was touched by tradition, history, ancient lore. It was a day's trip to the oldest wooden building existing in the world, the Horyuji Temple. The sound of the ancient city was with him always. His eye constantly fell on something touched by myth or legend. For example, the city is famous for stone lanterns, large and small, which sit around the shrines. Some of the shrines have hundreds of them. When all of them are lit in the evening of a high holiday one feels as if he were in the middle of the home of the soul.[6] One of these lanterns, which stands in the inner court of the Kitamo Shrine, is so old the granite has become rotten. It is called Toro, after the myth of Watanabe-no-Tsuna-Toro. Back in the old days, the legend goes, white fiends made raids on the town each evening to eat the men and steal away the women. Wanatabe-no-Tsuna was chief of the city's guard. He was patrolling one midnight across the Modoribashi Bridge on Ichijo Avenue when he came upon a woman of incredibly radiant beauty. His heart was struck; but then he began to wonder why a woman so beautiful would risk exposing herself to the fiends at night. Quickly Tsuna looked down at her reflection in the water, and there he saw her as the devil. He whipped out his sword. The graceful lady turned suddenly into his true form, snatched Tsuna up by the back of his neck and flew with him into the air.

He flew from the north of town to the south. As he crossed over Rashomon Gate, Tsuna summoned his courage, and with his huge sword slashed off one of the arms of the fiend as it clung to his neck. Roaring, the fiend flung him down beside the gate, where he lay unconscious. When he came to himself, he rose and looked about for the arm of the devil. It was missing; he couldn't find it. He began walking north looking for it, and then on the grounds of the Kitamo Shrine he saw it. It was a sign that Divine Providence had saved him, he decided; and he dedicated the lantern in commemoration of the event.

As a boy, Setschan once came upon the lantern. He tapped it lightly with his fist, and some of the bits of sand in the rotten granite fell away. "Look," he called to his friend, "the lantern is made of sand. It is no good."

6. There are, remember, 899 Buddhist temples in Kyoto, and hundreds of Shinto shrines. All of this still remains; the United States Air Force was under strict orders not to bomb Kyoto, out of respect for its antiquity.

Several years later he came upon it again. Now a brand-new tablet of white wood inscribed in superb calligraphy announced that it was the "Lantern of Watanabe-no-Tsuna – a National Treasure." Remembering his disrespectful gesture, Setschan blushed hotly. Then he made a respectful bow and vowed he would become a second Tsuna to rid the country of any fiends which remained.

So Setschan grew. Maturer emotions quickened in him. He began dimly to realize that there was, besides the visible world, another world in which resided grace and glory. Poems became vaguely intelligible. Words to songs began to have special meanings. Then, as if precisely on cue, his boyish romantic proclivities ignited.

The date was March 24, 1911; the occasion, most fittingly, the ceremony marking his graduation from primary school. Toward the end of the observances, the entire class joined in a song which celebrated the end of the early school years and the joys that nature held in store for them.

The singing of the song filled him with strong feeling, and it was still with him as he walked through the gate of the school for the last time, carrying the Chinese dictionary he had won as a prize for good conduct and assiduity. He did not want to go home, fearful that the old familiar objects would bring him down to earth. Filled with a deep, inexpressible, almost unbearable feeling of pathos, he wandered through Kyoto. Suddenly, as dusk began to descend, he found himself in front of the Kitamo Shrine, where he had once insulted the ancient lanterns. Plum blossoms scented the dusk air, and a soft breeze sighed in the trees. Around him the ancient lanterns were being lit, their points of light ripening all around. Now and then he could hear the clapping of hands inside the shrine as men began to pray. Swept with a sense of tenderness and beauty, he desired only to be where he was forever. His soul sighed; he felt that he had reached his eternal home.

Years later, when for the first time he opened the Bible to Psalm 84 and read it, the memory of that moment at dusk flooded over him again.

> How lovely is Your dwelling place, O Lord of Hosts. My soul longs and pines for the Lord's courtyards; my heart and my body sing out to the living God....

This, then, was how a Japanese was made. There was nothing about Setschan that marked him as different from his school fellows or that set him apart from thousands of other bright Japanese boys of good family. Raised in an ancient town replete with historical significance, he had been indoctrinated with a Shinto reverence for the Japanese past and a strong feeling for the virtuous way of the samurai. He was, like most good Japanese boys, eager to do right, to obey his father and his masters, to conduct himself always with honor and courage. And yet, within three years, this well-trained Japanese boy was to reject this training, cast it to the winds, and enter upon a long, arduous search through bitter doubt and anguished despair – a search which was to take him fifty years to complete

Chapter Three

It is now time for the author to drop the third person in speaking of himself. At the point in his life this story has reached, a change begins to take place in his mind and in his emotions. The psychology of a child begins to fade. Boyish sentimentality becomes true emotional response to the world of grace and glory around.

I want to remind the reader that I was not a boy gifted with a strong religious inclination, nor was I a religious genius. I was a simple, inexperienced boy, and that is all. However, I was stubborn and single-minded when I chose to be, capable of strong emotional responses to events and people, and both blessed and victimized by a strong sense of justice.

Yet although I was not especially religious in my attitudes, I was interested – sometimes deeply so – in the aesthetic virtues of the Shinto rites. From the fourth grade on I assiduously kept up the rite of kindling the sacred fire as my father had taught me. I rarely missed an evening. As the result of this love of the beauty of the old rites, and my parents' subtle education, I was being prepared for the religious experiences I was later to have. Even though I lived as a gentile, a passage was being opened inside me. Ironically, the efforts my parents bent toward making me susceptible to the call of Shinto had the effect of preparing my mind for the spark struck in it by my first look into the Bible. My parents were most cautious in their teaching. They managed to bring me to religion without creating in me any resistance to it. When the rites or observances are too complicated for children to grasp, they back away. When it is taught merely as an ethical code, without the appeal of color and sound to the senses, children find it dull. Furthermore, the reduction of religion to a mere ethical system can create a kind of religious anarchy, especially when the moral code changes with each succeeding era. But my parents avoided overdosing me with ethical teaching and complicated ritual; they adhered to the simple symbolic rites, and thanks to their wisdom, religious feeling blossomed in me and grew strong. Although they created in their son the feeling for religion, in the end Shinto did not satisfy that feeling.

Two important things happened to me in the years after my graduation from primary school. First was an injury which was to teach me considerably about bodily pain. The second was the awakening of my scholastic ambition. Both are important to my story.

In the Japan of my youth, students went from primary school to five years of middle school. I elected to take the commercial course, principally because it offered more English than the regular course. School started in the spring. The cherry trees blossomed, the migratory birds flew back from India, from Australia, from the South Seas and began to nest. The hills above the town burst into green; a mist blanketed their tops.

One Saturday morning during this lovely spring, I went to a nearby playground, where they had a piece of equipment called the *judo-enboku.* The *judo-enboku* is a heavy log about a foot in diameter which hangs two or three inches off the ground from heavy chains. It can swing back and forth, and the trick is to perform acrobatics on it. Some boys were riding it when I came in, and I decided that it looked like an easy and pleasant exercise. I got on, and we managed to get it swinging three feet high. Then one of the boys riding it slipped. He grabbed out instinctively to save himself and caught hold of me. The sudden jerk cost me my balance, and I tried to jump clear, but I didn't make it. The heavy log ground over my foot, crushing it against the ground. I touched my foot; it felt numb.

Fortunately, I was wearing heavy shoes; otherwise, my foot could easily have been completely crushed, leaving me a cripple. With the help of a friend, I dragged myself off to a corner and took off my shoe. My foot felt a little better; but then as the numbness began to wear off, an intense pain developed. I continued to sit on the ground, hoping that the pain would ease up. Instead, it grew worse. At the end of two hours, I was groaning aloud; at the end of three, as night began to fall, I was in anguish. The boys had left the playground one by one, leaving only me and an old friend. Now, as I had carried the boy up the mountainside so my friend lifted me onto his back and, struggling with my weight, carried me home.

It turned out that cartilage had been damaged. Proper ministration returned it to its place, but the deep, stubborn pain persisted. For five years following the accident the pain would leave in the spring, only to recur each winter. One never gets used to a pain like that. Winter after winter it clung to me, troubling me, and leaving me to wonder whether it would stay with me for the rest of my life. Without the encouragements of religion, as I developed them over this period, I could not have stood the pain.

Overshadowing this unhappy accident was a sudden surge of interest in my studies. For the first term in middle school I followed my usual course, I skipped homework and slid by on natural ability. At the end of the term, I ranked seventh in the class. I was reasonably satisfied with myself.

My older brother Genjiro, however, was not. He ridiculed my complacency. "You only managed to be seventh because nobody else in the class is any good," he jeered. "If you don't work harder, you'll drop even lower. You seem to be pretty satisfied with yourself, Setschan. Well let me assure you that saying you are fairly good is just another way of saying you are fairly bad. It's time you stopped being lazy and learned to study."

Genjiro was ten years my senior; he stood almost as a teacher to me, and his words had a strong effect on me. Besides, he was a brilliant student and a hard worker. His attitude toward his studies began to fill me also. I decided that I would learn to work as hard as my brother, and he in turn said that he would coach me in my studies. I did work hard. During the entire fall term, as the persimmons reddened and the fragrant scent of pine mushrooms filled the air, I put aside all desire to play and sat in my room with a charcoal-filled *hibachi* beside me, grinding away at my studies, ignoring the lovely weather out of doors. My efforts were rewarded. In December, at the end of the term, I was named an honor student.

Spoiling some of the new pleasure I took in my studies was the revival of the stubborn, dull pain in my left foot. Feeling on the one hand an awakened confidence in my mental resources and on the other the drag of this annoying pain was a complicated emotional condition for a twelve-year-old boy. It is difficult to trace its effect precisely, yet I am inclined to believe that the pain I suffered for so long a period did subtle work in undermining the religious education I had gotten from my parents, for it was at about this time that I first became conscious of religious doubts. I continued faithfully to light the fire at the Shinto altar each evening, and I gave no indication aloud to anyone that I was beginning to have reservations about Shinto. As my mother, with great pleasure, watched me kindle the little fires each evening, she no longer saw a child but a modest and well-mannered youth. She had no inkling of what was going on in my mind. There was, I recognized, great religious-aesthetic value in the elegant simplicity of the Shinto rites. And yet, somehow, they seemed hollow. There was nothing behind them, no value underlying and supporting them, and I began to wonder in the privacy of my mind whether they could be worth anything at all. The lack of didactic elements in Shinto, the lack of emotional substance, worried me. Perhaps if somebody had shown me the relation between the rituals and the ancient life-and-death struggles of the forefathers I might have found the value I was looking for in Shinto. Nobody did, and my hunger, a hunger I did not precisely understand, for something deeper, something more significant in my religion, grew.

Yet I could think of no good reason for stopping my observances, especially the ritual of lighting the sacred fire every evening. There was nothing wrong or evil in Shinto, certainly, and there was always the aesthetic pleasure it offered. And so, I went on, the sense that there was something meaningless about my observances nagging at the back of my mind.

Spring came. I was thirteen, and with the blooming of the cherry blossoms the ache in my foot died away. My mind grew more cheerful, and my emotions deepened. Kyoto in the spring has the softest, calmest climate anywhere in Japan. There is virtually no breeze, and the air is balmy and sweet. That year, out of my growing emotional responsiveness, I experienced the city's bells for the first time.

There are hundreds of bells in Kyoto, mostly attached to the Buddhist temples. They are rung twice a day: once just before dawn and again in the evening. They are of all sizes and types, and they are perhaps the most famous in Japan. Some of them, like the ones in such temples as Chion-in, Kurodani, and Komyoji Zenrinji are extraordinarily large; the one at Chion-in Temple weighs seventy-four tons; it is the largest in Japan. The bells of Kyoto were cast by master founders, and according to the legend, gold was mixed into the bronze to give purity to the tone. They sound with deep, slow vibrations, and when they shake the tranquil morning air, their echoes ever widening like the spreading of a circle in a pool, the people wake from their dreams with a sense of the Infinite around them. Half an hour later, as the Buddhist monks begin their prayers, the red, beamless sun appears suddenly to jump up from behind the eastern hill. The effect, due to refraction of the light, is quite real. It was during the spring of my fourteenth year that I began for the first time to feel the magic beauty in the bells and to take pleasure in identifying them by their various pitches.

That summer, too, I finally satisfied an old ambition. I joined Butoku-kai, the famous classic Martial Arts Association, to learn the fascinating and difficult art of classical swimming. The Butoku-kai course did not teach the standard strokes like the crawl or the breast stroke. All the strokes are ancient ones and used basically for display. For example, during the feudal age in Japan, it was customary for a lord's soldiers to parade before him occasionally. For their part of the military display, the swimming unit actually swam in a special style with a special stroke, wearing full armor. At the Butoku-kai this same stroke was taught, and the swimmers wore replicas of the ancient helmet and armor. Learning this art may seem like a useless, not to say silly, accomplishment. However, it takes a good deal of athletic skill and conditioning to achieve it; no weak city boy could manage the course.

To begin, the trainee spends his first summer passing through two preparatory courses. As the residue of a feudal military system, army notions of rank and obedience were insisted upon. Boys in the preparatory classes were required to wear humiliating red caps and were allowed to swim only under orders. I didn't like the humiliation of the red cap, and I didn't like behaving like a dog on a leash. As the reader will remember, I already could swim to some extent. Between this experience and some determined practice, I was able to pass the examination to move into the second of the preparatory classes. Two weeks later I passed a harder examination and putting off the humiliating red cap, moved into the regular course.

Now I began to learn the traditional swimming strokes, and by the end of the summer I was ready for the long-distance swim on Lake Biwa, spending three hours and forty-five minutes in the water. The following year I swam for five hours and fifty-six minutes, and in the third year I managed over six hours – but not without trouble. About three in the afternoon, when I had already been in the water for several hours, some bread was thrown in to us. I was asked to distribute it, and I began to tread water as I collected it. Suddenly my leg cramped painfully. From the boat which accompanied us, the officials urged me to climb out of the water. My old stubbornness took hold of me, and I asked for first aid. The cramp left, only to return again a few minutes later. Again, they urged me to get out of the water, and again I refused. This time a judo expert dove in and gave me first aid. The cramp left but some pain persisted. When I finally climbed out in the evening, having swum ten miles in six hours and five minutes, I was exhausted. For the first and only time in my life I ate five bowlfuls of rice along with the rest of my regular meal.

My stubbornness was rewarded, however, for I was nominated an honor student and exempted from the regular tuition fee. More important, the rigid training of the Butoku-kai taught me how to discipline myself, an asset of great value later on when I had to drive myself through books of Hebrew studies; and it helped me bear up under the torture of the Kempeitai – the Japanese Gestapo – during World War II.

In any case, both physically and mentally I was stronger and more confident, a boy my parents could certainly be proud of. There was only one flaw in my life: the dimly-heard cry of hunger coming from the bottom of my soul. Thus I stood in the autumn of 1912.

Chapter Three

In the early fall, the great Emperor Meiji died. His body was brought back to Kyoto and buried with enormous pomp and splendor. On the day of September 13, the day the body left the imperial palace in Tokyo, General Count Nogi immolated both himself and his wife as tokens of love and respect for the dead emperor. The country, as a whole, greatly admired his act, and the suggestion implied in it of the great virtue of the man who inspired it. As a well-brought-up Japanese, I at first gave the matter little thought. The action was completely in accord with tradition. But then I began to wonder if I could undergo the ceremonial death with a calm and composed mind, and I could not but feel a flutter of the heart. And this led me to begin asking myself some questions. What was the meaning of life? What was it all about? Should one kill oneself, and if so, in what circumstances? I was in this mental state when I wandered into a secondhand bookshop looking for something to read. It was late autumn; the country was still in mourning for Emperor Meiji, and the quiet hills around Kyoto were showing a red heart as if in lamentation.

I had become something of a book hunter. I liked browsing in secondhand stores examining the books, wondering when I would be old enough to read the ones which were too difficult for me. On this day, most of the books I picked up were too difficult. I examined book after book on shelf after shelf but could find nothing I wanted to read within range of my limited allowance. Then I noticed on the shelf where the larger books like dictionaries were kept a thick, leather-bound book covered with dust, through which shone gilt letters. I was curious. Its queer title attracted my mind. I reached up and took it down from its shelf, and through that gesture Providence led me to the first step along a path which would take forty-seven years to traverse, until the mighty hand of the Lord completely grasped me in both mind and body.

The book, of course, was a Japanese translation of the Bible, and why such a thing existed at all deserves a little explanation.

Japan is a country with a relatively good record of religious tolerance. The average Japanese has no set prejudice against religions, and it is this tolerance which has mistakenly led proselytizers to believe that the Japanese can be easily converted. The truth is that the Japanese, while allowing you to follow your own religion, expect that you will let them follow theirs.

Both Confucianism and Buddhism were introduced into Japan in the sixth century, shipped from China along with other parts of the mainland's superior culture. Both religions became influential. Confucianism was not so much a religion as an ethical philosophy, which many Japanese used to supplement the generally ethicless Shinto. Buddhism became the country's second religion. There are, for example, over eight hundred Buddhist temples in Kyoto alone.

For about a thousand years the three – Confucianism, Buddhism, and Shinto – existed side by side in relative peace. The arrival of Christianity sounded a discordant note. The first Christians to touch Japanese shores were a handful of Portuguese traders, who drifted there in a junk from China, where they had begun to carry on a trade. The year was 1543. Only six years later the new and energetic Society of Jesus sent Francis Xavier into the country to preach the Gospel. Other Jesuits followed, and their success in converting the Japanese was considerable. They were helped partly by the fact that the Buddhist priesthood had become lax and corrupt and by the fact that the famous ruler Lord Oda Nobunaga threw his support behind Christianity, largely for political reasons, in the late 1500s. His successor, Lord Hideyoshi, continued the policy of tolerance for Christianity for a number of years. Then, suddenly fearful that the Christians, specifically the Jesuits, were getting too much power, he reversed the policy in 1587. For a while, the ban against Christians was not completely enforced, and the religion continued to exist in underground fashion. In 1612, however, after the death of Hideyoshi, the powers in charge razed all Christian churches. Two years later they expelled all Christians – Japanese-born and otherwise – from the country. Those who remained were summarily executed. Not only was the country closed to Christians, but it was also closed to all Westerners. The Catholic Portuguese were forbidden to enter the country at all. The only contact with the West was through the Protestant Dutch, and they were confined to a small section of the port city of Nagasaki. They were not even allowed to talk with Japanese, except through officials. Japan was tightly closed against the West, and Christianity remained only as a tiny, hidden seed.

It was reintroduced after the Meiji Restoration, when the country was again thrown open to the West. Nineteenth-century Christians were enormously aggressive missionaries. Hardly had the first treaty with the United States been signed when Protestant and Catholic missionaries swarmed onto the island. Curiously, when the first Roman Catholic church was built in Nagasaki, several thousand Christians appeared as if by magic. For ten generations the faith had been secretly nurtured in Japanese homes, mainly around Nagasaki.

Yet, despite this ardent proselytizing, only a very small percentage of the population has ever been Christian. The peak was reached during the sixteenth century, under Nobunaga, when some 200,000 Japanese were Christians. Today, about eight-tenths of one percent of the population is Christian; but since many of them are business and social leaders, Christian influence is stronger than the numbers suggest. It is growing currently at a rapid pace.

The Jewish religion in Japan has been virtually nonexistent. Although a few Jews came to Japan through China in the ninth century, and a few more with the Portuguese traders in the sixteenth, it wasn't until the nineteenth century that there was anything like Jewish religion in the country. After the Meiji Restoration some Jews from the Western nations settled in the country as businessmen and traders. By the time I first came across the Bible there were perhaps one hundred Jewish families in the country, mainly in Nagasaki and Yokohama.

The Bible I found in the secondhand store was a translation made by a Japanese-American missionary group nearly a hundred years before. How it came to be there I do not know; perhaps a backsliding convert to Christianity sold it. What matters is that I opened it, and standing there in the dusty book shop, began to read.

"When God began creating heaven and earth...." What God? I asked myself. What does the combination Lord God (*A-donai E-lohim*) mean in the second chapter? Puzzled but gripped, I read on through the third and fourth chapters. Chapter 5 confused me again. What was the point of this repetitive listing of the names and ages of strange people? I skipped a few pages, turning at random, and stopped without plan or design at Chapter 12. There my eyes fell upon the words "The Lord said to Avram, "Go – from your land, your birthplace, and your father's house – to the land that I will show you.... I will make you a great nation, and I will bless you and make your name great. You will become a blessing. And I will bless those who bless you, and those who curse you I will curse. And through you, all the families of the earth will be blessed."

At that moment something great and deep took hold of my empty mind. I knew almost nothing about Israel and her destiny, nothing of the history of the Jewish people. Yet the pages of the book I had read to that point seemed to culminate in this great call. The real story, I felt, began at this point, with the call of the Lord to Abraham. I did not understand it exactly, and I was not sure precisely what was meant by the blessing. Yet the notion of Abraham breaking away from his home to go on a journey from which he could not return, as the chosen instrument of the Lord, inspired me and moved me deeply. Reading the verse as a whole, it seemed to me that I could "feel" without needing to understand exactly what the blessing was and what the words expressed. My Shinto training, which had prepared my mind to understand the spiritual content of a word such as "blessing," helped me to grasp what I was reading. Religion, I saw for the first time, was not merely a matter of blind observance of traditional ritual, but primarily a vital response to the divine voice.

As I stood there in the shop, carried away by my feelings, the shopkeeper approached me. "Say there, young fellow, are you interested in that book? I'll make a good price for you. How about twenty yen?"

I had twenty yen, it is true; however, it was all I had, and in those days twenty yen was a fair amount of money – perhaps ten dollars in modem American terms. In any case, as the shop was about to close, I left a five-yen deposit to hold the book until I could collect enough to pay for it. It took several impatient days to save enough out of my pocket money, but I managed to contain myself. Finally, the money collected, I brought the book home. Evening after evening I did nothing but pore over its pages, slowly working my way through to the end. The experience absorbed me completely. It didn't take me long to get through Genesis. I took it in one breath, so to speak. This first reading of the Old Testament, though not as deep as later ones would be, gave me my basic understanding of the history of Israel and a general sense of its religion. No longer were such curious names as Abraham, Isaac, Jacob, and others strange to me. I came to know them, to be familiar with their personalities, with their ways. And it was Abraham, whose name I was forty-seven years later to take, who impressed me in that first reading as the greatest and most inspiring figure in the book.

It is interesting for me to look back on that first reading of the Bible. Some of the books etched themselves deeply on my mind; others did not. Fortunately for me – and other young readers of the Bible – Genesis stands at the beginning, for it combines with its spirituality an exciting story, which can hold that elusive thing known as a boy's attention. The general tone of the book is Oriental, through and through. There was something familiar about it to my young Japanese mind. For example, courteous and hospitable greeting to strangers which the Japanese practice is well represented in Chapter 18: "My lords, if I have found favor in your sight, please do not pass your servant by. Let a little water be brought so that you can wash your feet and rest under the tree. Since you are passing by your servant, let me bring a morsel of bread so that you can be refreshed before you go on your way." Such courtesy, with its overtones of noble humiliation, is truly Oriental.

So too is the piety of Abraham, his attitude toward the Lord in his many communications with Him, embedded in a similarly Oriental courtesy and hospitality. I loved and revered Genesis, reading it over and over time and time again.

Exodus moved me with its tales of the suffering of the Hebrews in Egypt and the ultimate creation of the nation of Israel. Leviticus reminded me of Shinto, except for its burnt offerings. In the Shinto rites there are no animal or fish offerings, though some of the ancient stories suggest that there may have been burnt offerings in ancient times; modern Shinto has only vegetable offerings, like *minḥa.* There is also a distinction made between holy and unclean, equivalent to the Hebraic *kadosh* and *tameh.* It is not an exaggeration to say that the religion of Leviticus is a land of Hebrew Shinto.

I found Numbers and Deuteronomy heavy reading, especially the latter with its teaching of the laws and customs. Yet I recognized even then the importance of these two books, because they tell us of the laws and regulations of the new religious nation.

In my first perusal of the Bible, it was these books – the Pentateuch – which had the greatest impact on me. Later, I was attracted to the prophets, especially Isaiah, a book I came to appreciate only after I was able to read it in Hebrew. The language – graceful, grand, and yet direct – is a brilliant example of classical Hebrew style, in some respects reminiscent of classical Chinese. Isaiah does not attempt to teach holiness, yet he teaches it in a few lines, where Ezekiel would use a hundred for the same effect.

Before I came to understand the prophets, however, I developed a fondness for the Psalms. Some of them touched my heart intensely, and not surprisingly, I later discovered that my favorites – the ones I found most moving – were the ones generally acknowledged as the greatest of them. I took courage from Psalm 23, which begins "The Lord is my Shepherd." Psalm 42 ("As a deer pines for flowing streams, my soul pines for You, God") touched me with the mysterious sorrow behind it. Psalm 84 ("How lovely is Your dwelling place, O Lord of Hosts") reminded me of Shinto, with its pleasant shrines and aesthetic sense. Psalm 51, which opens, "Show me grace, God, in Your loyalty; in Your great mercy, erase my offense; wash me well of my guilt; purify me of my sin," although striking me as a remarkable psalm, worried me with its emphasis on the consciousness of sin.

Another one I loved was Psalm 46, each verse of which is a gem in itself. ("God is our refuge and might, ever present to help in times of trouble.") Late one evening, while I was rehearsing this psalm over and over, I was led into a state of religious rapture and felt myself really at the City of God. While I was in this mood, my father happened by my private study and noticed that I was still up. He opened the door and told me I ought to go to bed. The mood broken, I felt something like righteous indignation, although of course I obeyed.

It should be clear, then, that even from my first reading of the Bible I was shaken deep to the bottom of my soul. My life was forever changed. Despite the similarities to Oriental thought and the Shinto religion I found in the Bible, my acceptance of it involved a great revolution, not only in the mind of one Japanese boy, but more especially in the Kotsuji family. For a millennium the Kotsujis were priests and good Shintoists. Now I was changing, and I was seriously troubled in mind by what was happening to me. It made me sad to think I was tending away from the ancient religion, and I lamented that Shinto had no great book to support it. The two religions are similar in that just as Israel and the Jewish religion grew into life together, so did Japan and Shinto. Yet Shinto is a religion basically lacking in documents. There are books of myths and legends, of course, but there are no religious books in the sense of the Bible. This lack of documents is one of Shinto's great weaknesses; it has nothing to offer which has the power to inspire like the Bible. Thus, I breathed in the great religious feeling of the Bible, for which Shinto could not provide a substitute.

Inevitably, the awful day finally came when I could no longer bring myself to perform the ancient duty of lighting the sacred fire at the revered altar. One evening – an evening I will never forget – I simply lost my courage. I could not perform the act. Folding up my knees decently before the dark altar, I was suddenly overwhelmed with tears. In the dark I wept bitterly.

My mother found me thus. "What is the trouble?" she asked tenderly.

I could not answer.

"Do you have a stomachache, or a headache?"

I seized on the lie and nodded feebly. I could not respond to her great affection with the truth. I was tormented by the knowledge of the grief my parents would feel when they learned of the family-shaking revolt occurring in my mind. How could I possibly manage to explain what had affected me so? How could I explain Abraham? How could I explain Moses, Pharaoh, Passover? Even the vocabulary would be meaningless to my family.

"Of course, you have a headache," she murmured. "So faithful, to continue your sacred observance even when you are sick." And to an oppressed and unhappy boy who could not manage to say that he was far from faithful, she offered affection and praise. "Don't worry about the fire. I'll do it for you today. God understands that your mind is sincere."

So she made me a herb tea and lit the fire.

On the following evening, I was almost exhausted by my inner mental struggle, and I had little difficulty looking feeble and ill. On the third day my excuses were harder to accept. Yet patiently my mother went on lighting the fire, growing increasingly puzzled and unhappy over my defection. Finally, at the end of the week, she could no longer avoid facing the truth, and she reported to my father that I had given up lighting the fire.

My parents had made it a principle not to involve themselves too deeply in the lives of their children. They felt that if the child was constantly faced with approval or disapproval, he would never become an independent being.

It is one thing, however, to take a child's success in stride; it is another to stand by and watch him rebel against the family religion. It is always a most painful experience for parents to feel betrayed by a child whom they love and cherish. My parents' desire to avoid meddling in my life was put to a difficult test.

Of course, they had many consolations in me. I was an honor student, I was an honor member of the classic Martial Arts Association, and I was a generally well-behaved boy. Despite this, noninterference must have been a hard policy. Yet it was the policy they followed. Whatever emotions of grief, anger, disappointment, or sorrow they may have felt, I never knew them.

It was undoubtedly especially hard on my mother. There is a Japanese axiom which says, "The youngest son will not be at the parents' deathbed." In her later years, my mother was sick much of the time; she felt she would die early, and she believed that according to the proverb I would not be with her. Considering all of this, her willingness to let me go out of the ancient religion is all the more remarkable.

Not long after this crisis broke in the family, she called me to her. Her voice was gentle, and I knew she was not angry.

"I'm not pressing you to resume the fire service," she said quietly. "I know the importance to you of sincere feeling, not empty following of ritual. Only for our ancestors' sake, tell me why you have stopped."

"I have found a higher way of worship in the thick book I bought called the Bible," I answered. "It is something like our worship, but I think it is a higher Shinto." Then I burst into tears, unable to find an explanation to relieve her mind.

"Don't worry about it anymore," she said quietly. "I know you aren't bad. Just tell me what we should call your higher Shinto."

I calmed my tears. "It's ... it's the Shinto of Israel."

"Israel?" She looked blank and uncomprehending. "Well," she said finally, "whatever the name and whatever the religion, I have faith in your good nature. You cannot grow up to be a bad man."

She did not understand; but she forgave. My mother was an intelligent, broad-minded woman. She was not highly educated, but her understanding of human life was often brilliant.

My father, in his own way, forgave me too. He never spoke to me directly on the matter, but my mother spoke for him.

"Your father admits that you are doing well these days. He thinks it may be due to the book you are so eagerly reading. He says that if this is so, it must be an excellent book and the religion in it good. And if God is only One, he would have it only that way. You may go ahead with your new faith. Only remember your ancestors, honor them, and be proud of your great heritage."

I nodded sincerely to show her that I agreed, for I hardly could have expected such gracious and loving treatment at her hands. My parting from the Shinto ritual was a grave loss for both her and my father; yet out of love for me they found the goodness to make it a peaceful one, one which did not rupture our relationship. Their intelligent attitude left me forever with a good feeling about Shinto. Even now I feel that I have not rebelled against the way of the ancestors but have only been carrying to a logical conclusion the ideas implicit in Shinto.

Chapter Four

I had broken from the religion of my fathers and taken up a new one. The new religion was, in some respects, a kind of religion of my own invention. It was not Christianity, for I had not yet reached the New Testament nor come across the name Jesus Christ. In fact, I didn't understand the words "Old Testament" at the head of the book I was reading and was completely unaware that the Bible is divided into two parts.

Yet if I was not studying Christianity, I was not studying Judaism, either, except in a vague way. My reading to this point had been confined largely to the first five books of the Bible, the Pentateuch, and even here I had inevitably missed a good deal of the meaning. Furthermore, although I assumed that the Israelite nation existed, I had no real idea of what it was. I knew no Jews, no synagogue, nothing of the Talmud. My whole notion of the Western religion was hazy in the extreme.

I was, however, soon to find out what it was all about. And at the same time, I was to begin a long, arduous internal battle with myself – and Christianity. For the next several decades I spent enormously of my spiritual strength straining to swallow portions of Christian doctrine I was never really able to digest. There were many parts of Christianity I was to love: the gentleness of spirit, the serenity, the peace it sometimes offers. But there was also too much doctrine I could not truly accept: Original Sin, Predestination, the Protestant insistence on salvation through faith. I had made my bed; but my long attempts to lie in it were to keep me in spiritual misery for half of my life. It was the Pentateuch – the Torah, the Law of Moses – which had brought me to this religion in the first place; it took me forty-seven years to return to it.

I had, even by the time I had given up the Shinto fire ritual, come to realize that teaching myself the Bible was an inadequate method. I missed too much, and today it is surprising to me that I had the patience to work my way through the entire first five books without giving up. Undoubtedly it was the inherent religious value of the Pentateuch that held me so long. In any case, I was groping about for some means of furthering my study of the great book when an old friend, Eitaro Ogawa – the boy who had carried me home the time I had injured my foot – told me that there was in Kyoto a place where the Bible was taught. It was, he explained, a Christian Extension Lecture House. The news astonished me, and on a cold Sunday evening Eitaro Ogawa and I joined an audience of perhaps thirty for a lecture on the Bible.

The lecture house was run by the American Presbyterian Mission, but the lecture that evening was hardly typical of Presbyterianism. The speaker was the Reverend Shimagoro Chira, a soft-spoken, quiet man with a pale face set off by a beautiful long black beard. His attitudes, as I reflected on them later, were more Confucian than Presbyterian. He was not doctrinaire, but serene. I discovered later that he was not an ordained minister, but merely a licensed preacher.

It is a curious thing that my first experience with organized Christianity should be at the hands of so atypical a speaker. Had he pressed on his listeners some of the doctrine – predestination or the divinity of Jesus, say – which a more standard preacher would have concentrated on, I might have walked out of the lecture hall, finished with Christianity forever. But instead of presenting the doctrine which I was never able to accept, he talked in a Confucian spirit of supreme ethics, and I was entranced, utterly absorbed. He spoke mostly of the story of Moses leading the Jews out of the wilderness, a story with which I was familiar, and he used the name of Jesus Christ only in the prayer at the end of the sermon. I was carried along with him.

When the sermon was over, an American missionary jumped into the pulpit. He had a foxy face, and he was showing a broad smile. "My name is Gorbold; now let's all sing a happy song." And he taught us this simple song, which seemed to be his main accomplishment.

> I'm so happy,
> I'm so happy,
> I'm so happy,
> Happy all the time.

He sang this refrain three times, and then asked us all to join in. Coming immediately after the meditative sermon, this obvious little song had a blatantly disruptive, almost hysterical effect. Then, when the song was finished, he distributed cards on which we were to write our names and addresses and followed this with an announcement that he would supply a bibliography for Bible study to anyone who wanted it. The whole thing was done so quickly and in such a businesslike fashion that there was hardly a chance to say no.

I was beginning to feel sorry that I had come to this odd gathering, and as I wandered toward the door, I was having second thoughts about Christianity. Then, at the door, Shimagoro Chira, the Japanese preacher, approached me, full of grace, and kindly spoke to me for a few minutes. He was glad I had come, he said, and asked me what school I went to and inquired a little bit about my background. I was caught by his magnetic personality, and that was enough to hold me. And so, the next Sunday I returned to the lecture house.

For the three weeks following I took great inspiration from the sermon of this wonderful speaker. He spoke calmly but convincingly, usually basing his sermons on Old Testament stories with which I was already familiar. Then this happy experience ended. Shimagoro Chira was replaced by a younger, tougher preacher. His name was Senji Hashimoto, and he had been a policeman on Formosa. Changing his course in life, he had studied at Tokyo Shingaksha Theological Seminary and been sent to our chapel as preacher. His old policeman's instincts stuck, apparently, for he was one of the most argumentative men I have ever met. His sermons bristled with theological arguments, and they usually lasted nearly two hours. (With the two-hour sermon, singing, reading of the text, and the informal prayer Protestants like, the service often took three hours; the unfortunate women present were often late getting home to cook the midday meal for their equally unfortunate husbands.) He also liked to shake his fist or pound his hand on the lectern to reinforce his arguments, and the noise he created was frightening. Once he slammed his fist so hard that the huge pulpit Bible fell off onto the floor, breaking its spine. Obviously somewhat ashamed of himself, he stood silent, expecting one of his audience to pick up the book and return it to the pulpit. We were all too awed by his furious manner, and none of us dared dash forward to replace the heavy book. In the end he came down rather sheepishly himself and picked it up. The incident was typical of the man.

It seems to me that it was typical of early Christian missionaries, too. Mission societies preferred to send tough, aggressive preachers into Japan, rather than more meditative, religious people. These missionaries were inclined to attract Japanese converts of the same type, and the Christian religion, as it developed in Japan, had a driving, propulsive quality, which was undoubtedly effective in some way. On the other hand, it had a tendency to call forth a stubborn resistance in Japanese who valued the traditional culture. Curiously, after World War II, when the traditional culture broke up, taking with it the resistance to Christianity of the population at large, Japanese Christianity itself became soft. The old zeal died. Apparently, it needed the pressures from outside to keep its driving force alive.

Senji Hashimoto had an enormous influence on my development. He was the man who taught me Bible and Christian doctrine. Though he had many virtues, I regret having come under the hand of so tough and argumentative a man at such a crucial age in my life. I was in middle adolescence. During this period boys are naturally disposed to rebellion. Although there had been always an element of stubbornness in my character, I had been fundamentally gentle and obedient. Experiencing the argumentative character of Senji Hashimoto at this time served to turn my stubbornness into argumentativeness, my adolescent demand for independence into outright revolt.

For all his shortcomings, Senji Hashimoto had his good points. For one thing, he spoke often on the Old Testament, which he knew well, and which was familiar to me and easier for me to grasp. Many Christian ministers do not know the Old Testament very well. Once I met a full-fledged minister who could not find the Book of Nahum for several minutes. But the Reverend Hashimoto knew the Old Testament, and I benefited from his teachings.

Secondly, Hashimoto was always ready to serve his parishioners. He willingly performed all his ministerial duties, including tending the deathbed and washing the body, even when the deceased had died of tuberculosis or typhus. He was also good at making marriages.[1] When Senji Hashimoto decided on a match, a wedding march was inevitable. He liked to bring complementary people together. Once, for example, he married a middle-aged midwife to a widower physician. Another time he picked a servant girl for a Nishijin weaver. Nishijin weaving is considered very beautiful, and the weaver presumably had a well-developed aesthetic sense. Unfortunately, the girl was short and dumpy. But when the weaver balked at the match, Senji Hashimoto lectured to him for hours on the meaning of marriage as put forth in the Bible, pointing out that what counted was not beauty or the lack of it, but the fulfillment of the Divine Will, until he finally convinced the poor weaver.

He had, furthermore, a good grasp of the young mind. A bachelor, he made it a practice to invite young men from his congregation to his house after Sunday morning worship. He would cook sukiyaki for them, a great favorite among Japanese, and see to it that everybody had a lively time. Between these tactics and his good services during times of sorrow he continuously added new members to his congregation. Yet as quickly as new people came, he drove the older members out by roaring theological arguments at them during the sermons. In sum, he failed to understand the Japanese. The long schooling Japanese of the day received in exaggerated courtesy and the masking of feelings led him to believe that his fierce sermonizing was being accepted. The reverse

1. At that period in Japan, a man did not court a woman; he, or his family, arranged for a go-between, who presented the man's case and arranged questions of dowry and the like.

was true; his audience was merely covering its resentment of his high-handed approach. They dropped out as soon as they politely could.

Yet I remained, constantly torn between those frightful sermons and the goodness he often displayed outside of the pulpit. Two things kept me going. One was the knowledge that I would lose face with my parents if I gave up my new faith so soon after espousing it. A second was the kindness and decency of a woman named Mrs. Hideko Yamamoto, who worked part-time for the congregation. She lived in an apartment above the meeting hall, and she took a motherly interest in me. She often took me up to her rooms after meetings and found books for me to read, especially pamphlets on the Old Testament, which she knew was my special interest. She cheered me up when I became downcast because of the difficulties of the road I had chosen, and she warned me against falling into the minister's tough-mindedness.

"You're a good Kyoto boy," she said to me. "Don't grow up to be an argumentative man."

So I drove myself on with my studies. There is a Japanese saying which goes, "A hundred readings will make it clear," and that was my method. Working without commentaries, I read the verses over and over. I wondered at the contrasting pessimism and burning patriotism of Jeremiah, and felt an inward cry that I was the same; I found Ezekiel difficult, but full of matter similar to Shinto; I was shaken and elevated by Isaiah. And I came finally to the New Testament, which created mixed feelings in me. The Gospel according to St. Matthew struck me as most familiar because it was the most Hebraistic of the four gospels. But aside from the Synoptic Gospels – Matthew, Mark, and Luke – the New Testament did not interest me much, except as a history of the Jews during the period of the Roman rule of Palestine. I was convinced Jesus intended only to be a reformer, and he died as Jesus, the Jew. I felt that to be a Christ was far from his intention.

Thus I made my studies. By the time I was nearing fifteen I had covered the entire Bible and felt that I had come to a thorough understanding of God. I was beginning to develop the rudiments of a philosophy, a manner of thinking about God and life. In those two years, from thirteen to fifteen, my life received its profoundest influences. I was changed forever, and my way was fixed.

It shouldn't be thought, however, that I was concerned only with my religious experiences. I was still an adolescent and, like most young people, needed physical activity. I had begun to study fencing. Classic Japanese fencing is nothing like the European type. It was developed by the samurai nobility during the Tokugawa feudal period in the 1600s. For sport, a long, heavy rod of bamboo is used as a substitute for the broad samurai sword. The swordsman attempts to attack the forehead, throat, trunk, and hand. As practiced in my youth, it was intended mainly as a character builder, rather than for the development of any physical skills. With eight other boys I would line up at seven o'clock in the morning in an unheated hall, where temperatures often went below zero. We fought for an hour on the freezing floor in bare feet. Three of us survived the two-week ordeal and were cited by the schoolmaster. Then one day he brought in an assistant teacher to duel with us as part of our advanced training.

He was a tall man in his twenties, tough-looking and eager to show off. I was merely a boy of sixteen, not yet fully grown. We started dueling, and then suddenly he took a position called *dai johdan-no-kamae* – the "great upper hand" position. It is one of the boldest and riskiest of positions in Japanese dueling. The fencer raises the *shinai* – the bamboo sword – as high over his head as possible, leaving his waist open and unguarded. If his opponent doesn't react quickly enough to strike at the unguarded midsection, he will be pounded hard on the top of his head. Fencers as a rule wear strong face guards made of steel, but the tops of their heads are covered only with a thin pad. This man had no business presenting such a position to a novice, but there was nothing I could do about that, and, in desperation combined with indignation, I dashed forward, aiming for his neck. My sword struck; and at the same moment he backed up a step and slammed his *shinai* onto the top of my head. Ashes filled my skull, and I felt the shock to the soles of my feet. Then I collapsed.

When I came to fifteen minutes later, my comrades were bent over me anxiously, and the fencing master was checking my pulse.

"Are you all right? Are you all right?"

"Yes, I'm all right," I said. I wasn't, however. I had suffered a slight cerebral concussion. Had my opponent been a few pounds heavier, I would have been the beneficiary of a beautiful school funeral, complete with speeches by the schoolmaster and the mayor. Fortunately, the Almighty did not allow me this honor.

Still alive, I walked up to Mount Hiei above the town and sat down on a rock overlooking both Lake Biwa and the city of Kyoto, and contemplated my fencing future. I understood now how people had been killed in the sport. (A prince was one of them.) Sitting there I remembered a maxim of Confucius: "A wise man does not approach danger," or, to give the English version, "Discretion is the better part of valor." Thinking this, I began to feel dimly that yet hidden out of sight, life held out a purpose for me. In my ear I suddenly heard one of the phrases I had rehearsed so often: "The Lord is your guardian; the Lord is your shade at your right hand." Someday I would hear a clear call from the Lord; until then I must cherish my life with a little more care than I had heretofore. I decided not to continue at the fencing school.

I was now approaching sixteen, and my mentors in Christianity were urging me to join the church formally. The status of the lecture hall had been raised; it was now known as the Juraku Church. Even now I doubt that I was really ready to join. My knowledge of the New Testament was extremely weak. I knew the Gospels fairly well, but the Pauline Epistles, which comprise the real heart of New Testament doctrine, I had not read. Nor was I emotionally any better prepared. My feelings about Christianity were in conflict. There was much that bothered me, much I had not settled in my thinking about doctrine – such as the divinity of Christ – which were to plague me for years afterward.

In the hope that I might come to a better understanding of Jesus, I asked my Japanese minister to tell me something about Israel and the modern Jewish nation. He told me that the nation no longer existed, that the Jewish people had been dispersed and had melted into other nations as a stream of water disappears into the desert sand.

The answer surprised me; moreover, it struck me as somehow odd, so I asked Mr. Gorbold, the American missionary, for a better explanation. He gave me roughly the same answer: the Jewish nation was dead. This, he explained, followed the prophecy of Jesus, who had said, "Behold, your house is left unto you desolate. For I say unto you, Ye shall not see me henceforth, till ye shall say, Blessed is he that cometh in the name of the Lord" (Matt. 23:38, 39).

I still found the story hard to believe. Israel, as a nation, was so vivid and alive in my mind that I could not accept the fact that it had died.

Eventually, because the Old Testament, which I loved, was one of the two wings of the Scriptures, I was led to Christianity. I was baptized, and I answered the ritual questions. My head was sprinkled three times, and I became a Christian.

As a new, young member of the church, I was a source of joy for the elders. They put me to teaching Sunday school. As part of this task, I had to instruct the younger children in hymn singing; and out of that job, so carelessly taken on, sprung not only my first real understanding of music, but a chain of events which led ultimately to an irreparable rupture with my family.

Using the church hymnal as a text, I began working out for myself the meanings of the black lines and dots on the pages. I was too shy to ask the organist for help. Struggling painfully by myself, I gradually mastered the notes. Then I turned my mind to the organ, a small portable one the missionaries had shipped from America. This was more difficult; but we now had a new organist, a woman only a few years older than myself, and I had the courage to ask for help from time to time. During the summer vacation I had taken advantage of my free time and worked over the little organ. By fall, I was able to play any of the five hundred simple four-part hymns in the book. When I consider that I learned the rudiments of organ playing virtually by myself, I am astonished, looking back, at my accomplishment. Undoubtedly my childhood experiences with the quaint harmonies of *gagaku* music laid the groundwork for my triumph. (Later on, I was organist for my college chapel.)

Now that I could actually perform, my early love for music sprang up again with great force. I took enormous happiness in playing. At seventeen years of age, it seemed to me that to be a musician was far more than a mere means of earning a living; it was an ideal life, and I approached my father with the idea that I should go to music school. He was sympathetic to the idea, as he had been to my early desire to study horticulture. But the old pattern repeated itself; he began asking relatives for advice. Genjiro, my eldest brother, was solidly against it. An uncle, Kichinosuke, a prosperous gold brocade and damask dealer, whom my father asked next, was even more vehemently against the idea. Both felt that music was an effeminate profession, hardly suitable for a boy from as ancient a family as mine. (It was somewhat the same as an American boy suggesting to his father that he become a ballet dancer.) Unfortunately, my father had no real knowledge of the matter, and quite naturally he refused to let me study music.

I despaired. I had been determined to dedicate my life to music, and I was thrown into a deep misery. Inconsolable, I simply did not know how to deal with my unhappiness. Finally, I stopped going to school. For twenty days, just before final examinations, I spent my time wandering aimlessly through the woods and fields of the hills around town, watching the maples come to leaf and the flowers blossom.

Then one day, for no apparent reason I climbed up into the attic of our house, which was used, like American attics, for storage. There I came across a group of ancient ritual swords and daggers which had been handed down from generation to generation of Kotsujis. I picked one up and drew the blade from its scabbard. The steel was unstained. It shone with a queer, enticing glitter. I stared at it, transfixed, seeing my own face reflected in miniature on the shining surface of the blade. The notion of suicide passed across my mind. I could turn the knife on myself very simply. Then the power of my emotion forced me to take a deep breath, and the momentary spell was broken. In shock I dropped the dagger to the floor, where it landed point first and stood upright in the wood.

The suicidal impulse of that brief moment awoke my common sense. I ended the days of brooding over my parents' not permitting me to become a musician and returned to school. Yet for years the regret lingered. It wasn't until I was thirty that I was able to conclude that I was better off in other occupations. In the world of music there is endless strife and struggle, constant bitter competition. I love music still; but perhaps my enjoyment is all the greater for having remained an amateur.

At the time, however, I felt only the tragic loss of my great ambition. I began to entertain feelings of bitterness and resentment toward my family. Twice now I had been prevented from following a career I loved; twice I had been thwarted in a laudable ambition. And gradually, out of despair and anger, I began to form an audacious plan. I would break with my family. I would go to live in Tokyo, where I could be free and unfettered.

To understand what this meant, you must realize what a powerful position the father held in the family in that society. There is nothing comparable in American history. Not even the Victorian father of the last century controlled the life of his family as did the Japanese man of my youth. The children could do very little of importance without his consent, and this situation continued until long after they were grown up. The father had a strong voice in the occupations his sons chose, and he selected husbands for his daughters. His wife had very little influence on him. She was very much confined to a secondary role.

The idea, therefore, that an adolescent boy should leave home to strike out on his own was unthinkable, especially against his family's wishes. There was, in fact, a Japanese ceremony called *kando* to symbolize the cutting of the relationship between a father and son. It was normally used in cases of a prodigal son, who often would be given a last sum of money and then sent away from the family house forever.

Before I could break away, however, I had to have some place to break away to. Inevitably I sought the advice of my Christian mentors – Dr. Gorbold and the Reverend Senji Hashimoto. Just as inevitably, they suggested that I might be able to get a scholarship to the American Presbyterian College in Tokyo, a school run by a coalition of Dutch Reform and Presbyterian missionaries. I broached the idea to my parents. My mother objected. It made her unhappy to lose her baby from the nest.

But my father was the important one, and his reaction surprised me. Instead of objecting, he simply washed his hands of me. I had been rebellious. I had broken from the ancient religion. Now I wanted to break from the home itself. I could go to Tokyo to study at the foreign college, I could do whatever I wanted. The conditions he made were quite specific. I would be exempt from any interference from family or relatives, in return for which I was not to make any financial or other demands on the family. My father could not legitimately perform the ceremony of *kando* for me because, after all, I was not a prodigal; I was a youth with a very good record in sports and school. The effect, however, was the same. I was, quite simply, cut adrift. My personal integrity and the burden of tradition produced an inevitable conflict in my soul. But I managed to save my honor. The loss of traditional protection was the price I had to pay, and great sorrow was my lot.

That spring, at sixteen, I graduated from high school.[2] A soft rain fell almost silently when, on the evening of April 7, 1916, I went to the Kyoto railroad station with my mother and boarded the train for Tokyo. As the train melted into the darkness, my mother stood in the station weeping bitterly. On the train I also wept. I would not return to Kyoto for seven years, nor would I see any of my family for that long time.

---

2. Primary school ran for six years, middle school for five, high school for three.

Chapter Five

American Presbyterian College stands on a piece of high ground in Tokyo called Shiba-shirogane. Founded in 1869 by Dutch Reform and Presbyterian missionaries, it introduced baseball to the Japanese. It is built around a quadrangle. In my day most of the buildings were wooden, many in the Japanese style, with an admixture of Western-style brick buildings. Some of the buildings of the theological seminary were made in the style of the eighteenth-century Dutch and the chapel was nineteenth-century Gothic. The college emphasized the teaching of English; half the teachers were American. (One of them was the father of America's former ambassador to Japan, Mr. Edwin Reischauer.)

The dormitory to which I was assigned was called Severance Hall, after the man who paid for its construction. A low, wooden Western-style building, something like a barracks, it was largely cut off from the sun. It was always dark, dank, and gloomy; no sun fell through its windows. To a boy from a city like Kyoto, where natural beauty was everywhere, the contrast could not have been more vivid. The depressing atmosphere was hardly calculated to enhance the feelings of a young boy torn for the first time from his home. Beautiful weather was rare; whenever we had a bright, warm day the students did not attend their classes, but went off together to have a sukiyaki party.

As a rule, the students attended classes six hours a day and spent most of the rest of their waking hours studying in their rooms. The classes were, for the most part, taught entirely in English from English texts, which made our work doubly difficult. It took a stubborn and determined student to finish the course.

Here at the college, I began a seven-year ordeal, which, however much it taught me about the virtues of patience and fortitude in the face of adversity, scarred me for the rest of my life. I marvel yet that I survived. My financial condition was frightful; I lived in abject poverty. The college supplied my room and my food for nothing. I ate in the main dining hall. It also supplied me with a scholarship which purchased an occasional candy bar. I couldn't buy any clothing; I had to depend on the compassion of my mother, who despite my father's views, occasionally sent me a kimono. I had difficulty getting the books I needed, even at secondhand prices, and of course there was nothing left for entertainment or travel. Occasionally, later on, I was able to earn a few extra sen tutoring American teachers or their families in Japanese, but this income was spotty and meager.

I could have borne the poverty, however, had it not been for a worse tribulation: the collapse of my health. I began, during the first year of my stay at the college, to feel inexpressibly fatigued. My throat was chronically inflamed, and I seemed to be suffering from an ailment similar to malnutrition. As the second year passed, the condition worsened. Exhausted most of the time, I found work of any kind difficult. I had to drag myself through my studies, and I was forced to cut down heavily on my tutoring jobs, which served to worsen my financial plight.

The crisis came during the summer after my third year in Tokyo. I was staying in Tokyo for the holidays. One summer night I slept at a Buddhist temple in the room of a friend of mine who boarded there. In the morning, we had a cup of breakfast tea together, and then he went off to his duties. Shortly after he left, I felt a constriction in my throat. I coughed to clear it. Still the constricting feeling persisted. I coughed again, and gradually I began to notice that I was having difficulty breathing. Something was clogging my lungs. Then I realized what it was. In sudden fright I dashed to the old granite sink and there I began to vomit blood. Standing by the sink I coughed again and again, hoping I would avoid being strangled by my own blood. I wondered how long I could live; for it was now clear that I had been suffering from tuberculosis for years.

Then, miraculously, the hemorrhaging stopped. I lay down on my friend's mat, exhausted and weary, my chest and lungs aching painfully. Then, when I felt enough strength to move, I crept back to my own room, collapsed on my bed, and lay there, hardly daring to move lest the bleeding start again. For twenty-four hours I lay still; when I finally dared to move again I felt as if I had risen from the dead.

I went then to a doctor. He told me solemnly that I must take three years of absolute rest if I were to survive. I despaired. I knew that if I did any such thing I would forfeit forever the opportunity of studying at the college and with it chances to make something of my life. I sat in my room, considering. Finally, I made my choice: I would take my chances with the tuberculosis, for what was the point of clinging to a life I did not want?

In the end, the hemorrhaging proved beneficial. I grew somewhat better; but still the tuberculosis lingered, keeping me weak and tired all of the time.

I was still in this condition three years later, as I approached the end of my university schooling, when a kind of a miracle occurred, as if the Almighty had decided to intervene in my case. There was in Tokyo a Dr. Shusaku Fukui, who claimed to have invented anti-tuberculosis shots. Not only could his serum prevent the disease, it could produce a cure in a few months if the disease was caught in the early stages. Naturally, people were skeptical. To erase popular doubt, Dr. Fukui said that he would have another specialist take X-ray photographs of his patients before the treatment and again when he felt the disease was cured. It was public skepticism that kept him from publishing his cure, despite his own confidence in it. He was, he said, a simple general practitioner. Unless he had overwhelming proof of the efficacy of his treatment the medical profession would still his small voice, and he planned to wait until he had ten thousand cures to his credit before he made his findings public.

I heard about his work, and his confidence in it impressed me. I decided to try it. He began by giving me six shots in the back. Almost immediately my appetite picked up. As he continued giving me the shots, my temperature dropped to normal and stayed there. Within five months I was completely healthy. Incredibly, my tuberculosis was cured.

Even in these days of antibiotics and miracle drugs a cure like this would not be taken for granted. At that time, it was astounding. Why did the cure never become popular? Four months after I regained my health Dr. Fukui was crushed under his house by the Great Earthquake of 1923. His wife and his assistant died with him. With him also went his medicine and his records, totally destroyed by the quake and the fire which swept through the area in its wake. Such are the accidents of chance. Had he lived to publish his cure he might have become one of the world's great benefactors. As it was, he saved only a few people. I was one of the last.

My six-year fight against tuberculosis, though the worst of my troubles, was hardly the only one, particularly in those first days away from home. During those beginning months in Tokyo, I was often struck by a deep remorse over my break with my parents and a powerful desire to be home again in my old, familiar surroundings, a feeling my constant illness had fed. Yet I could not return without great loss of face. In Japan of that time – indeed up until World War II ended – a youth who left home against the desire of his parents could return only if he came heaped with honors and accomplishments. Then his parents would take him back with tears of joy. No homesickness, no regret, was strong enough to override that loss of face.

Then one morning toward the end of my third year, I awakened to hear ringing in my ears the great Psalm of David: "I lie down to sleep; I wake again, for the Lord sustains me." My fragile life, I then understood, depended not on parents, no matter how compassionate, but on the Lord God of life. Suddenly I felt the strength to sustain myself for my studies, no matter what trials beset me. The thought of retreat to Kyoto was gone.

A second problem I faced in my early days was the absence of the kind of comradeship I had been used to at home. I was a little frightened by the tough country boys who came to the college from odd, remote places, and I was ashamed of my Kyoto accent. The difference between Kyoto and Tokyo speech is somewhat like the difference between the accents of the North and South in the United States. Kyoto is softer and slower; Tokyo is sharper, more precise, and often caustic. The vocabularies are slightly different as well. My Kyoto drawl, because it was soft, set me apart from the majority and made me an easy mark for teasing. I attempted to change my accent to the Tokyo fashion, but I found the task virtually impossible. It is not a matter of accent alone, but of vocalization. I gave it up as a bad job. As the years passed, I was not sorry, for it began to seem to me that the Kyoto vocabulary has deeper significance in its nuances than the Tokyo one.

As studded with misfortune as my college years were, they were not entirely without their joys. Primary among these was my increased experience with music. My voice was good, and I joined a male quartet called the Gregory Band, after Pope Gregorio I, who created the famous Gregorian chant. I sang first tenor, and in those days, I could produce the high G. My experience with this group is one of my fondest memories of college. Those of us who belonged to the band developed strong bonds of loyalty and friendship. We stuck together as much as possible, united by our love of music. Ultimately, two of us became professional musicians.

Along with my singing, I developed my organ playing. In time I was asked to be the organist for the college chapel service. The organ, compared to the one I had learned on in the Kyoto church, was enormous, equipped with two keyboards and a set of foot pedals. It was not pumped electrically, but by hand. One of the janitors, a man whose name I remember as Ohkubo, was required to pump it. Ohkubo was short and bald, and he did his pumping behind a small screen next to the organ, which was supposed to hide him from view of the congregation. The screen, however, was about an inch shorter than Ohkubo, and as he pumped, his bald head appeared rhythmically above the screen. During fortissimo passages, when he had to pump very hard, he made a quick little jump on each stroke, so that the louder I played, the larger a section of his bald dome flashed above the top of the screen. The sight, needless to say, was not conducive to the solemnity expected in chapel.

My desire for musical expression must have been insatiable. Organ and voice were not enough. I had a burning desire to learn the violin as well. Fortunately, the conductor of the Gregory Band was the assistant professor of violin at the Academy of Music at Uono. He liked me, and he promised to give me free violin lessons, if I found an instrument. The offer excited me; more important, I knew where there was a violin for sale. In a tiny secondhand shop near the rear gate of the campus, I had seen an old, dusty violin hanging, which was probably very cheap.

"Three and a half yen," the owner told me.

I despaired. Even this infinitesimal price was more than I could afford. Three and a half yen would pay for ten days of rice. Five yen – the tiny pittance I had in my pocket – was reserved for some medicine I was supposed to be taking for my debilitated condition. I walked slowly out of the shop and down the street with heavy steps.

The violin acted on me like a magnet. It pulled me, tugging me back toward the shop. I stopped, turned, and walked a few paces back toward the shop. Then I remembered my medicine, and I turned sadly around again and went on a few paces, when the magnetic lure of the instrument stopped me again. For fifteen minutes I walked up and down the street behind the campus, first tugged this way, then that. Finally, I made my decision. I might recover my health without medicine, but I could never learn the violin without an instrument. I returned to the shop, bid the price down to three yen, and took the dusty, battered violin home with joy. Thereafter I studied with my violin teacher friend for four years. Those three yen were an investment of incalculable value. For the rest of my life the violin has been a source of solace and great joy.

Despite my devouring interest in music, my studies were of primary importance. I spent a total of seven years at the university. The first three at the college were devoted basically to languages. In addition to English, I labored over Latin, German, and Greek, which I studied for seven years. I excelled in languages and was often at the head of my class. The heavy emphasis on languages, especially Latin and Greek, later enabled me to read the Bible and early theological writings in their original tongues. I became interested in comparing various translations, and it occurred to me that when my command of the language was good enough, I would prepare parallel translations of the Bible in the five languages I knew: English, Japanese, classical Chinese, Greek, and German. It was not until I studied in America that I became aware of the Polyglot Bible, in which Hebrew, Greek, Latin, English, and German versions exist in parallel order.

The last four years of my study in Tokyo were at the seminary school attached to the college. Here I began to face the doctrines which had bothered me from the moment of my first contact with Christianity. My life there was difficult, for a deep intellectual crisis was added to the problems I already had with poverty and poor health. Despite my tribulations, I must be grateful to the seminary. There I laid the foundation for the later studies which were to become the heart of my life. Without the seminary teaching, much that I did later would have been impossible. Not only did it enable me to develop my English into a workable instrument, but it gave me the opportunity to learn both German and Greek. Through Greek I was able to look into the Septuagint and other Greek translations of the Scriptures, an experience which widened my views of the Bible immeasurably.

My study of Hebrew alone disappointed me. I was very anxious to start with Hebrew, and during my first year at the seminary I found a course in the ancient tongue. I signed up for it eagerly. But after a few classes I began to have an uneasy feeling that the teacher had no real command of the language. His grammar did not seem to make sense, and his method of pronunciation filled me with doubt. I resigned from the course.

A few days later, as I was walking through the halls of the seminary building, I heard somebody call my name.

"Mr. Kotsuji."

I stopped and turned. It was Professor Tsuru, the Hebrew teacher. He spoke sharply. "Why did you leave my class? Don't you care for Hebrew?"

I was trapped. "Yes sir, my desire to learn Hebrew is serious."

"Well then, why didn't you keep it up?"

I hesitated, searching for words. "I'm sorry sir, I just wish to be excused from the course." I did not have the courage to say anything further.

Professor Tsuru frowned. "Why do you dislike my class?"

"Because... because...." At that moment the president of the college came down the corridor. I appealed to him with my eyes, and he joined the conversation and saved me, both from the situation, and from being forced to learn Hebrew incorrectly. It was, undoubtedly, presumptuous of me to question my professor's competence on so scanty a knowledge of Hebrew as I possessed, yet fortunately my insight was a correct one. None of the students who took that course ever learned to translate correctly a single chapter of the Scriptures from Hebrew. It may seem odd that a Christian seminary should teach a biblical language so incompetently; but I have since discovered that Hebrew is often badly taught in seminaries.

Of course, the main interest of the seminary I attended lay in the teaching of the life of Christ. It was taught with reverence, sympathy, and understanding. I responded sympathetically to the life of Jesus. Despite all of his accusations against the scribes and Pharisees and despite his burning desire to correct the evils of his age, it was as a Jew that he lived and died. He wanted the Jews to abandon their blind observance of law and ritual, which he felt lacked spiritual significance, and substitute genuine faith in God.

Although I responded to Jesus, I could not accept Pauline theology. Paul was a Jew by birth and education and thus a real apostate. His major doctrine of salvation by faith bears a close resemblance to the mystic religion of Mithraism, which was widely practiced in the Greco-Roman world around the time of the birth of Christ.[1]

I reacted similarly to Church history, which was not surprising in a Protestant seminary in that time and place. The history of the Catholic Church was presented as little more than a series of bloody controversies, quarrels among church leaders, and vast persecutions, with the Spanish Inquisition at the summit. It seemed that the teachers were more interested in justifying the Protestant revolt than in exploring the continuity of Christian thought.

As a result of my seminary studies, one fact came home to me clearly: Christianity is not genuine monotheism. All the major branches of the religion – the Roman Catholic, Greek Orthodox, and a few Protestant groups – accept the Nicene Creed, which, among other things, defines Jesus Christ as "very God of very God." I felt that Christianity was contradicting itself, that it could not consider itself to be a monotheistic

1. Mithraism, a sort of reverse Christianity, was based on a myth that described the Son of God – represented by Mithra – as killing the father – represented by a bull. Much of the content of its ritual is startlingly similar to Christianity.

religion and at the same time maintain the Godhood of Jesus. Curiously – or perhaps not so curiously – neither the students nor the professors at the seminary liked to debate the contradiction I saw here. They shied away from the whole subject.

I could not ignore the matter. Finally, I went to Professor A. K. Reischauer, who lectured on systematic theology, and who had written a highly reputable book, *Studies in Japanese Buddhism.* I caught him just as the students were leaving his lecture room.

"Professor Reischauer, I want to ask a question which is very important to me," I began seriously.

He noticed the gravity of my demeanor and halted at the door. Smiling his usual sardonic smile, he turned and led me back to one of the long classroom benches, where we sat side by side, a discreet neutral space between us. "Well, young man," he said, "let's have your question."

"May I speak bluntly?"

"Of course."

I gathered my forces. "When you use the word 'Lord' in your prayers, who do you mean?"

"I mean the Lord God," he said.

"But you pray in the name of Lord Jesus. Please, one of these two Lords must be the true one, the other merely a name."

He hesitated. "Well . . . ."

I took a deep breath and plunged ahead. "Jesus taught, 'No man can serve two masters: for either he will hate the one, and love the other.' Jesus was a Jew, who believed in one all-powerful God, and yet Christianity has this dualism of Father and Son."

Dr. Reischauer was often quick tempered, although in theological discussion he invariably remained calm. Now, vastly to my surprise, he simply burst into laughter. When at last he pulled himself together he said, "You're right, Mr. Kotsuji. Theoretically Christianity is essentially a dualism. The gap cannot be bridged."

I was startled to hear a Christian teacher of theology so frankly and openly admit to a contradiction in his religion; yet, despite my admiration for his openness, I continued to press the argument.

"You say Christianity is theoretically a dualism; what about practically?"

He sobered a trifle. "Practically, Christianity offers monotheism." He watched my face quietly.

"The contradiction is still there, Dr. Reischauer. Who handed down the practice?"

"Jesus himself."

"Then Paul, who founded Christianity, must be an apostate. Is that not so?"

He smiled sardonically again. "That's up to you."

"But if you rule out the Pauline documents from the New Testament, along with the doctrine in them, you won't have much left."

I was disappointed – not with Dr. Reischauer, but with Christianity itself. This good teacher recognized my disillusionment. "Don't let all this contradiction dishearten you. Christianity is a practical religion in the end. Resist the temptation to split theological hairs and someday you'll make a fine preacher." He leaned forward, bringing his face, now serious, closer to mine. "He that increaseth knowledge increaseth sorrow," he said quietly.

Despite Professor Reischauer's kindness and concern, the crisis was not resolved. As I came to the end of my studies at the seminary it began to dawn on me that I had not yet found a career for myself. My health was still poor. It was clear that I was not strong enough to undertake the rigorous training necessary for a musical career. By the same token, it did not seem possible for me to teach. Considering the condition of my lungs and throat, it didn't seem likely that my larynx could stand four or five hours of daily lecturing. That left very little other than a career as a Christian minister open to me; and my worries about the contradictions of the Christian religion seemed to disqualify me. My essential belief that Jesus was a humane Jew or at most a devout Jew was the result of my interpretation of Christian doctrine. Thus, it seemed to me that all roads were closed.

Troubled, I pondered the problem for a long time, and then I decided to discuss my worry with Dr. Ibuka, president of the seminary, a sober and sensible man who had always looked on me with understanding. I went to him and asked him to help me find a life's work.

"Well," he said, considering, "there is a call from a Presbyterian church in Asahikawa, on Hokkaido. It's a hard climate. The temperature goes down to thirty below zero in the winter. But it's healthy."

"I'm not worried about the climate. What bothers me is my lack of conviction in Christianity."

"Don't worry. No minister has perfect conviction. Most are just striving to reach it. Don't press for pure orthodoxy. It will come to you in time. You have been a conscientious student. Take it easy, enjoy the pastor's life and get your health back."

Deadlocked as I was, the advice made good sense. At that moment I decided that I would teach my strong belief in One God and His loving-kindness; what else was necessary for salvation? Once more I set my eyes on the Old Testament, and all the doubts and struggles about the contradictions in the Christian faith seemed to fly away. I decided to accept the call from Hokkaido.

Chapter Six

The kind, wise words of Dr. Ibuka helped me to cope with these growing theological doubts to the extent that I was able to undertake Christian work. But kind words could not win for me a battle with the church authorities.

In order to graduate from the seminary, it was necessary for the student to write a theological dissertation on a theme selected by the examining committee, which was chosen by the general congress of the church, as well as to give a sermon. The theological paper caused me no trouble. It was essentially a matter of scholarship. The sermon, however, was a matter of faith. To escape the contradictions in my Christian belief I wrote a purely theistic sermon that failed to mention Jesus at all.

The sermon caused an inevitable uproar among the university officials. Some understood my doubts, felt sorry for me, and wanted to pass the sermon. Others were simply angry. But I could not disclaim the sermon; I could not change my mentality. In the end the missionary groups felt that the sermon ought to be passed, but the Presbyterian Examining Committee, which had the final word, refused to accept it. This solved nothing, and finally a compromise was reached. I was to pass conditionally, with the proviso that I study more about Jesus Christ for a year. I felt ashamed to have been turned down in that manner, but this did not prevent me from leaving the university and starting on a career.

I had accepted the call from the church in Hokkaido, but before I went, I had a sentimental journey to make. I had left Kyoto as a boy of seventeen. I had not seen my home, my family, or the places of my youth since that rainy spring evening in April 1916. Now, seven years later, it was time to return.

I went back to Kyoto. My mother wept to see how thin I was; if she had seen me six months earlier, when I was still suffering from tuberculosis, she would have despaired. Tears streaming down her face, she held my *tatami* mat in her hands, examining it. When I had left home it had been a plump three inches thick. Now it was a hard-packed inch. How cold it must have been to sleep on all those years. Why hadn't I written her for a new one? I knew there wasn't any point in trying to explain to her that I had endured that cold for an independence I would not have traded for a new sleeping mat.

I told the story of my seven years; my mother laughed and wept. I saw my brothers again and my uncle, Kiichiro Ishida, for whom I had great respect. They gave me some clothing and new bedding, and then, toward the end of April of 1923, I left Kyoto by train and headed for Hokkaido. I was finally and at last a man, an independent citizen of Japan.

Hokkaido is the northernmost of the four main islands of Japan. About 250 miles square, it is the second largest, the most sparsely populated, and by far the coldest part of the country. The climate and topography are similar to those of Canada or the northern United States. In the winter, temperatures go down to thirty or forty below zero. Pine trees cover the hills, deer and bear roam the forests; there is splendid cod, herring, and sardine fishing off the coasts.

For hundreds of years Hokkaido has been the home of the Ainu, the original settlers of Japan. They are rather European-looking people with abundant, curly hair and stocky physiques, and about fifteen thousand of them remain on Hokkaido. Hunters and fishermen, they are looked upon by the Japanese as the remaining Indians are regarded by Americans. Once they were the sole inhabitants of Japan; but as, over two thousand or more years, newcomers streamed in from Korea, China, and other parts of Asia to create the population of modern Japan, the Ainu were driven north to Hokkaido. But even here they found no peace. After the Meiji Restoration in 1868, serious efforts were made to colonize the empty spaces of Hokkaido. An overpopulated nation like Japan could ill afford to let a quarter of its territory lie empty.

Thus, when I reached the island in the spring of 1923 it still bore the scarring marks of recent colonization. It must have resembled – in feeling at least – the frontier towns of the last century in Oregon and lower Canada. Asahikawa, the town to which I was called, had very much of a frontier look. At that time supporting perhaps twenty thousand people, its streets were unpaved and the roofs of its rough wooden buildings were largely thatched. There were hardly any automobiles there and those few belonged to the military contingent stationed in the town. Even if there had been many cars, they would have been unusable half the year; in winter the snow piled up in ten- and twenty-foot drifts. Transportation around the city was by "street car" sledge. The Ainu, who lived around the outskirts of the city, were usually visible in the streets, but even for them there was nothing to do. There were two small movie theaters in town; that was the extent of its amusement center. For pleasure, people walked in the woods, hunted, fished, and ice-skated. It was a simple life and in many ways a good one. The cold was excellent for one's health. (The old-timers like to boast of the year it went to forty below and the petroleum froze in cans.) During my stay in Hokkaido my health improved rapidly, until I was finally, for the first time in many years, a completely well man. I even learned to skate, although I was never very good at it.

My church was a big barnlike building, which seemed more like a warehouse than a church, for it was totally without ornament. It was, however, big enough to hold several hundred people. My job was to fill it. I discovered on my first Sunday that this task wasn't going to be easy. When I came out into the pulpit, I stared down at twenty faces looking lost and lonely in the huge spaces of the building. Afterward I expressed my astonishment to one of the elders.

"The church is thirty years old," I said. "How is it possible to have such a small congregation?"

The elder shrugged. "We made an effort to get all active members to attend your first sermon."

"You have a lot of inactive members, then?"

"Yes," he said. "At least a hundred."

I was surprised. "What happened? How could you possibly lose so many members?"

The elder shrugged again. "They were proselytized in a hurry, before they had much idea of what Christianity was all about. They backslid almost immediately."

The general tedium of life in Asahikawa helped me to solve the problem of my empty church. With nothing to do in their leisure time, the people inevitably took an interest in the new Christian minister who had arrived from Tokyo. I was young and passably good looking; I was educated; I could speak several languages; I played the organ and the violin. All of this impressed the people of Asahikawa, and soon I was something of a minor celebrity in the city. My church began to fill up, especially with young, marriageable girls. A group of them circulated a photograph of me among themselves; it was obvious that most of them were looking for husbands.

However, the dullness of life in Asahikawa had its evils, too. It helped to fill my church; but at the same time, it turned the minister into something like a part-time entertainer. I was expected to be available for conferences whenever anyone wanted to drop by, and far worse, I had to make that constant round of visitations which are the bane of Christian missionary life. Ministers in Japan suffer more than others in this respect. Each visit calls for a cup of green tea. The poor minister can't refuse it, for fear of offending his host. By the end of the day, I was often nauseated. Generally speaking, the practice of daily visitations is an enormous waste of the minister's time. A man of God ought to have maximum time to devote to study, to meditation, to communing with the Highest. Adding to my difficulties was the fact that my stock of entertaining material ran short after a few months. When I first arrived in Asahikawa I had much to talk about: my youth, my college experiences, stories about what I had seen and done in the great cities of Kyoto and Tokyo. When my storehouse of stories was empty, however, my parishioners began to grumble. "He told that same old story, again," they complained after I had left.

I was urged especially by the elders to make regular visits to the rich men in town, in the hope of recruiting them for the congregation, and they asked me to preach on the subject of charity. I was supposed to point out to the members that God would reward them for contributing to the church. Another time a church elder wanted me to play my violin in the theater he owned. I refused to follow these orders. I preached that the material blessings, prosperity, and pleasure, didn't matter, that they are evanescent, and easily lost. I told them that the true blessing is to feel God's hand on your soul.

I hoped to become a righteous person, so internally beautiful that people would want to emulate my religious example. I wanted to be a religious as great as Samuel, a preacher as powerful as Isaiah, a leader as bold as Abraham. But this was impossible. The elders felt that they could not raise money to support the church unless I carried out the Christian ideal of service, with its constant visitations and its emphasis on social work, charity, and relief of the poor. I grew to hate the myriad details which interfered with my pursuit of religious knowledge.

Feeling as I did, conflict with the church elders was constant. Part of the trouble, it seems to me now, was inevitable in a small congregation. Where only a handful of people provide the minister's support, each is likely to feel that the minister is in his own employ and that he has a special right to his services. It did not take me long in Asahikawa to begin to feel that perhaps I had made a mistake and that perhaps my natural bent was not right for the Christian church. The thought depressed me. Instead of the optimistic viewpoint a Christian minister needs I became pensive and questioning.

Yet all was not without hope; my emphasis on pure religion helped me to develop a following among young people and those who were troubled and sorrowing. The young people came to me for help with family troubles, with the pains of love, with those nameless longings of youth, and sometimes even with stories of crime. From this devoted following I took much solace; it was the most meaningful thing in my religious life in Hokkaido.

My public life was not always happy; but fortunately, my private life began to improve radically shortly after I came to the church. During all my years at the university I had avoided the company of girls. I had felt that since my health was very poor, I ought not to risk marriage, or even a close association with a girl to whom I could bring only sorrow.

In effect, I lived like a monk, tasting neither the joy nor sorrow of love, and in recompense, I enjoyed the sweetness of a composed mind.

When I came to Hokkaido and my health began to improve, this frozen peace of mind began to thaw, and I decided I wanted to marry.

Despite some changes in the old traditional ways, most Japanese marriages were still arranged in the 1920s. Usually the parents of the young couple settled the matter, working through a go-between, but sometimes, especially when the parties were adult, a friend or mutual acquaintance might act as middleman.

Dating between the young couple was very much frowned upon as vulgar and unmannerly. Usually, the bride and groom were barely acquainted on their wedding day.[1]

Mineko Iwané was the daughter of a wealthy landowner of Sapporo, the capital city of Hokkaido. It is about seventy-five miles from Asahikawa, a city surrounded by flatlands and low hills. Her father, Seiichi Iwané, had been born into the nobility in the 1850s, before the Meiji Restoration. A good-looking youth, he had sat at the right hand of his feudal lord and would certainly have grown to be an important figure among the samurai.

The Meiji Restoration changed all that. When the feudal system was abolished at one stroke, Iwané found himself without a future at sixteen. Striking out on his own, he took advantage of the efforts of Emperor Meiji to colonize Hokkaido. He was assigned to the first pioneer mission on the island. In time the local government sent him abroad to study stockkeeping and then appointed him head of the meadowlands belonging to the Imperial household. He was just twenty. By virtue of his natural abilities he continued to rise in the world. When I came to Hokkaido, he owned a private meadow of one thousand acres and lived almost like a tribal chieftain.

I had decided not to marry any of the girls in Asahikawa, in order not to create jealousies and petty envies. Mineko Iwané was a Presbyterian, and I met her at a party in Sapporo, in June 1923, and was immediately struck by her beauty. Graceful, pretty, with exquisite manners, the

1. Kissing, of course, was unheard of. It was introduced into Japan only after World War II, by the American occupation troops.

daughter of a wealthy, aristocratic man, she was obviously able to marry someone better than a poor Christian minister. Yet after the party I could not forget her. Simply looking at her gave me a clean, fresh feeling. The host of the party suggested the marriage, and according to the old tradition I was to allow him to do all the negotiating. Instead, I began to write to her. She answered my letters. This correspondence was indeed unconventional. After a few more letters, however, we grew bolder, and I met her in Sapporo occasionally. We did nothing more than walk around the countryside a bit, but even this took great courage, for it simply wasn't done. Our love flowered, and we decided to marry.

Although her father was willing to permit the marriage, a good many of her relatives were against it. Mineko's sisters had married into wealthy families; why should she not do likewise? Why should the last girl be consigned to a poor scholar? As a matter of fact, it was something of a source of wonder to me that I had succeeded with so well-placed a girl. Of course, my family heritage was good; there could be no complaints on that score. What really swayed Miné in my favor, however, was my scholarship. Everything about the situation fired me with new ambition to become a great scholar, so that I could justify my wife's faith in me against the opinion of her relatives.

We were married on October 1, 1923. Normally marriage in Japan is a civil matter, conducted at home. Since we were both Christians, we were married by a Christian minister. My parents were not present, for the recent earthquake in Tokyo discouraged them from travel. After a honeymoon in Tokyo, we made a brief visit to my parents' house in Kyoto, and then we returned to Hokkaido, where we moved into the parish house next to the church. It was a cold, small, dismal place, and I felt sorry for my wife, who had been raised in luxury. She never once complained, and I was very grateful.

Happy as I was in my marriage, however, my religious work continued to trouble me. The pressure on me to search out wealthy parishioners and to preach agreeable sermons continued. Moreover, I was beginning to discover that there were some people in my church who did not want any new members at all. The older people in my church dwelt upon the time when the church was new and belonged to a handful of people who worked together and built it. Of course I could sympathize with their feelings. Yet if they had their way the church could never grow. I had to overrule them as well as I could, and the result was constant friction.

Making matters worse was a general anti-Christian feeling which blossomed after the United States Congress passed the Immigration Act of 1924. The act, which grew out of a feeling in the United States that a flood of post-war immigration would change the country's complexion, virtually shut off immigration from Asia. The Japanese people felt insulted, and the entire country became violently angry. They transferred their negative feelings onto Christians, whom they identified with America. Hokkaido did not escape the hysteria, and there was strong anti-American feeling among the members of my church. I tried to calm them, and inevitably my words were interpreted by the local military authorities as favorable to the United States. They sent an inspector to my house to question me about my activities and beliefs. Fortunately, I had my family lineage to fall back on. When the inspector realized that my Shinto ancestors were closely connected with the imperial house, he lost his nerve, made a polite bow, and left.

It was beginning to grow clear to me that I would have to make a change in my life if I was really going to do effective work. Already forming in my mind was the thought that I ought to leave the church; the seed was as yet small and undeveloped, but it was there, and it might have grown to fruition then, had not a wind blown events from a different quarter.

One noontime, as I sat in silence with my wife, contemplating the possibilities for my future, my wife said softly, "What are you thinking about so hard?"

I merely shrugged.

"Too much knowledge increases sorrow," she said quietly. "Stop thinking for today. Go to a public bath, relax, and let go of your worries."

Pleased by this sensible advice, I went out. In the public Japanese bath of the day there was a tub in the center of the room, surrounded by a wide stretch of floor space. One never washed in the tub itself. The washing was done on the floor; then one sat in the tub and soaked in very hot water afterward. The heat was excellent for circulation, and it acted as a tonic for the spirits.

This day, happily, only one old man was in the bath, and he began a conversation immediately. Much to my astonishment, he spoke with a Kyoto accent. In a moment we were talking together like old friends.

"I take you for a scholar," he said. "Am I right?" "Partly," I told him. "I am a minister." He shook his head. "A man like you ought not to stay in as rude a place as Hokkaido, when he could live among the shrines and temples of Kyoto."

So we talked about Kyoto, and I told him of my ancestors who had been priests at the Kamo Shrine.

He shook his head sadly again. "It's too bad you're a Christian, instead of a Shinto priest. With your lineage you could have been a great success." He paused. "Have you ever been to Gifu?"

I said I had not, although I had heard of the place.

"It's like Kyoto," he said, "only more so. Kyoto has hundreds of shrines and temples, of course, but in Gifu the people of the town really live religious lives. The town is a big center of Buddhism, and the religious spirit is everywhere."

The old man's words sparked my imagination. Living in a town dedicated to religion in such fashion appealed to me greatly, and I said so.

He nodded. "You're young, you can still head in any direction you want."

We conversed a little longer, and then we parted saying, not *sayonara,* but *sainara,* in the Kyoto fashion.

My meeting with the old man was prophetic. A few days later I received a scroll letter written in the traditional brush-stroke style. The penmanship was familiar, evoking old memories; it was in the hand of the Reverend Hashimoto, the argumentative preacher whom I had met in my adolescence. I read the letter, and to my astonishment discovered that there was an opening at a Presbyterian church in Gifu for a minister who knew not only Christianity but Buddhism as well. Gifu was crowded with dignified and scholarly Buddhist priests. The Christian church needed a man who could command the same respect from the people of the city. My lineage was as ancient as that of any of the Buddhist priests of the city and my scholarly training as good. I seemed like an obvious choice to the Reverend Hashimoto.

I was overwhelmed. I did not think I measured up to the responsibility, and I wondered if I could manage it. At the back of my mind was still the thought that one day I might leave the ministerial profession, a profession for which I was not certain I was suited. Yet many forces prompted me to accept the offer: the problems I was having with the elders in Hokkaido; my desire to take my wife to a warmer, happier land; and above all, the curious meeting with the old man in the bathhouse. After some mental struggle, I decided to accept the call.

Gifu is a middle-sized town in central Japan near the port city of Nagoya. It is only about seventy-five miles from my hometown of Kyoto; it is one of the prettiest towns in the country, and today it is something of a tourist attraction. It lies along the Nagara River, a swift, scenic stream above which rises a hill known as Kinkazan. On top of the hill is an ancient castle, and because of the castle and the beauty of the river scenery the river has been called by Westerners the Japanese Rhine. Gifu is noted for two things: paper lanterns, a local manufacturing specialty; and cormorant fishing. The cormorant, a bird which looks something like a duck, is worked by fishermen from a long tether during the nights from May to October. The birds snatch up a little fish called *ayu* from the river; because of a ring around the bird's neck, it cannot swallow the fish. When the bird has filled its gullet with twenty or so *ayu*, the fisherman hauls it in, and squeezes out the catch. The birds are highly trained and seem to take pride in their work. All told, Gifu is a charming and fascinating town. The two years we spent there were happy ones, and the extraordinary beauty of the city contributed not a little to the joy my wife and I felt there. I think that if I could have lived right at the riverside I might never have left.

Moreover, I was now earning sixty yen, which at that time was a good salary for a minister and enough to keep us in comfort. Thus, virtually everything about the change was an improvement. My wife was delighted to leave the cold, comfortless atmosphere of Hokkaido, and I found Gifu, filled as it was with highly cultivated Buddhist priests, a great challenge. During the time I was there I studied hard and was especially proper in my behavior in order to compete with the Buddhist priests. We worked hard, and we enjoyed ourselves. We liked to climb the hill up to the castle, and we liked to go and watch the cormorant fishing. In all, the experience in Gifu was deepening and enriching.

My experiences in Hokkaido had taught me something, and I had brought some resolutions with me to Gifu. The first of these was that I would readily and instantly give up my post without regret the moment I felt that there was any dissatisfaction with my preaching. This determination was important, for it freed me for my second resolve. It was that I would preach boldly and honestly, without soft-pedaling the messages of the Bible. This turned out to be an excellent decision, for the reaction was far better than I had expected. My boldness brought me far more respect than I would have received from a lifetime of ordinary ministry. I said to my parishioners right at the beginning, "God is not asking you to become members. You must ask if you can join. Nobody is required to stay. Anyone who wants can leave this church." They stayed.

The old man had been right about Gifu. It was a thoroughly religious town. There were expensive gold-plated altars in the windows of many of the stores. The religious experience was a common one; religion was everywhere and people were accustomed to turn to it naturally for solutions to their problems. Priests and ministers were constantly visited by people who in other places were seeking the advice of psychiatrists or lawyers. Criminals came for help, star-crossed lovers for advice, the mentally ill for solace. In Gifu I sometimes had to deal with genuine schizophrenics and paranoiacs.

From this point of view, life in Gifu was exciting. Religion filled my days. I studied a great deal, and I fell into the habit of meditating with the Most High in one of the densely wooded hills around town, even in the dead of winter when the air was full of snow.

In Gifu, too, my wife and I were blessed with another happiness, the birth of our first child, a beautiful little girl whom we named Aiko. She was never to grow up; but our tragic loss brought by her death in later years was in part compensated for by the pleasure we took in her while she lived.

We had much to enjoy in Gifu; yet, despite the charm of the place and the excitement of its religious atmosphere, there was still a shadow over my happiness. At the back of my mind, the old problem of my belief continued to nag at me. How could I continue to be a Christian minister when I could not accept so many of its major doctrines? I tried to believe, I tried to accept, but much of the Nicene Creed – the virgin birth, the trinity of the Godhead, the ascension of Christ, and much else – was merely words to me. I found the stories of the birth of Christ as recounted in Matthew or Luke beautiful and poetic. Yet I could not take them for more than an emotional fabrication based upon one tiny fact.

A change was inevitable, and while I was in Gifu two things precipitated that change. The first involved my reading. I had become interested in archaeology, and I had studied as many books on the subject as possible. Inevitably a good deal of what I read was about explorations in the Holy Land and of the work archaeologists had done there. And as I read, it gradually dawned on me that the true, original religion of the Bible actually existed. Judaism was alive. As this realization grew in me, I was filled with enormous elation. It was astonishing to me that I had never known it before; surely somewhere in my studies I should have found this out. But I hadn't, and now the knowledge moved me deeply.

I was in this state of mind – excited by the discovery of Judaism and perplexed by Christianity – when a small incident occurred which pointed it all up. Early one winter evening I answered a knock at the door, to discover a leper standing there. Gifu is often visited by lepers, who count on the sympathy of its Buddhist population for help.

"I'm sorry to bother you so late, but I'm ashamed to walk around during the day," he said.

"That's all right," I said. "How did you happen to choose my house?"

"Because we have met before."

I stared into his deformed, horrible face. "What is that? Who are you?"

He pronounced his name. "I was with you in college. I was studying English literature when you were at the seminary."

I was startled and speechless. He was trembling with cold. "Come in, come in and get warm," I said.

"No, I don't want to come into the light. I'm too ashamed of my face."

I remembered his gay student days, and I thought of the torment of shame he was undergoing as he stood on my doorstep, and the tears blurred my eyes. I remembered, then, a story about Dr. Kagawa, a great Japanese religious leader, sometimes called the Gandhi of Japan. Once

Dr. Kagawa took into his home and bed a beggar who was suffering from trachoma; Dr. Kagawa then contracted the disease, from which he suffered the rest of his life. Should I do likewise? Yet what, after all, had the great man given that beggar!

"What can I do for you?" I asked.

"I need clothing."

"Of course," I answered. "And you could use some money, too."

He nodded silently. I took from my chest the clothing I had bought for my own winter use and gave it to him, along with enough money to keep him going for a few weeks. "Where are you headed?" I asked.

"No destination. No end. No tomorrow, but it's a long, impatient way."

Then I told him I would help him to get into a leprosarium, where he might at least live more peacefully, and sent him on his way.

And it was then I felt ashamed. I was supposed to be a religious leader, and yet what could I do for this poor man?

I could not take him into my bed; I could not take him into my house. I wanted only to send him on his way. For what else could I do? What use was my religion? I searched my soul.

And so, the time came when I knew that I must turn away from the religion of the New Testament and turn back to that of the Old. I determined that I would go to America and take up the study of Hebrew.

Chapter Seven

When a young man reaches the age of twenty-eight he ought to be settled in his work. For me, this was not so. Twenty-eight was my beginning, not an end; for it was with my trip to America that I came alive to the things which were to become so important to me.

My decision to go to America was occasioned by the fact that during the two years in Gifu I preached almost exclusively on the basis of the Old Testament texts. The New Testament interested me less and less, the Old Testament more and more. It was clear to me that no matter how strongly the New Testament had been presented to me by my spiritual overseers, my heart lay with the book of Israel. The sensible thing for me to do was to become an Old Testament scholar, with the ultimate hope of teaching it. Such study was impossible in Japan, of course; America was the obvious place for me to go, for many reasons. In the first place, I knew English better than any other foreign tongue. In the second place, my church connections would help me secure admission to a college. Last but not least, I had retained a childhood yearning for a chance to visit this great country which had appeared so gay and free-spirited in my elementary textbooks.

The decision seemed sensible and easy enough to make. But to finance the trip was another matter altogether. I was naturally not inclined to ask my parents to help. I had come this far without them, and I did not want to do anything to jeopardize my independence. I felt, however, that I could safely ask them for enough money for second-class passage for my family. Once in the United States, I assumed that I would be able to survive. They sent me enough money for third-class passage. My brothers were able to add a little more; but the real help came from an unexpected source – my wife, Mineko.

One evening as we sat considering the matter she said, "I know of a way to raise some money."

"Oh?" I replied.

"I will sell my kimonos."

The offer meant a great deal more than it may seem. One of the largest portions of a Japanese woman's dowry was her kimonos. A wealthy man such as Miné's father gave her kimonos as presents from time to time, and she added to them herself later on. They were both her most significant property and a symbol of worth and status, comparable in a way to the flat silver a Western woman inherits, or gradually builds up over the years. My wife had several dozen kimonos. Therefore, she was a rich woman; to sell her kimonos for her husband was an act of great sacrifice.

"No," I said, "I can't allow you to give up anything so important to you."

"Did Abraham's wife carry many kimonos with her when she followed her husband from Ur?" she demanded.

"No," I admitted.

"Then I will follow the example of Sarah," she said. "Besides, it would be a waste of money to ship them all to America."

"A woman's regret can linger long, Mineko," I said.

"Please don't think of me as Lot's wife," she answered.

She was clearly serious, and I let the subject drop in order to give her feelings a chance to quiet down. If she did nothing further about it there would be nothing to regret, and I would have the gift of her desire to be helpful to me.

She said nothing further; nor did I. A few days later she came up the street accompanied by a fat, middle-aged man carrying a *juroshiki* – a kind of carrying cloth used for making bundles. I understood, but I did not interfere. She saved only a few of her favorites. The dealer carted away the rest. She never once complained or looked sorrowful. In fact, I was more depressed than she was; it was a sad thing for a Japanese woman to part with her kimonos, each representative of a piece of her parent's affection for her.

Because of her sacrifice and the money my family gave us, the trip to America was now possible. Through officials of my church, I was matriculated at Auburn Theological Seminary, then at Auburn, New York.[1] A generous scholarship was granted me, and in the spring of 1927 I advised the elders of my church that I was leaving. They were surprised – even shocked – for I was just beginning to get a thorough grip on my work in Gifu. They tried to dissuade me, but my mind was made up. I left, feeling deep inside me that I would never return to the ministry, and on July 23, 1927, my wife, my child, and I boarded the *Tenyo-Maru* at Yokohama, bound for the United States.

We landed at San Francisco; our stay was brief, but it included one important event. We were met by the Reverend Dr. Hata, one of my superiors in the Presbyterian church. I asked him, in conversation, what he knew about the living religion of the Old Testament.

He knew very little about it. Once, he explained, he had been invited to attend a Jewish service. He told me about some of the rituals and customs. "I uncovered my head in order to show respect for the congregation," he smiled. "There was a bit of a flurry. In the synagogue men are supposed to remain covered."

"But that's exactly what they did in the ancient religion," I said excitedly. To me, this simple fact was a stirring piece of news. It was confirmation that the religion of the Old Testament was alive, was immediate, and was practiced in some measure at least as it had been thousands of years before. But Dr. Hata's information was limited. I was still outside the Jewish religion, and I knew of no way to get in.

From San Francisco we took a Panama Line boat to New York City. Everything was new, exciting, and bewildering. We slid into New York

1. It has since been moved to quarters on the Union Theological Seminary grounds in New York City.

harbor at dusk on a September evening. The huge buildings towering above us appeared to be gigantic monsters with golden eyes; to a simple tourist they were living creatures, awesome and mammoth.

From New York we took a sleeper – another new experience – to Auburn and there I began my real education.

Auburn is a typical upstate New York small town. It sits on Lake Owasco, about twenty-five miles from Syracuse. The seminary was run jointly by the Presbyterian and Congregational churches, who picked Auburn for their college when it seemed likely that the town was to become the state capital. The hope did not materialize, and as a result the seminary, sequestered as it was in this sleepy American town, developed a homey, family air, which however charming, was not conducive to great scholarship. A second drawback for a man in my position was that Auburn offered little in the way of part-time work; and of course there was no companionship for my wife, at least at first. I would have been far better off in New York City, where I would have had a wider variety of courses available to me and where I probably could have earned a little extra money translating or doing other scholastic chores. Today I still regret that I did not make the change. If I had made the Jewish friends then that I have made since, my path to Jerusalem might have been thirty years shorter.

But I did not know, and I matriculated for the Bachelor of Divinity degree at Auburn. We were virtually paupers; and I had to live apart from my family. I moved into Morgan Hall, a dormitory where I could live rent-free, and my wife and child went to live with a professor who had a house on campus. That period was the only time I have ever had to live away from my family. It was lonesome for us all, but it had one virtue: undistracted by family demands, I was able to study long hours without interruption, and I accomplished a great deal.

My studies were mostly confined to Hebrew and the Semitic languages. Because I had already taught myself a good deal of Hebrew grammar, I was allowed to start with the second year. In order to really grasp the language, I decided to follow the same method I had used to learn my native tongue. Like all Japanese children, I had learned Japanese from my mother, who had spoken it to me day in and day out. By the time I was old enough to speak, I had already developed a sense of the language. Over the years, hundreds of hours had gone into developing that sense, and I decided that in order to develop the same sense of language in Hebrew I would have to be exposed to it for many, many hours. In addition to skill and methodical study, I would have to devote to my studies considerable time. I resolved then to steep myself in Hebrew for six solid hours every day. As I had other subjects to deal with, I had to study my Hebrew from eight at night until two in the morning. Since breakfast at the seminary was served at six sharp each morning, my regimen allowed me only four hours of sleep. I adhered to this rule the entire time I was in the United States, over four years in all. There is no question but that such a method of study is dangerous for one's health, and I warn students against imitating it. But I survived it and inevitably the effort showed up in the quality of my work.

The man whom I worked most closely with and who taught me my Hebrew was the professor of Semitic languages, Dr. William Hinke. He offered courses in Aramaic, Arabic, and Assyrian; and he specialized in Hebrew archaeology.

The school offered no course in the Talmud, which I was eager to study, and I asked Dr. Hinke if he might give me a brief introduction to it.

"Christian students don't need the Talmud. It's a waste of time for you."

"I thought you would say that" I said. "But didn't Jesus study the Talmud?"

"I assume so," he responded. "He was, after all, a Jew."

"Then why shouldn't I imitate Jesus?"

After that he gave me a few private lessons in the Talmud, quoting to me bits and pieces of the great text. It was a great experience for me; for it marked my first real glimpse into the world of Jewish lore. Dr. Hinke's knowledge of Hebrew was profound, and his understanding of the Talmud was sure. I have always suspected that he was born a Jew, although I didn't, at that time, dare to ask him. Because of my timidity, I again perhaps missed a chance to shorten my road to Judaism. I had discovered that there was a synagogue in Auburn, and I occasionally walked past it; but just as I could not bring myself to ask Dr. Hinke if he was a born Jew, I felt that I would have been intruding if I had entered the synagogue. During my entire stay in Auburn, I never had the courage to investigate it.

In the end, my stay in Auburn lasted only a year and a half. Auburn's limitations became obvious to me. I had covered all the courses in Semitics and the Old Testament that the seminary offered, and I was anxious to go further. I had heard of Professor William Frederic Badé, a noted biblical scholar and archaeologist, who had made several expeditions to the Tel-en-Nasbeh diggings near Nablus, north of Jerusalem. A Dutchman, Dr. Badé was one of the most brilliant archaeologists of his day and a formidable linguist besides. He knew all the Semitic languages, the Romance languages, and his grounding in German was so solid that he had lectured at Göttingen University.

Dr. Badé taught at the Pacific School of Religion in Berkeley, California. Originally organized as a Congregational theological seminary, it had been turned into an interdenominational school. In practice, it was virtually nondenominational. Its administrators were broad-minded enough to allow Jewish rabbis to speak occasionally, and once a Japanese Buddhist studied there. It seemed like the logical place for me to go; and in the spring of 1929 I made arrangements to transfer to Berkeley.

To travel there was a more difficult matter. Train tickets were beyond our means. Instead, I got a friend in Auburn to give me driving lessons. I practiced for a week, and then bought an old Oldsmobile for forty dollars, loaded my family into it, and headed west.

The car was overpriced, even at forty dollars. If I had known anything at all about automobile mechanics, I would have never undertaken the venture. The wheezing Oldsmobile could not go over twenty-nine miles an hour, and it was a strain to do that. In this time-worn vehicle I expected to cross the Great Western Plains and climb the Rocky Mountains.

We had hardly left New York State when the car began to fall to pieces. As we wandered through the Midwest, we left behind us a trail of broken parts, along with small portions of our meager supply of money. Nearly every day a small repair had to be made. By the time we crossed Kansas and Colorado, we had only a few dollars left. As we entered New Mexico we had only sixteen carefully hoarded pennies to our name.

Feeling desperate, we drove down a mountain road when suddenly an Indian stepped out of the shadow and, blocking our path, stopped us. Visions of every Western movie I had ever seen rose up in my mind, and I nervously looked at his belt for scalps.

He fumbled in his pocket and drew out a can. "He wants canned food," I whispered to my wife.

"We haven't any," she said. "We have hardly any food left. What can we give him?"

"Opeen, opeen," the Indian said, holding up the can.

We began to laugh. I handed him our can opener. He grinned broadly, nodded his thanks, and stepped out of the way of the car.

We were winding down out of the mountains into Gallup, New Mexico, when the motor made a peculiar noise, one I had never heard before. We lurched down the road, into town. The noise grew louder. As we came into the middle of Gallup the car suddenly gave its death rattle and stopped dead on the main street. Simultaneously the gas ran out. Despair in my heart, I looked around and saw that I had been vouchsafed a miracle. The car had given up the ghost directly in front of a Japanese restaurant. During the several days we spent in Gallup, waiting for money to come from a friend in Berkeley, the townspeople received us cordially and took good care of us. If they still live, my gratitude goes out to Mr. Yoshimi and Mr. Hayashi, of Gallup.

Although I had the largest possible scholarship at Berkeley, we were still extremely poor. I managed to find an attic room for twenty-five dollars a month, and we managed somehow. I was able to do a little tutoring from time to time, especially in Greek, and that helped. Still, an extra five dollars a week would have been a Godsend, we were so close to destitution.

Dr. Badé was extremely generous to me, to the point where envious students began to comment. He permitted me to use his private library, and although he was required to teach only four hours a week, he used half of them to offer a course in Semitic epigraphy for me alone. He kept warning me that I would ruin my eyesight and my health in general if I did not cut down on my studying, yet undoubtedly it was the long hours I put in on my books that moved his scholarly conscience to help me in any way that he could.

Within a short time at Berkeley, I completed my work for the Bachelor of Divinity degree and began working toward my doctorate. I chose to specialize in archaeology, partly because of Dr. Badé's influence and partly because I had become more and more convinced that, contrary to the opinion of the day, archaeology would testify to biblical truth. Poor biblical scholars, meaning to be devout, shy away from archaeological fact because they fear it may contradict the biblical message. My own feeling is that dodging such contradictions will only serve in the end to undermine confidence in theology.

My studies, however, were only part of my Berkeley experience, for something else of considerable importance happened to me while I was there. One day I took my courage in hand and walked into a synagogue. It happened to be Temple Emanuel in San Francisco proper, a large Reform synagogue. I had begun to know a little more about the Jewish religion, and I chose the Reform synagogue in part because I knew that it was fairly difficult for outsiders to participate in an Orthodox service, due to the complicated siddur and *tefilla*, as well as traditional customs. Partly I chose Temple Emanuel because it was close to a streetcar line convenient for me to ride.

On that first day I walked in and asked one of the ushers if I could buy a prayer book. He looked at me with interest. "Are you a Japanese Jew?" he asked. He was full of curiosity and goodwill, and I might have told him I was.

I said instead, "No, I'm not. As far as I know there are no Japanese Jews."

"Can you read Hebrew?" he demanded.

"Yes," I said.

"Really? That's interesting. Come in, come in." He took me into an office and, full of curiosity, picked up a prayer book from the shelves. Opening the page of "*Shema Yisrael*" (Hear, O Israel) he handed it to me and begged me to try it. Of course I read it without faltering.

He was astonished. "Wonderful. Are there no Jews in Japan? How did you develop an interest in Judaism?"

Briefly, I recited my history. He was delighted. He refused to let me pay for the prayer book, and he urged me to attend service any time. From then on, I attended the synagogue every Sabbath. At the same time, I seldom attended the Christian church. I was not a Jew, I was a Presbyterian minister, and my obligation should have been to Christianity. Yet I was drifting away from it, and there seemed to be nothing to prevent me.

Dr. Badé was a wise man and right about many things. One of them was the matter of my health. For three years it stood up to the rigors of my studying regimen, but inevitably lack of sleep and overwork caught up with me. In the fall of 1930, as I was making the final push to complete my doctoral dissertation, I caught a cold, which rapidly developed into a stubborn bronchial cough I could not shake off. I dosed myself with cod-liver oil (today it would have been vitamin pills) but I did not slow the pace of my studies.

To make matters worse, Dr. Badé had arranged a job for me. At the time I was in Berkeley, he was continually receiving case after case of archaeological fragments he had dug out on his recently completed expeditions to Nablus. He gave me the job of unpacking these objects and restoring them. They came packed in straw chaff, and when I worked with them, straw dust was in every breath I took. Furthermore, the solvent used to restore the objects contained ether. This too I breathed in. Therefore, with the lack of sleep, and breathing in ether and dust, I became desperately worried that my tuberculosis would recur; the effect was only to make me work harder. I raced against my health to finish my dissertation.[2]

The kindness and great human spirit of a man named Tokinobu Mihara saved me from total collapse. He was the thirty-seven-year-old editor of a small Japanese-language paper for the San Francisco area, called *New World.* Despite my scholarship, my job in the Palestine Institute, and my occasional tutoring work, I was constantly pressed for money. Tokinobu Mihara, whom I had met in the San Francisco Japanese colony, befriended me. Watching my health gradually give way under the strain of my studies, he concluded that I would simply ruin

2. Among the articles I restored was an incense burner dating back to the time of David. When in 1960 I visited the school as I passed through San Francisco on a lecture tour, I saw the incense burner in the exhibition hall of the school's Palestine Institute.

myself unless something was done. He was not a well-paid man himself; nonetheless he managed to spare some of his salary for me every week. When I finally finished my work and went to speak to him about returning the money, he shook my heart with his words.

"I don't want the money back. If you want to do something sometime, pass it along to other poor scholars who need it." His kindness was overwhelming. Not only did he give me money, but he also arranged for me to lecture on the Old Testament in Christian Japanese churches and put himself out in other ways for my benefit. The example of his lofty spirit and great humanity has remained with me always.

In the spring of 1931, I finally finished my work, defended my thesis on "The Origin and Evolution of the Semitic Alphabets," and prepared to end my American experience. For my wife and my family it had been a turbulent, busy time. For one thing, our second daughter, whom we named Mary, had been born in Berkeley in February, 1931. That in itself had been an experience. My wife's English was poor; the doctor asked me to stay with her during childbirth, to act as translator, something never done in Japan.[3]

America itself had been a great experience. Contrary to what we had expected, we found very little anti-Japanese feeling or prejudice. People for the most part were kind and generous to us, and we were given the opportunity to remain here. The University of California offered me a position teaching Japanese language and history. My wife begged me to take it. She wanted to stay in the United States forever. In truth, America is a far better place for women than is Japan. It shocked me, when I first arrived, to see men rise when a woman came into a room, to see them take off their hats when a woman walks into an elevator. The women, for their part, seemed to accept the courtesies as their right, rather than as a gift. Brought up believing that women held a distinctly second place, I was annoyed by their attitude. Once, when some of us at Auburn had been invited to the president's house to hear a recording of Beethoven's Fifth Symphony and I failed to rise when five girls came in late, I was criticized; but I replied, "Which deserved the homage, Beethoven's Fifth or

3. In fact, in Japan the man does not even come to the hospital but waits at home for the news.

five girl stragglers?" They could not respond. Today, now that I have seen more of America, I am no longer so shocked and angry by the behavior of women. I suppose this means I have become a little Americanized.

The basic difference I feel between the Western world and the East is the Western habit of analyzing, verbalizing, abstracting. This kind of thought process makes Western science possible, but it seems to me that there is a loss of some of the beauties of life. The Eastern mind works figuratively. The Oriental is intuitive, subjective. Where the West is prosaic, the East is poetic. Where the West analyzes, the East symbolizes. Western poetry, for example, is inclined to be long, narrative, and explicit. Eastern poetry is very short and indirect, implying much by saying little. It is understandable, then, why the Old Testament, with its strong Oriental mystery and symbolism, fired my Japanese mind while the directness of the New Testament failed to strike a spark.

I left America as a Jew more than a Christian.

Chapter Eight

We left San Francisco in September 1931. It was a prophetic time to return to Japan and an ominous period in the history of the entire world. We were still on the ocean when the Japanese army marched into Mukden and the Manchurian Incident – the harbinger of fifteen disastrous years of world history – began. I will have more to say on this subject later; for the moment, let me turn to personal matters.

We had been gone from Japan nearly five full years. I had seen my parents and close relatives only twice in fifteen years – once after my marriage, and once more before we left for America. Both of those occasions had been unceremonious. But now I was returning from five years of study in America with a doctor's degree, *magna cum laude,* and fluency in several languages. I had gained the honors necessary to reunite me with my family. When we landed in Japan, I took my wife and children directly to Kyoto. The family welcomed me back into its bosom. They honored me with a banquet given for all our relatives, and they praised my work. It was a source of deep satisfaction to me to have proven myself in their eyes.

Honors, no matter how pleasant, do not feed a family, and jobs were not necessarily easy to find, even for PhDs. That fall, Japan was in a turmoil. The depression which struck most of the world during the early thirties crept up on Japan as well. Prices fell, and people were out of work. Propagandists on the left and the right battered the public ear; rioting in the streets grew more common; and a Communist organizer was shot down in the Tokyo station. Japan did not escape the ferment and turmoil which led to revolution in Spain, Nazism in Germany, and Fascism in Italy.

Fortunately, I came home just at a time when the Theological Seminary at the Aoyama Gakuin University in Tokyo was looking for a man to teach the Old Testament and Semitic languages. It was not precisely what I had hoped for. I preferred teaching ancient history or peripheral studies at a non-Christian university where I might avoid doctrinal problems and be able to teach what I wanted as I wanted. However, because of the incipient depression, Japan's colleges and universities were all trying to economize. One does not get everything one wants in life and consoling myself with the thought that if Israel could eat the bread of Egypt for four hundred years, I too could wait for the time God may prepare. I decided I had better accept the position at Aoyama Gakuin University, and I moved my family to Tokyo.

The two years I spent at Aoyama Gakuin University in Tokyo were possibly the most placid years of my adult life. They were a moment of calm between the ardors and tribulations of my Christian years and the storms which were to follow.

Prior to my coming to the university, study of the Old Testament had been pushed off into a corner. As in many Christian seminaries, concentration was on Christ and the New Testament. In my inaugural lecture I took advantage of the opportunity to create an interest in the Old Testament by making my lecture as stimulating and exciting as possible. I was successful, at least in part, and I began to attract students. I was able to bring fresh, sound scholarship to subjects which my poorly trained predecessors had made either dull or too difficult. Unhappily, my success occasioned some resentment among some of the Old Testament scholars in Tokyo, many of whom were simply inadequately prepared.

It was during this period that our third daughter, whom we named Julie, was born, on July 4, 1932. We were now a cozy family of five. I took pleasure in my work. I was doing well enough, and after the tribulations of fifteen years I felt I deserved a respite from trouble. I did not get it.

One midnight, early in October 1933, our eldest daughter, Aiko, aroused her mother from sleep, complaining of a pain in one of her fingers. She had been perfectly happy during the early evening and had eaten a good supper, so that nobody was especially alarmed by anything so minor as a sore finger. Mineko comforted her and went back to bed. But when I looked in on Aiko at six o'clock in the morning, our usual arising time, she appeared weak and flushed.

"I can't raise my head," she whispered. She could hardly speak. I immediately took her temperature. It was over 104 degrees. In extreme alarm, we called the doctor. He diagnosed the case immediately. Our six-and-a-half-year-old daughter had a type of children's dysentery, cholera infantum, very common in Japan at that time. The disease works extremely rapidly and is usually fatal. Poison created in the intestines moves quickly to the brain, finally paralyzing the heart action. We despaired. All that morning she lay still on her bed, exhausted. Her temperature continued to climb. By the afternoon she showed signs of cyanosis; by nightfall she was unconscious. All that night the doctors gave her camphor injections and managed to keep that small heart beating; but at daybreak it stopped.

In Shinto it is taught that the spirit of a good person goes close to God, and there is solace in that for the bereaved. In Christianity, the consolation of Heaven is less concrete, less easy to grasp, less solacing. Even so, in any religion it is difficult to face a personal loss. The death of Aiko was so real. We felt so alone, and the biggest solace was the people who came in and wept with us. When one is lonesome, those who join us in sorrow are most precious. Judaism says that a visitor to a sick person takes away one-sixtieth of his illness. Yet it was many years before my wife and I overcame the sorrow of the death of Aiko. Finally I understood that the loss had given me this virtue: I was able to console people who had suffered a similar tragedy. I think that it is better to smile when you visit someone who is in mourning, for a sad face simply gives the bereaved a heavier load to carry.

Two weeks after the death of Aiko, my wife and I, still suffering from the burden of our loss, were out walking with our two babies, Mary and Julie, still in the carriage. Suddenly I began to feel odd, as if cold water were running through my body. I was instantly uneasy.

"Mineko, let's go home."

"What's the matter?"

"I feel a little strange," I said, "but it's nothing."

We rushed home. I tried to eat but couldn't manage it. Feeling suddenly weak, I slumped down heavily on my bed, and, as if on cue, my temperature started to rise. For a week it fluctuated wildly, and then the doctor diagnosed my disease as typhoid fever. I was taken to the quarantine hospital, and a municipal employee went through the house, disinfecting everything. My wife, in an agony of horror and disbelief, could only stand and stare blankly at him as he went through her rooms.

Typhoid fever has one peculiar side effect. It often works havoc with the memory of the victim. One man I knew, recovering from typhoid fever, could not recognize any of his family. Sick as I was, it never occurred to me to worry about a possible memory loss. To pass the time in the quarantine hospital, I rehearsed Hebrew verses hour after hour. I did not do the same with my English, and one day, not long after I had been discharged from the hospital and was resting at home, I picked up an English book and began to read it. Startled, I discovered that I was stumbling over passages I had always read easily. To test myself, I began to read aloud.

"Mineko, my English doesn't sound right to me. Listen, please."

She listened while I read a bit. "No. No, you used to read it better." She paused. "For God's sake, what about your Hebrew?" I snatched up a Hebrew Bible and began to read. Her features relaxed. "Yes, your pronunciation is as good as ever."

It was a relief that my Hebrew was saved, for my livelihood depended on that. Still, it was a year before my normal facility in English returned. Nonetheless, I was not able to return to my teaching job. Once again poverty stared at us.

Gradually, over a period of three or four months, my health and strength returned. I was feeling almost like my old self when I noticed an intermittent pain in my stomach, or side. I did nothing about it for a week or so, but it persisted, and I was thinking that I would have to visit a doctor, when my wife fell ill with pleurisy. This last in the unbelievable chain of disasters almost ended matters for us. For weeks she lay helpless in bed, while I nursed her. At odd moments I washed, cooked, cared for the two little girls, and picked up whatever part-time work I had the strength for. All the while the pain in my side persisted. It had been diagnosed as chronic appendicitis, and I had been told that I must have my appendix removed immediately. But until my wife was able to care for our children this was of course impossible. For three months my wife lay helpless in bed. Then, as she began to recover, I hired a maid, spent ten days training her in her work, packed a suitcase, and went off to the hospital to have my appendix removed. It had been a year of torture, but it was over.

At times like these, when the foundation of a family is shaken by disaster, many couples move toward divorce, holding each other responsible for their trials. That is the time, however, when the marriage bonds – the oath to love in sickness as well as health – ought to be remembered. Mineko and I remembered.

One other virtue came from the disasters. During the time that Mineko was sick and I was forced to remain at home, I began to write a Hebrew grammar, the first one ever put into Japanese. I had the time, and it served to distract me a little from the ache of my appendix.

Now, however, I was faced with reestablishing a way of life. Given a choice, I would have wished a lectureship in Semitics, but there was no such thing offered at any Japanese university. A second choice would have been the chance to teach the Old Testament for its own sake, rather than as an adjunct of Christianity. But there seemed little likelihood of that.

I considered: What is a university? Is it the scholars? Or the buildings? Or its institutional status? The answer was obvious: A university is its faculty. I thought of the private scholars of Chinese philosophy and literature, who, during the feudal period, were so respected and renowned. I thought of the poor rabbis of Jewish history. I thought of Yoḥanan ben Zakkai, the founder of the *beit din* at Yavneh. Was it for his wealth or his learning that he earned his place in history? Again, the answer was obvious; and from that moment on I knew that the solution to my problem was to establish my own school – an Institute of Hebrew Studies, where I could teach as I pleased.

With the help of a few friends, I was able to organize the Institute of Biblical Research. Through the favor of Mr. Auler, a broad-minded and sympathetic man who had charge of the Bible House on the Ginza, Tokyo's main street, I was able to use the eighth floor of the building for my lectures, and on October 1, 1934, I opened the doors for the first time.

I had only a handful of students that first night, but the number increased rapidly, until I had fifty on my rolls. In Japan it is not usually difficult to find students if you have something to offer them. I drew on theological students from the Christian institutions who wanted better teaching in Hebrew studies than that offered at their own colleges. Many students came from Tokyo University, especially religion, history, and education majors. In Tokyo there was considerable interest in Hebrew studies, which had been stimulated by Christianity. Besides, it is the sort of study that Japanese like. I lectured only in the evening, and I concentrated on the basic course, the Hebrew language and the Old Testament. At last I was able to teach that great book without Christian interpretation.

I never expected to get rich from my work at the Institute, and I did not. Each student paid only a small tuition. It was enough, however, to enable me to support my family in comfort, something I had not done very often. In addition to what I earned from my teaching, I earned some money from the sale of my Hebrew grammar, which was published in 1937, and from the publication of my doctoral dissertation, which had been well received in the academic press.

Yet the envy I had stirred up among Old Testament teachers during my stay at Aoyama Gakuin University continued to plague me. Because I had studied the Old Testament from an archaeological point of view, I was able to fill my lectures with details about biblical life and times which made them more colorful and exciting. Inevitably, I drew students away from the seminaries, and this only served to worsen matters. No university likes to lose students to a private teacher, and one evening, when I went to open the doors to my classroom after an absence of a few days, I found the doors locked tight.

I went immediately to the janitor. I had been lecturing in the building for three years at that point, and it seemed to me there must be a mistake. I asked the janitor to open the doors, but instead of doing so, he put me off.

I got angry. "Why won't you open up the door for me?"

"I...I...." He looked away timid and apologetic, and I understood that something had happened while I had been gone. "Mr. Auler has authorized me to use this floor, you understand that, don't you?"

"Yes sir...but...."

"But what?" I demanded sharply.

He bowed several times and remained silent.

"Did Mr. Auler order you to lock the doors?"

He nodded, looking unhappy.

"I don't believe it. Mr. Auler isn't that kind of a man. You believe in the Bible don't you? Tell me the truth," I said sternly.

"He...was...pressed by...people."

So the whole story came out. A number of Japanese Christians of various denominations had apparently brought pressure to bear on Auler to close the building to me. When I finally persuaded the janitor to open I saw that they had gone even farther. All of my Bibles, papers, letterheads, and other pieces of small equipment had been thrown into a broom closet, where they lay in a heap in the dust. With tears streaming down his face, and trembling in fear of the sacrilege he feared he had committed, the janitor helped me to rescue my Bibles and wipe the dust off them. I got my possessions back; but the right to use the Bible House building was permanently withdrawn, and I ended up lecturing in whatever quarters I could find.

On a larger scale, however, events were working out to make my problems academic. By 1938 Hitler was in Austria. Japan was at war with China and had cemented its alliance with Germany and Italy, creating the so-called Rome-Berlin-Tokyo Axis. In Japan, the average citizen – and I was an average citizen – knew very little of what was actually happening in the world. The military clique had taken a firm grip on the country. The newspapers were rigidly censored; we were told what the military wanted us to know and nothing more. Things had reached beyond mere politics in Japan by February 1936, when a group from the militarist clique had raided the houses of a half-dozen top government officials and assassinated them. But because of the censorship, we had only a very poor notion of the flame spreading across the world. For example, I understood the war between China and Japan to have been instigated by the British, supposedly to impoverish and weaken both countries so that England could maintain its trade rights in the East.

The matter of most importance to me was the Nazi persecution of the Jews. I knew nothing about the details until much later, but the little I knew began to touch my life before that time.

What happened was this. With the signing of the German-Japanese pact, and the establishment of the Rome-Berlin-Tokyo Axis, the Nazis put immediate pressure on Japan to adopt the German policy of Jewish extermination. As far as Japan proper was concerned, the policy was relatively unimportant. There simply weren't enough Jews in Japan to constitute a "problem." But it was different in Manchuria and China.

To be very brief, Manchuria, although naturally and historically a part of China, has for the past seventy years or so been pulled back and forth between Russia and Japan. Each country has felt it belonged in its sphere of influence, and each has managed to gain the upper hand at alternate times. Russia, furthermore, was notoriously vicious toward the Jews, millions of whom lived among its people. During most of the past two hundred years, Russian czars periodically carried out pogroms against the Jews, slaughtering them by the tens of thousands. Pressure on the Jews to leave Russia was unremitting.

During the early part of this century, to encourage Russian colonization of Manchuria, Czar Alexander permitted Russian Jews to settle there, principally in the rough new city of Harbin, located in the central part of the country. A few other Russian-Jewish soldiers remained after the Russo-Japanese war. Other Jews fled into Manchuria, especially Harbin, during the Russian revolution of 1917, taking advantage of the upheaval to flee the country. By the time the Japanese came to Manchuria in 1931, there were 300,000 Jews in the country. About thirteen thousand of them lived in the city of Harbin alone. They owned businesses there, including banks and newspapers, and lived a relatively happy and prosperous life.

When Japan came to power in Manchuria, it was faced with governing a country full of minority groups – White Russians, Jews, Koreans, Chinese (who constituted the bulk of the population), and Japanese. Japan wanted most of all to create an orderly, well-organized society in Manchuria. Occupied with a war in China, it wanted no upsets in Manchuria, or Manchoukuo, as the country had been rechristened. Japan was especially eager to remain on cordial terms with the Jews in Manchuria, for this and for many other reasons. Japan had never been an anti-Semitic nation, and it had no intention of becoming one. Yet Japan was in alliance with Germany, and Germany wanted pressure brought on the Jews. Japan, thus, was caught in something of a quandary; and it is to its credit that on the whole, it resisted Nazi pressure and maintained throughout the war honorable, if perhaps slightly strained, relations with the Jews under its rule.

In 1938, the Nazis sent some SS men to Japan to make Nazi propaganda, specifically anti-Jewish, in the country. One of their devices was an organization called *Seikei Gakkai,* or Political-Economic Association. One day its president got in touch with me. Japan was faced with a growing "Jewish problem" he explained. I was undoubtedly the man most expert in Jewish matters in Japan. Would I be willing to help the group in its research work?

There was no reason for me to refuse. I signed up and began to attend their meetings. I also made translations of a few articles on international affairs from English for them. In a short while, however, a few things became obvious about the organization.

One was that although the association never seemed to put any money in the bank, it was always able to draw out as much as it needed. A second was that the organization was violently anti-Semitic. It published a journal called *Researches into the Secret World Power,* which was essentially a vehicle for translations of anti-Jewish pamphlets. They were full of the ancient notion that there was a conspiracy of Jews to take over the world, stated in the usual hysterical accusations. Occasionally a Dr. Pausch, who belonged to the SS, spoke on the Jewish conspiracy.

I withdrew; but the organization continued, to startling effect. Japanese officials first laughed at it, but the Germans began producing cleverly forged documents supporting their contentions that the Jews were indeed conspiring to rule the world, and some of the officials grew convinced of the justice of the charge.

The whole matter of Japanese attitudes toward the Jews, then, was exceedingly fluid. It was in this fluid state in January 1939, when, vastly to my surprise, I received an invitation from the president of the South Manchuria Railway Company to work for him in the capacity of an expert in Jewish affairs.

The South Manchuria Railway is far more than a simple business. Like the British East India Company of a century ago, it was virtually a second government in the country. The South Manchuria Railway owned coal mines, foundries, and shipping companies; and it ran its own hospitals, medical colleges, and technical schools. It was the single biggest concentration of capital in the entire Japanese economy, and it acted like a small welfare state toward the thousands of people who were employed by it. Imagine that the ten largest corporations in America were gathered under a single management, and you will have some idea of its importance to Manchuria, and indeed to Japan.

The head of the South Manchuria Railway was Yosuke Matsuoka, later one of the Class B War Criminals. Like any other official in Manchuria, he had to deal with Jews and Jewish matters daily, and he needed somebody to advise him. He had apparently heard of me through my books, especially my Hebrew grammar, and he urged me to come to work for him.

I flatly refused. I was happy with the Institute of Biblical Research. I was doing what I wanted to do, and I was content to continue. Furthermore, there is a feeling among Japanese scholars and people of the upper classes that it is degrading to go into the world of commerce. I did not like the idea of selling my scholarship for money. But Matsuoka did not give up easily. He raised the first offer of three hundred yen to three hundred and fifty, and when I refused that, he raised it again. I still refused, and this game continued for several months.

Yet my refusals began to trouble me. It seemed certain to me that Nazi anti-Semitism would eventually reach the East, and that the Jews in Manchuria would suffer for it. I thought: Is all my learning merely a matter of cold knowledge, or is it for love of the people of the Bible? If I can do something to help the Jews, shouldn't I do it?

By this time Matsuoka had raised his price to five hundred yen, a salary so enormous that the personnel department of the South Manchuria Railway refused to authorize it, telling Matsuoka that he must offer it on his own authority.[1] I discussed this with my wife, and it was decided that I would accept.

1. Five hundred yen was a salary a top corporation executive might make.

Chapter Nine

Dairen – now called Talien – is a town of about a half million people on the Liaotung Peninsula just north of Port Arthur on the Yellow Sea. The southern terminus of the South Manchuria Railway, it came under Japanese control after the Russo-Japanese war in 1904. The home office of the South Manchuria Railway is there. It is the most northern year-round port on the Chinese coast, and it is connected by rail with the Chinese Eastern Railroad, which in turn branches off from the Trans-Siberian Railway. It is connected, thus, with every important city in Russia and Northern China, and has therefore been a city accustomed to receiving immigrants and refugees from the West. Harbin, to the north, where the Chinese Eastern and South Manchuria Railways joined, was the center of Russian – and Russian-Jewish – groups in Manchuria. Dairen, however, had a Russian-Jewish colony of considerable consequence.

In general, Japanese policy toward the Jews in Manchuria during the years just before the war was colored by the feeling that friendly relations with the United States, France, England, and other Western nations might be disrupted if Japan was harsh toward the Jews. There was also the hope that Jews might be persuaded to invest capital in Japanese enterprises. Despite Nazi pressure and propaganda, there were very good reasons for Japanese kindness toward the Jews, and since the Japanese had never been anti-Semitic there was no emotional reason for persecuting them. Indeed, many Japanese officials, especially on the lower levels, were almost totally ignorant of the existence of the Jews as a special group until they became a refugee problem. To them, Russians were Russians, Germans were Germans.

Yet despite all of this, as early as 1938 the Nazi propaganda machine had infected numbers of Japanese with anti-Semitism. This was especially true among the military, who admired German methods. Typical of those practicing this attitude was Ohshima, a former high army officer who had been ambassador to Germany before the war. Although Ohshima must certainly have known of the Nazi persecution of the Jews, he cooperated with the Germans in keeping the story from being made public in Japan. In any case, Japanese policy toward the Jews was sometimes contradictory, although in the main it held to one of tolerance – in Manchuria, at least.

I arrived in Dairen on October 14, 1939, tense with expectation. Just over forty years of age, I had spent all of my life in the cloister, either as student or teacher. In practical affairs, I was an innocent. During my stay in Manchuria, I was to come down out of my ivory tower and learn the hard facts of life. Not only was I connected with a powerful institution which viewed everything pragmatically, but life in Dairen itself had the quality of that on a military outpost. There was not much cultural entertainment. Consequently the people drank constantly, and the men spent much money on women. The sight of a man destroying himself through high living was not unusual.

At no other time in my life was I so materially comfortable as during our stay in Manchuria. The company supplied us with a first-class house, snug and well heated. My salary was high, and I was allowed to travel first-class at company expense sixty days a year. The South Manchuria Railway trains had four classes. The lowest class was for the coolie.

Yosuke Matsuoka, the president of the South Manchuria Railway and the man to whom I was directly responsible, was a badly misunderstood man. Short and stocky, he wore a heavy mustache and projected an attitude of self-importance, but he nonetheless was basically a good-hearted man. It is true that he played a major role in persuading Japan to sign the anti-Communist agreement with Germany. Nonetheless, his attitude toward the Jewish people was correct and even warm to some extent. He had spent part of his boyhood in America, had studied at the University of Oregon, and was friendly to the United States. He fervently opposed war with America – partly because he didn't think that Japan could win – until the very last.

When I arrived in Dairen I reported to him immediately. I was of course curious about him, and I was especially curious about the South Manchuria Railway's policy toward the Jews. Matsuoka was the first man of real national importance I had ever had a chance to know well, and as we sat in his office, I took advantage of the opportunity to understand something of what was going on in the minds of Japan's leaders. How, for example, did Matsuoka justify Japan's treaties with both Communist Russia and Nazi Germany, two nations with contradictory outlooks?

Matsuoka was amused by what must have struck him as a naive question, and he laughed. "One is the bear, one the leopard. When you train a tame bear, you feed him only vegetables from babyhood, and he will never bite. However, once you begin giving him meat, he will start biting."

"And Russia has had a taste of meat?"

He nodded. "Russia is no longer a tame bear. Sooner or later it may bite Japan, irrespective of our neutrality treaty."

"Then why bother with a treaty?"

He shrugged. "Mainly as a gesture to indicate that we don't want war, that we're not a threat to Russia."

"And the leopard?"

"Germany is the leopard. He'll bite, no matter what you feed him. It's in the nature of the beast. The bite perhaps we needn't fear. He's too far away. But he'll try to use us, just as we'll try to use him, against Russia. Thus another good reason for the treaty with Stalin. We want to placate him, if possible."

He looked thoughtful. "Personally, I don't like the leopard very much, but I've got to get along with him. I was raised in America, I went to school there. I like America very much. If it will only keep silent until the China Incident is closed, Japan can have a fine future. But if America chooses to interfere.... " He looked somber and grave, and I understood that he had touched upon what he considered to be the heart of Japan's international problems.

I changed the subject. "I think I ought to know what your point of view toward the Jews is, in view of your support of the treaty with Germany."

He nodded. "It's very simple. I support the anti-Communist agreement, not anti-Semitism. These are quite different things, and Japan must be clear minded on this point."

Matsuoka was not dissembling. He was eager to win the Jewish people over to the Japanese viewpoint. My task was to advise him, to tell him what the Jews wanted, and how best to obtain their good opinion.

I was fortunate in being able to establish my own position with the Jews shortly after my arrival in Manchuria. There had been in 1937 and again in 1938 meetings between Japanese and Jewish leaders in Manchuria. An important figure in these meetings, and indeed in all Jewish-Japanese relations in the Far East, was Colonel Senko Yasue, an army specialist on Jewish affairs. Yasue, about whom I will have more to say in a moment, had helped to arrange the conferences in order to smooth out differences between the two peoples, and when the third conference was scheduled for late December 1939, I was asked to speak, as a representative of the South Manchuria Railway. The conference – called the Third Far-East Jewish Conference – convened on December 23. There were various speakers, including Dr. Abraham Kaufman, perhaps the most influential Jewish leader in Manchuria, who later became a friend of mine. When it was my turn, I gave only a short speech, entirely in Hebrew. The Jews in the audience were astonished, and they gave me a standing ovation. The news that there was a Japanese Hebrew scholar who could talk to them in their own language spread rapidly among the Jewish colonies of the Far East. Indeed, the incident was even reported in a Hebrew paper in Jerusalem.

With that introduction, I was able to make many friends among Manchuria's Jews, and my work was that much easier. I had, of course, no authority of my own. I worked for the South Manchuria Railway in an advisory capacity only. Nonetheless, because of my personal relations with Matsuoka, I was able, over the months, to make myself useful to the Jews in a number of ways.

The man who helped me most in this respect was Lieutenant Yoshinori Shirahama, one of the best of men. He was a member of the military police mission, had been at the Far-East Conference, and was altogether a kind man. I came to know him and his family well and had lunch with him often. On one occasion he helped me save a Jew who was about to be arrested for smuggling. In another case I told him the story of a Jew who was being unfairly taxed. Again, he helped. A third time he helped me bring a Jew who needed an operation into a hospital.

But even with the South Manchuria Railway behind me and the cooperation of decent people like Yoshinori Shirahama, I was at constant odds with the military.

The military mission was headed by Colonel Yasue. He was considered by Jews, familiar with his work in Manchuria, a real benefactor, and it is perfectly true that he helped the Jews in many ways. Yet he and I had trouble from the start for I was fully aware of his not-too-innocent past. Despite his protests of friendship for the Jews, in his earlier days he had published a book called *Inside the World Revolution,* which was essentially a translation of the notorious anti-Semitic work *The Protocols of the Elders of Zion.* Even as late as 1936 he had published statements accusing the Jews of wanting to take over the world. Most of this writing had been published under the pseudonym "Hokoshi." I knew the true facts because once in Tokyo he had proudly presented me with a copy of his book.

As a result of this activity, he had in military circles come to be considered an expert in Jewish matters. This explains why he was stationed in Dairen. The military did not care what his personal feelings were. They had established the policy of getting along with the Jews in Manchuria, and they expected Yasue to carry out that policy. It hardly mattered to them – or to Yasue for that matter – whether or not he was a true friend of the Jews; and the fact that so many Jews familiar with the situation considered him sincere in his dealing with them merely indicates how well he carried that policy out.

Unhappily, Yasue was well aware that I knew of his previous writing. If his earlier views had become public, his position among Manchurian

Jews would have been impossible. To allay his fears, I pretended to have forgotten his book completely, but he remained almost neurotically suspicious of me. However, we might still have managed to work together, if it had not been for malice on the part of an unfavored South Manchuria Railway official named Oyama.

Oyama had been educated at Nicholai Seminary, a Russian and Greek Orthodox school in Tokyo. This irregular education worried his South Manchuria Railway superiors, and although they found his excellent Russian useful, they failed to promote him. When I arrived in Dairen as a high-ranking official, he became jealous of me and began to play upon Yasue's neurotic attitude toward me.

Finally, Oyama came to me and said, "Mr. Kotsuji, the Chief of the Military Mission, Colonel Yasue, wants to see you."

I was instantly suspicious. "What for?"

He shrugged. "How would I know?"

There was something portentous about his manner that became understandable when I appeared at the Military Mission. To my surprise, instead of taking me to a conference room as usual, Yasue guided me into one of the examination rooms. I realized that I was in trouble, but I remained calm. "Colonel, if you want to see me, there is a proper routine for asking me. You need not use Oyama. I work for the president of the South Manchuria Railway, not for him." Yasue's face twitched. "Please remember that I have the authority to arrest you – or even have you killed by the police under me."

"Perhaps you could explain how I have offended you?" "Don't argue," he shouted. "Now listen to me. From now on you have no direct contact whatsoever with any Jew."

"I don't understand," I said blandly. "Do you wish to have the monopoly on my friendship?"

He slammed the floor with the end of his saber. "Didn't I make myself clear? Don't you realize what I can do to you?"

I felt certain then that he was about to arrest me; yet at the same moment I suddenly understood how to handle him. "Of course you have the power to arrest me, and if you decide to do so you will. I want to point out, however, that I am not merely a simple citizen here. All the Jews in the Far East know about me and they like me. If you do something rash, word will get out instantly that the Japanese military are being ruthless toward friends of the Jews." I paused. Then I added quietly, "I've always spoken highly of you. Somebody has slandered me, isn't that so?"

His manner suddenly softened. "I may have spoken out of turn. Don't be offended."

I met his gaze and stared into his eyes. "I mean to be offended so long as a high-ranking officer like you can be influenced by so mean a man as Oyama."

That ended the matter, and smiling in friendly fashion, he let me go. Despite his bluster, Colonel Yasue left a good record of protecting the Jews in Manchuria during the war. It is too bad that even he was not free of the tendency toward stratagem and deceit which characterized the entire Japanese military system of the period. I learned later that he died in a Siberian prison camp a few years after the war; some say he was shot by a cunning stratagem.

On the credit side, he did attempt to help the Jewish refugees in Shanghai. Shanghai's Jewish colony dates back to 1843, when the city was first opened to the West. Under the influence of the Sephardic Jews, and especially the fabulous Sassoon family, the Shanghai Jews developed a prosperous and highly cultivated colony which was perhaps, by the 1930s, seven thousand strong. Shanghai was an international city, an easy place to enter. Between August of 1938 and August of 1939, some thirty thousand Jewish refugees from Nazi Germany poured into Shanghai. Despite its efforts, the Jewish colony could not take care of them all. Thousands of them had to be established in the Hongkew area of Shanghai, which was largely rubble because of the fighting between Japanese and Chinese troops. Here, in barracks and in camps, some eleven thousand Jews lived hard lives.

In May 1940, a group from Manchuria went down to Shanghai to inspect conditions there. It included Colonel Yasue, a Navy representative, Captain K. Inuzuka, the consul Ishiguro from Japan, and me, representing the South Manchuria Railway.

As a whole, the Shanghai Jews were relatively well taken care of, compared to what they had suffered elsewhere in the world. There were complaints, of course, for there was no variety in the diet and in some cases people were hungry. Young people, especially, found the food inadequate.

When our party walked through the community kitchen in one of the camps, which was guarded by a high wire fence, young men and women outside stood staring hungrily at the huge pots bubbling on the stoves. I asked one of the girls how old she was.

"Sixteen," she said.

"How are conditions here?"

"I'm hungry," she said, and glanced again at the cooking pots. "I want to get out of here, to find work as a housemaid. Please, take me into your house. Please help me."

I was deeply touched by this hungry girl. When we left, I told a high Japanese official about her, and he was able to find a place for her. To my regret, we left to return to Dairen before she was released, and I lost track of her. Perhaps if she reads this, she will have the courage to write to me some day.

The most enjoyable aspect of my life in Dairen, and the most valuable to me, was the many new friends I made. Later, these friendships were to become of life-and-death importance to me; but during those South Manchuria Railway months it was a happy matter of getting to know a large number of the Jewish people. There was a restaurant in Dairen called the Victoria, which was run by a Russian Jew. Here both Jews and higher South Manchuria Railway officers usually ate lunch. Nearly every man in the restaurant had a story to tell. There was, for example, the old man everyone called "The General." Since he was poor and aging, I assumed the name was a rather bad joke, until I discovered that he had once indeed been a general in the czar's army.

Another man whom I met in the Victoria was a Jew named Becker, who had fought at Mukden with the Russian army which had been badly mauled by the Japanese army in 1905. He didn't mind talking about it all.

"Most of the Jews," he told me, "had no stomach for a war against the Japanese. We shot in the air most of the time. It was either the front lines or the pogroms at home, and consequently our morale was very low. But then the morale of the whole army trapped in Mukden was low. On the last day of battle a strong, sandy wind blew into our faces. We couldn't keep our eyes open. And then there arose on the distant horizon white figures like ghosts. We couldn't explain it. It was God's will that Russia be defeated."

Japanese soldiers who had fought in this battle had also referred to these white ghosts, and they were presumably real. What made them so frightening to the Russian Jews in the army was that the word for "the ghost of darkness" in Hebrew is *tohu* – very similar in pronunciation to Admiral Tojo's name – and therefore they refused to admit that the curious figures might have been sand dust stirred up by the wind.

Perhaps most important to my understanding of Jewish life were the stories I began to hear everywhere of Nazi persecution. I made a point of asking people what conditions had been like under the Nazis: they were glad to tell me. There was, for example, Karl Rosenzweig, who had been director of the Coal Division of the Danube Navigation Company. A young man in his office had served him faithfully as secretary. One morning, shortly after the Nazis marched into Vienna, Karl Rosenzweig walked into his office to find the young man sitting at his desk.

"I'm director now," the man said boldly. He had been working with the Nazis all along. Ultimately Rosenzweig was forced to flee to Manchuria. He was living with an uncle in the suburbs of Dairen, and we became friends. The war finally separated us, and he seemed lost to me forever. Then, twenty years later, I found him again in Vienna – an importer of cultured pearls from Japan.

I knew another man named Weinberg, who had been one of the 67,000 people arrested in Vienna on the eve of Hitler's arrival there. Because he was able to show that he was not an important person, he was ultimately discharged from prison. As he went out, the jailer shot him in the arm – merely out of pique.

From these people, I was able to piece together the true story of conditions in Europe. I was able to give Matsuoka the clearest idea of what was really going on. As for myself, I began to develop a hatred for the Nazis and began to find myself thinking and feeling more and more like a Jew, as if there were a Jew living inside me. There was, it seems to me now, a prophetic spirit residing in me.

But my South Manchuria Railway days were almost over. Late in 1940, Matsuoka was appointed Foreign Minister of Japan and resigned from his post in Manchuria. In such cases it is usual, as a sign of loyalty to one's superior, for a subordinate to resign. Moreover, Matsuoka told me he would give me some kind of diplomatic post in the course of time.

It seemed as if my resignation was in order. I resigned, and we packed to go back to Japan.

The two years in Manchuria had affected me considerably. For one thing, I had experienced the world outside the ivory tower, and I had participated in large events. For another, I had finally come to be familiar with the Jewish people, to make friends with them, to understand their ways. I was closer than ever to Judaism.

Chapter Ten

In July 1940, after a little short of two years' service in Manchuria, I brought my family back to Japan. As was customary, I had received "retirement money" amounting to twenty months' pay from the South Manchuria Railway – severance pay which would keep me comfortably for a year or more. I took a summer house in a resort town called North Karuizawa, near the volcanic Asama-yama, in central Japan, and here I worked revising my Hebrew grammar for a second edition. I had also, during my spare time in Dairen, translated the Canticles into the classic Japanese thirty-one syllable verse form, and I worked these over in hopes of finding a publisher for them. Then, in the fall, I moved my family into more permanent quarters in Kamakura. Kamakura is a small village about thirty miles down one of the arms which form Tokyo Bay. A historic town,[1] it is an important beach resort today. It is especially noted for the Daibutsu, or "Great Buddha of Infinite Light," a giant bronze statue of the Buddha which weighs 103 tons and stands over forty feet high. It is considered one of the finest examples of this kind of statuary

1. It was the *de facto* capital of Japan in the twelfth and thirteenth centuries.

in Japan. In fact, because of its antiquity the town is rich in shrines and Buddhist temples. It is indeed a very pleasant place to live.

The house we took was directly on the water, separated from the beach only by a small road – a point which was to have significance later on. The house was not large; but it commanded a view of the whole bay down to Miura Point, where the famous lighthouse stood. At night the revolving light flashed dimly into our bedroom. I loved taking my ceremonial tea there, where I could look down the bay to that distant light and point of land.

I came to Kamakura looking forward to a peaceful time, when I could concentrate on my Hebrew studies and enjoy my family and the wonderful sea air. I had been there exactly two weeks when I got a telegram which put an end to this serene way of life. It was from some Jewish leaders in the Japanese town of Kobe, asking me to meet with them in Tokyo. I did, and suddenly I found I had a problem involving five thousand people.

Kobe lies toward the southern end of Japan, not far south from Kyoto, on the inland sea locked in between the islands of Honshu and Shikoku. It is pressed against the water by a string of mountains rising above it, and it has been forced to expand lengthwise, to curve along the coast. Westerners have called it the "Japanese Rio." Having a population of one million, it is the second-largest open port in Japan, and it is the sixth largest city. It is not a town of temples, especially, and it lacks the antique flavor of so many Japanese towns. It has instead a modern, cosmopolitan air.[2]

Kobe is also one of the main centers of what little Jewish activity there is in Japan. A few Jewish traders from Iran and Iraq had established themselves in the port city before World War I, and a few more families had come in after the 1923 earthquake which had destroyed their settlement in Yokohama. Some White Russian Jews had come in after the Russian Revolution. By 1940 there were perhaps fifty Jewish families in Kobe, with both Sephardic and Ashkenazic temples. The little community was prosperous and on good terms with the Japanese citizens of Kobe.

2. As an example, there is a Kobe folk dance called the Philosophers' Dance, or *Dekanso* – De-Kan-So – which stands for Descartes-Kant-Schopenhauer.

In July 1940, the quiet of their lives was suddenly shattered by a flood of refugees pouring in from Vladivostok. They were coming from various places, but most of them were Polish and Lithuanian Jews who had managed to get Japanese visas in Kovno, Lithuania, from a sympathetic Japanese consul, Sugihara, who later disappeared, possibly assassinated by the Germans. By 1940, of course, European ports were all shut tight. These Jews had come east on the Trans-Siberian Railway. Many of them literally had come on the last train out of Europe. They were mostly men; the women and children were often not up to the rigors of the journey, and it was felt that it was the men who stood the greatest risk at the hands of the Nazis. They came by way of Harbin, where the local Jewish community fed them and sent them on, usually to Vladivostok, where they took a boat to Tsuruoka on the Japanese coast and from there went by train to Kobe.

The Jewish community in Kobe was assisting them, but it was clear that fifty families could hardly handle the flood of refugees. Money coming from America – largely from the Hebrew Immigrant Aid Society – helped, but the need was to get the refugees out of Japan, into other lands where they could rebuild their lives. Arrangements could be made to have them admitted to the United States, Canada, Jamaica, and various other places. The difficulty was that their Japanese entry permits were temporary. They could stay in the country for ten days only. Ten days was far too short a time to arrange to place them elsewhere. Some, in fact, who had come without entry permits, were in an even worse plight. They could not get off the boat at Tsuruoka and went back and forth from Japan to Vladivostok.

The Kobe Jewish Committee had heard of me through my work in Manchuria, especially because of my well-publicized speech in Hebrew before the Far-East Congress. Was it possible, they asked, for me to intervene with the government and get the entry visas extended?

I knew it was not going to be easy. Since my return from Manchuria, I had become increasingly aware of the rise of anti-Semitic feeling, especially in military and government circles. Anti-Semitism meant little to the average citizen, for few had ever seen a Jew, or even knew what one was. Those who had, like the people of Kobe, were not much fooled by government propaganda. Yet there was a general wariness among the people. One well-connected man who had visited the Jewish Committee in Kobe and had promised to help had been threatened by a militarist and had never shown up again. Many Japanese were sympathetic to the plight of the refugees, but because they lacked courage they closed their eyes. (Adding to their fear was the fact that most of the refugees were Eastern Jews, who were heavily bearded and appeared somewhat strange compared to the local Kobe Jews.)

I determined, however, that I would do what I could and use what influence I had to help. There is a *Bushido* saying which goes, "It is cowardice not to do, seeing one ought"; running away from the trouble went against the grain of my youthful samurai-trained notions of honor and pride. Further supporting me were words of the Old Testament: "Grass dries up, and shoots will wither, but the word of our God stands firm; always."

I commuted to Tokyo almost daily to press my suit with the Foreign Ministry. Time after time I appealed to any official who would listen. In a few days the unfortunates who were riding back and forth between Vladivostok and Tsuruoka were given tacit permission to land in Japan. What part my pleas played in this and what other factors were involved I do not know.

In any case, there was still the problem of getting the visas extended. The Foreign Ministry simply refused to respond to my supplications. Finally an official at the Ministry warned me not to press the matter any further.

Disappointed, indeed heavy hearted, I still took hope from the fact that I had not yet played my trump card: my old superior, Yosuke Matsuoka, now Japan's Foreign Minister. Matsuoka, I was aware, had the pistol of the military at his head. He had to consider their attitude to everything he did, especially when it involved so touchy a problem as anti-Semitism. Still, he was my last hope.

I went to him and told him my story. "I have been trying desperately to awaken the conscience of my country," I said. "It appears that I have not succeeded."

He nodded. "I'm sorry, Dr. Kotsuji."

"So now I have come to the minister himself, to tell him of my sorrow, for he is my superior."

My sad eyes and his sympathetic ones met and held for a moment. Then he leaned back. "Dr. Kotsuji, can I give you a tip?"

"Of course."

"But wait," he said. "Not here. I speak as a friend, not as a ministry official. Let's go out to lunch."

In a quiet restaurant a good distance from the ministry, I detailed the entire story to him.

He listened quietly. Then he said, "Further pleas by you or the Jewish committees will be useless. The ministry has set its policy, and the pressure is on us to keep it unchanged. But there is something that can be done. It is possible that you can get the local prefectural government in the Kobe area to extend the refugees' visas. If you can, I promise you that the ministry will look the other way. The central government in Tokyo simply will ignore whatever action the local government takes."

Heartened by this good advice, I went down to Kobe to see the Jewish committee, which was headed by Mr. A. Ponevejsky, who later became a naturalized American citizen. The refugees were sleeping on borrowed mattresses on floors, eating what they could, and spending most of their time on the street in front of the Jewish Community Center, where their European faces and long black beards stood out vividly in the Oriental city.

The problem now was dealing with the local officials. The easiest way was to buy them, not by obvious bribery, but with liquor, parties, and small gifts. All of this would take money; and I had very little of my own.

It might have been possible to get funds from the Jewish relief agencies, but that would have been dangerous. All of my dealings with national and local officials had to be kept quiet, for the plan could only work so long as the right hand failed to see what the left hand was doing. A little gossip at the wrong time, a letter in wrong hands – and negotiations would have collapsed.

I turned, then, to the only other source of money I knew: my wealthy brother-in-law. A millionaire by inheritance, he had never done very much for me. "You must make your own way," he had always told me. "However, you'll have better luck if you dress well," he would add. On this principle he had for years given me his hand-me-down clothes, so that even when I was poor I had always dressed like a slightly worn millionaire. This was the sort of man he was – getting money from him would not be easy.

I went down to Osaka and called on him at his door.

"Come in, come in," he said. "What are you doing these days?"

"I'm trying to help some old friends," I said. "In Manchuria my work was mostly with the Jewish people. They need me now, and I want to keep faith with them." I told him the story of the refugees and my plan for helping them. "You have said I should wear your old clothes so as not to lose face. Now I need money so as not to lose face."

"Is it important to you?" he asked.

"It is not for me, it is for humanity's sake. Look, you told me that you once lost a million yen overnight when the stock market fell. Money means nothing to you; it is only counters in a game. You can do something."

"I'll think it over tonight," he said.

In the morning he gave me 300,000 yen, a handsome sum of money in those days.

My pockets bulging with currency, I hurried back to Kobe and registered at the Oriental Hotel, the best and most expensive in the city. Then I went around to the police chief and introduced myself as somebody concerned with Jewish affairs. "Something has to be done about these refugees," I said. "Why don't you and some of your section heads drop in at my place this evening, where we can discuss it."

Five or six people came that evening. I took them out to the best restaurant in Kobe and fed them a luxurious Japanese dinner: shellfish soup, lobster in soy sauce, seaweed with vinegar and bean jelly, and plenty of sake along with it all. We had a *geisha* girl with us to play the guitar-like *shamisen* and to sing to us. The officials sang, laughed, and got uproariously drunk. I did not touch upon the refugee problems at all.

Two days later I invited them to dinner again; but still I did not mention the refugees. Finally, at a third dinner a few days later I brought up the question of the homeless Jewish men. The visa extensions were granted.

The local officials would not grant visa extensions for more than fifteen days at a time. Over the course of the next several months I became a great friend of the Kobe police, seeing that they were constantly my companions. I traveled from Kamakura to Kobe – a trip of twelve hours – once or twice a week. I spent a night or perhaps two buying lunches and suppers, and I talked with the Kobe Jewish Committee to see that things were going properly. The police became most cooperative. They allowed the refugees to open a *talmud Torah* and were as helpful as they dared to be. It took about three months to get a man out of Japan. The flood of refugees began to dwindle in the spring of 1941, and by the fall of that year most of them had passed safely out of Japan, either to Western countries if they had visas, or to the open city of Shanghai if they had not. Though the hospitality of Japan toward the suffering Jews was nothing to boast about, because of the propaganda efforts of the Nazis, the country at least tolerated their presence until they could find a way to move on to safety.

Occasionally in the years since then I have run across people who were in Kobe at that time. In 1959, on my trip to Jerusalem, I met a young woman who said that she had been in Kobe when she was four years old and that she could remember some scenes of Kobe still. In 1960 I met the wife of Rabbi Shlomo Poupko in Brooklyn and discovered that she was also in Kobe when she was four. She still can sing a Japanese song she learned then.

Another young man, Rabbi Pinchas Hirschprung, had published in Canada in 1944 a short history of Jewish refugees entitled *From the Nazi Vale of Tears (Fun Natsishen Yomertol)*. He dedicated the last chapter to "Der Japanischer Professor Avram Kotsuji." He concludes with the information that I was assassinated by the militarists for my liberal views. It was true that I was later marked for assassination; how that information came to Canada I do not know.

In any case, by the autumn of 1941 nearly five thousand refugees had passed through Japan, and the flood was over. I settled down in my lovely house, once again hoping for a period of tranquility. I had two months of it. Then one morning I went out for my daily paper, only to discover that it had not arrived. I intended to go up to Tokyo anyway to look for some books I needed, so I walked down to the Kamakura railroad station. It was a pleasant walk; the day was sunny and warm for December.

At the station there were newspapers. I picked one up. The headline read: "This morning our Navy has entered into a state of war with the battleships of the United States."

Chapter Eleven

By the Japanese calendar the war between the United States and Japan began on the eighth of December with the bombing of Pearl Harbor. The people of Japan were nearly as unprepared for this attack as were the people of the United States. They were shocked and dumfounded. They were not told at first of the surprise attack on Pearl Harbor, but merely that there had been a battle between United States and Japanese naval forces. The story of Pearl Harbor and the subsequent invasion of the Philippines came out bit by bit over the next several days.

Despite their initial shock, the Japanese of course rallied to the support of their country – encouraged by the thought of victory following victory, as was the case in the early days of the war.

A militaristic tone began to creep over the country. Men were urged to wear combat uniforms, and they were required to wear puttees as they went about all day. Small shopkeepers were forced into the factories, rationing was instituted, charcoal-burning taxis began to appear in the streets. The country began to resemble an armed camp. The military, already firmly entrenched, now became absolute masters of the country. The civil police were helpless against the military police, the

Kempeitai, who as the war progressed became as ruthless as the German Gestapo. My own position in Japan was extremely ambiguous. For one thing, since my wife and I had lived in America we felt friendship and gratitude toward the country. For another, my feelings toward the Jews made it impossible for me to accept Japan's German allies. Beyond this, my always stubborn nature revolted against the banzai-crying spirit adopted by the masses. I refused to go into the factories; I would not wear the puttees, camouflaging their absence by tucking my trousers into my socks. I was a Jeremiah, crying "Woe" to my nation. Perhaps I was unpatriotic. My attempts to rouse the conscience of my country against the anti-Semites seemed more patriotic to me than the so-called banzai patriotism of the masses.

At the time the war broke out I had been out of work for a year, and my severance pay was nearly exhausted. My refusal to work in factories might have been disastrous had I not experienced another of those coincidences which have marked my life. One day, about three weeks before the Pearl Harbor attack, I was in the Yokohama station waiting for a train to Kyoto, when I heard somebody call my name. I looked around and saw a couple I had known in Manchuria, Lewis Zikman and his wife. He had pioneered the sugar refining business in Manchuria and owned a factory at Ajho, about an hour away from Harbin. He stopped to chat. The Zikmans were sailing for the United States the next day, and they were now on their way to the customs house to make sure everything was in order. They needed some help, and after a moment's thought I decided that I could easily postpone my trip for a day in order to shepherd them through customs. The next day they sailed for San Francisco on the *Tatsuta Maru,* but they never reached their destination, for at the time of the Pearl Harbor attack the ship turned around and came back to Yokohama. Troubled and upset, Zikman called on me. A short time later he put me on his payroll to teach him Japanese and to advise him on his business ventures in Japan. Both he and Mrs. Zikman were kind and grateful, with a deep understanding of the Japanese mind; they were God-given friends and a great help to me during the confusions of the war years.[1]

1. The Zikmans finally reached San Francisco, many years later. I met them there again in 1960 during a lecture tour.

My main involvement during the war, however, was in the struggle against anti-Semitism. It is a curious matter that such a movement appeared in a country that had virtually no Jews. The fault lay entirely with the Nazis. Hitler had sent a man named Dr. Pausch to Japan expressly to stir up anti-Jewish feeling, and he had ordered his ambassadors in Tokyo and China to continue to press for the deportation of the twenty thousand Jews in Shanghai to the places they had come from. This of course meant condemning them to Hitler's gas chambers, and fortunately Japan did not succumb to this pressure.

The people most concerned with the so-called Jewish problem were two or three military people – Colonel Nosuke Yasue and Captain Inuzuka among them – and such civilians as U. Wakamiya, Atsushi Akaike, and Masao Masuda. Most of them were in no sense the experts they claimed to be, but merely translators of anti-Semitic documents. They would not have had much luck extending their influence, except that they were heavily supported by some mysterious financial source, presumably a Nazi agent. The target of the anti-Semitic program was not the tiny handful of Jewish families in Kobe; it was the twenty thousand people in Shanghai. It was useful to the Germans to try to justify some of their actions to the Japanese, for the Japanese were not unsympathetic to Jewish people. Nevertheless, many among the Japanese military group were taken in. It was helpful, too, for the militarists to claim that the United States was under the thumb of such Jewish capitalists as Carnegie and Rockefeller, both of whom were gentiles; for many Japanese had relatives in America and were otherwise sympathetic to the country.

Despite the influence of the military, there were a few bold men, showing great courage in the face of the military, who stood up against the anti-Semitic propaganda. One of these was Mr. Tanzan Ishibashi, who after the war became Minister of Trade and Industry, and for a short period, Premier. Ishibashi was president of an organization called the Economic Club (not the Political-Economic Association mentioned earlier) with branches in the chambers of commerce of thirty-five major cities and headquarters in Tokyo. It supplied lecturers to all its branches at least once a month. In order to handle the demand, Ishibashi hired a man to deal with the so-called Jewish problem. He was Toshio Shiratori, and he had once been ambassador to Italy. To Ishibashi's vast surprise, the man turned out to be one of the most violent anti-Semites in the country, and he went from branch to branch pouring out Hitlerist poison in his lectures. Ishibashi fired him of course, but he could not stop Shiratori from continuing to lecture around the country.

At just about that time, a conference of scholars in various fields was called, with a view to supplying the Foreign Ministry with expert opinion on a number of topics. The speakers included Professor Kiyoshi Miki, who later died in the hands of the Kempeitai, and Dr. Kotaro Tanaka, former chief judge of the Japanese Supreme Court and one of the former judges at the International Court in The Hague. I was among the speakers; and I took advantage of the opportunity to counter some of the anti-Semitic propaganda so prevalent in government circles. I began by pointing out that the Nazi notion of *Rassenschande* – racial shame – was absurd, since no civilized nation in the modem world is composed of a single original race. I pointed out why Hitler was so interested in promoting anti-Semitism in Japan and added what other details I knew. As it happened, Mr. Ishibashi heard my lecture. Immediately afterward he came to me and asked if I would be willing to undertake a tour pursuing the footsteps of the anti-Semitic Shiratori. I was delighted and accepted the offer immediately. For the next several months I crisscrossed Japan, giving people an insight into the true nature of anti-Semitism and into the Jewish people. I opened eyes everywhere. People who heard me speak usually believed what I had to say, despite the Nazi propaganda. On one occasion, when I was speaking at Hakata on Kyushu Island, a corporal from the military police, wearing a pistol and full uniform, strode into the lobby of the hall where I was to lecture and asked to be admitted to the lecture, even though he was not a member of the chamber of commerce, which sponsored it. I was alarmed by his presence, for the appearance of a military official was usually a prelude to trouble.

Nonetheless, I nodded politely and said, "You're welcome to join us. I'm delighted that you want to hear what I have to say."

He smiled politely. "Will it be all right if I take notes, Dr. Kotsuji?"

I nodded again. "Certainly. I appreciate your great interest."

When I rose to speak, I decided not to give an inch. I gave my usual lecture, in the firm belief that if the facts convinced ordinary citizens, they would convince the military too. At the end of the lecture, I walked off the rostrum and down into the hall where he was waiting for me, surrounded by the anxious officers of the sponsoring committee.

He bowed politely. "I enjoyed the lecture very much. It was very enlightening. Thank you, Dr. Kotsuji."

The sponsoring committee – and I as well – drew a sigh of relief.

The lecture tour, unhappily, ended a few months after it began, because civilian travel was curtailed and railroad tickets became impossible to buy. Although my lectures had necessarily reached only a small portion of the population, they had reached an important portion – business leaders, academicians, local officials – and much had been done to counteract the Nazi-spread anti-Semitism.

I felt, then, that perhaps I could do something more. A book on the subject seemed to be the obvious answer, and I cast about for a means of getting it published. As it happened, a friend of mine, a professor of Chinese literature at Kyoto University, knew some people at the Meguro Publishing Company in Tokyo, which was then issuing a series called "The Nations and Cultures Series." I told them what I had in mind, and they offered to publish it, an act of some courage considering the state of mind then prevalent in official circles.

I wrote the book, a 350-page volume which I called *The True Character of the Jewish Nation,* and delivered it to the publisher. The book was essentially a history of the Jews and a discussion of their religion and mores, but it also contained an analysis of Hitler's anti-Semitism and the admonition that Japan should not be misled by European propaganda.

Shortly after I turned the manuscript over to the publishers, I was ordered to appear before the director of the intelligence bureau of the central government, who was in charge of the censor's office through which all books must pass.

The director came to the point immediately. "Dr. Kotsuji, do you mean to publish this book as it stands?"

"Why yes, of course."

"Then you will probably be arrested," he said bluntly.

"Why?" I demanded.

"Believe me, I don't want to stop publication of this book. It is the first solid, well-balanced history of the Jews offered in Japan. Therefore, I want to warn you that there are a few changes you'd better make. You've criticized Hitler and the Nazis outright, and you've made some remarks which might hurt the feelings of the Italians. You have criticized both of Japan's allies. Isn't that so?"

"Yes," I agreed.

"The Kempeitai will probably arrest you if I let them see the book. In fact, I didn't have to tell you any of this. I could have let the book go. I respect you, however, and I want to ask you to make the cuts."

There was certainly no point in bucking the government; I would be jailed, the book suppressed, and nothing would be gained. I took out the direct criticism of Germany and Italy and let the book stand as a history and analysis of the Jewish nation.[2]

The book was an immediate success. The first printing of five thousand copies was sold out by subscription before it appeared in the bookstores. Then the book began to suffer a series of misfortunes. First, just as the publisher was considering a second printing, paper was rationed. Then his offices were bombed out and the plates lost. My own manuscript disappeared during the war. Secondhand copies are very scarce today and will sell at thirty times the original selling price. Judging from the mail the publisher got, most of which was congratulatory, the enterprise was still a considerable success.

Shortly after the book was published, I was visited by two men from the Kamakura police station. They belonged to a branch called "Special Higher Service," a group responsible for keeping a watch on intellectually suspicious persons – in other words, a kind of thought-control police. One of the men began to question me immediately.

"You have recently published an excellent book, I understand, Dr. Kotsuji."

"Thank you."

"We understand that the Jews of Kobe are extremely grateful to you?"

"Is that so?" I said.

---

2. Incidentally, the item which the censorship office thought would "hurt Italian feelings" was the indisputable statement that the Romans were responsible for the fall of Jerusalem in 70 AD.

He played his trump. "You must have made a lot of money on it," he said casually.

"Why yes, I made some money from the book."

"Who paid it to you?" he asked.

"Why, the publisher, of course."

"No, Doctor, not the publisher. The Jews."

I laughed. "Come on, that's nonsense. You're victimized by the current spate of anti-Semitism, just like so many others. You prefer to believe Hitler and not your own countryman. Suppose I was a foreigner, would you have better faith in me?" I pointed around at my tiny house. "If the Jews were paying me a lot of money, would I be living so simple and frugal a life?"

He frowned, but looked abashed; evidently, he decided that there was no point in pursuing that topic. "What are you writing these days?" he asked, as if merely being polite.

"I am beginning a history of Jewish literature."

"Very interesting. I'd like to see the manuscript."

"I'm still thinking out the plan for the book. I have nothing to show you."

At this point my wife brought in cups of green tea, and the conversation ended. I was aware now that I was being watched, and that I was marked as suspicious. I had espoused the cause of the Jews. I had spent four years in the United States, had been educated there, and had friends across the country. Finally, I had been (and was still, at least nominally) a Christian. All of these things conspired to mark me as a suspicious person.

By early 1944, as the tide of the war began to turn against the Axis nations, conditions in Japan worsened. The government did not conceal our defeats from us, although they did gloss them over as much as possible. There was a feeling of doom and despair in the air; and yet, the idea that we might lose was somehow unbelievable. The people clung to straws; there would be a miraculous deliverance yet. Meanwhile, American troops crept inexorably closer to the chain of islands, from the Solomons to the Marianas to Okinawa to Iwo Jima.

Food grew scarce. The rations were not enough to fill the stomachs of children, and the purchase of black market food direct from the farmers became the general rule. This meant walking for miles out into the villages and farms with a rucksack on your back, begging from door to door to be allowed to buy some rice. The farmers grew arrogant. They refused money but demanded kimonos and other valuables. Once as I walked through a village, I found a man who had a full bag of flour for sale. I bought it, and staggered home under its heavy weight. The stuff turned out to be inedible, and all *I* had for my pains was a stiff and swollen shoulder. My wife and I decided that our children came first. We held back only a single handful of rice for ourselves and gave them the rest to take to school for their lunches. Boiling the rice with some ill-tasting seaweed and salt sea water, we were able to fool our stomachs. We were, in fact, slowly starving. My wife was pale as death, and my face was swollen. In Nagoya, a well-known court prosecutor actually died of starvation because he refused to deal on the black market.

Nearly everything was in short supply. Women stopped wearing kimonos and pretty dresses, and put on *monpes* – ugly bloomers – mostly because social pressure demanded that people be serious and grave. The draft age rose to forty-five, and it seemed that I might have to fight. The yen fluctuated wildly, finally dropping to about a fifth of its usual value. It didn't matter – nobody wanted to buy anything but food and the basic necessities. I sold a typewriter for the unbelievably low price of five yen. It was possible to pick up fine furniture for virtually nothing. In fact, after the great air raid on Tokyo that March there were hundreds of pieces of fine furniture for sale at three and four yen.

By 1944, the air raids became a fairly regular occurrence. Sometimes, as I walked on my lovely beach at Kamakura, I would see the huge American planes, darkening the distant northern skies like masses of birds in flight, as they headed inland to devastate Yokohama or Tokyo. Once as I watched such a mass flight, speculating on its deadly beauty, I thought of Jeremiah watching the Chaldean army invade Jerusalem. A few minutes later the flight so blasted Yokohama with incendiary bombs that the town was reduced to ashes. The fire department of Kamakura disappeared for a week, and we knew that they had spent that long time helping to dispose of the corpses scattered everywhere in the streets.

One day in the fall of 1944 I returned from a walk along the beach. My wife was out, my girls were in school. I opened the front door to enter and saw a note which had been pushed under it. I picked it up and read: "Dr. Kotsuji: You are requested to appear at the Kempeitai headquarters at the earliest opportunity." I knew I was being honored; usually the Kempeitai just came to arrest one. They were giving me the chance to turn myself in before they came.

I stood for a moment in a state of shock, my heart pounding, unable to think. Men who visited the Kempeitai often simply disappeared. Later, Professor Kiyoshi Miki, my philosopher friend, was to die at their hands during the ten-day period between Japan's surrender and the arrival of American forces. This was a time when the Kempeitai killed at random. My wife and daughters suddenly seemed remote and distant from me, as if I had already been carried off to my death. I could refuse to go; I could attempt to run; or I could wait for them to come and arrest me. Terror grew in me; then, suddenly, I remembered the ringing words of Jeremiah: "Whatsoever I shall command thee thou shalt speak. Be not afraid of them; for I am with thee to deliver thee, saith the Lord."

I decided I would go the next morning without telling my family; there would be grief enough for them later, and it would spare us all a difficult farewell. So I left in the morning, telling them I had business in Tokyo. A great love welled up in my heart, and I said to them silently, "Goodbye forever." The hour train ride seemed to last only minutes, and those thirteen steps up to the entrance to the Kempeitai headquarters were a heavy climb.

I went to the desk and showed my summons. A young lieutenant came and took me to a gloomy, windowless, secluded room. Then he began to question me. What work had I done for the Jewish underground? Who were they? How did they work? What were their agents' plans? He was quite clearly gripped by the delusion that Jews were everywhere, plotting to take over the world.

At first, I tried to show him his mistakes, and then I simply began to deny his charges. He pressed me with wild, insane stories of Jewish intrigue. I denied them. An hour passed, and then a second, and then a third. He continued to question me relentlessly. The pounding monotony of his questioning made me drowsy. When I began to relax, he jerked my hair to snap me erect. I still denied his accusations. He resorted to physical torture.

He started with a most simple trick: He put a pencil vertically in the V of two of my fingers and squeezed them in his hands. This may sound mild, and compared to other forms of torture, it is. But it is still extremely painful.

What he wanted of me was the single word "yes." I was determined not to say it, even if I had to die for it, for not only would it wrongly indict the Jewish people, but it would be a mark against my pride, a stain on my soul.

The hours passed. They gave me nothing to eat or to drink. Thirst came, then hunger, and the pain continued. I became weak, and my mind grew dim. I dimly remembered something I'd heard about Captain Alfred Dreyfus in France. After a long, monotonous period of questioning, Dreyfus had reached a trancelike state where he answered "yes" without even knowing it. I now understood how such a thing could happen. My battle was no longer against one young lieutenant, but against trance. I mustered every effort to stay alert and awake, and I continued to say "no."

He continued to press me. I had been there nearly ten hours. The young lieutenant was threatening me with the water torture, and I was coming to the end of my strength. Then suddenly the door opened, and there stood Yoshinori Shirahama, my old friend from Manchuria, now wearing the insignia of a colonel.

"What's going on here?" he shouted. "Kotsuji, what are you doing here?"

"I am being tortured for no reason," I gasped out weakly. And then I collapsed.

Shirahama turned on the young lieutenant. "You get out of here," he shouted. "Out."

The lieutenant stood his ground. "In a moment, sir. The examination is almost finished."

"Examination? What examination?"

"About this man's connections with world Jewry."

"You idiot," Shirahama shouted. "Get out of here, or I'll have Professor Kotsuji examine your brain." He paused. "Leave the case to me, lieutenant. Your superior is under my command. I'll take charge now. You can leave." The young lieutenant understood and reluctantly left. Then

Shirahama, tears of rage and shame running down his cheeks, stepped to the examination table, picked up the report, and tore it to pieces. "If I'd only known sooner," he said.

I began to recover myself a little and sat up in my chair. He sat beside me. "It's been a long time, old friend," he murmured.

"You came in like the whirlwind to save me," I said, still dazed by the turn of events.

"I understand your book is doing very well," he said.

"How is the military taking it?" I asked him.

"Very well," he said. "You are bringing some of them out of this insanity. But there are still some mad dogs like this young lieutenant among them." He paused. "I'm sorry for you, Kotsuji. You are the conscience of your country, and your courage is more than the courage of the soldiers at the front."

When I heard these words, all the pain and tribulation I had endured seemed worthwhile. But Shirahama would not pursue the subject further. "You'd better leave right away," he said. "Keep out of alleys, walk only on the main streets. Go right to the station and get on the first train home."

I struggled to my feet and staggered after him down a corridor to a rear exit. "Grab a taxi if you can. I'll watch you from here until you're out of sight. Tomorrow I'll try to think of a way to protect you, but there is nothing I can do tonight. Good luck."

With great physical effort, I left the building, my body aching with pain and exhaustion, and reached the main street, where I was able to get a cab to the station. When at last I was seated safely on the train, my heart throbbed with joy and my thanks burst forth as I murmured the twenty-third Psalm in Hebrew: "*A-donai ro'i lo eḥsar....*" ("The Lord is my Shepherd; I lack nothing...."). The Jews repeat this psalm at funerals, but it is more than a euphonic liturgy. The verses are filled with the emotion of deliverance from the horror of death. I felt as if the psalm had been written for me at that moment.

When I arrived home all the houses around were blacked out; there seemed to be no sign of the human world, just the myriad sparkling stars and the roaring of the waves sounding the beat of the eternal universe. I was hungry, exhausted, and disturbed; yet I had never seen the natural world so beautiful, nor felt so moved by the sight of it.

I told my family very little about my harrowing experience, just enough to explain my lateness. I didn't want to distress my wife, nor cast a blackness on the innocent minds of my two children.

This experience at the hands of the Kempeitai marked me. I had read many times of the massacres of millions of Jews during the Middle Ages by the Crusaders, during the Inquisition, and by other groups and peoples. It had always seemed a horror to me; but after my own small ordeal, the persecution of the Jews over the centuries had a reality for me it had lacked before. I now knew what persecution was, and I had discovered that in the face of torture, I could not abandon my belief in the One God as my Lord and Citadel. I felt closer than ever to the persecuted people of Israel. I knew that someday I would become a Jew.

By the beginning of 1945, there was a feeling abroad in Japan that an invasion by the American forces was imminent. In February of that year, I had a curious, illusory experience. I was standing in front of my house looking down Kamakura Bay, where the cove waters meet the Pacific. The surface of the water was dead calm, and mirror-like. Suddenly there appeared on it ships and hundreds of landing barges bearing in rapidly toward the shore where I stood. I was shocked and gasped in astonishment. Then as quickly as it had come it all disappeared, leaving only the calm sea and the growing realization that my beautiful little beach would be an ideal place for an invasion. The water was calm, the beach flat, and the capital city only thirty miles away. If the invasion should occur at Kamakura, my small house standing only twenty-five yards from the water would certainly be devastated and my family along with it. I began considering ways to move to some safer place.

A week later a sailor walked into our front yard, and asked if he could eat his lunch there. He was a country boy, obviously away from home and lonesome, apparently hoping to spend a day in a peaceful setting away from the rigors of the naval base. We made him welcome and offered him such hospitality as we had. We gave him a bit of our valuable rice, and a bottle of beer – the only one we were allowed each month.

He was grateful, probably more for the kindness than for the beer or the rice, and in return he gave us a piece of confidential information. The whole area on which my house stood was to be evacuated by government order in a few months. The military, too, had decided that Kamakura would make a fine landing beach.

It was now clear that we were going to have to move. My first thought was that we should go to Manchuria. I had many Jewish friends in that country, and to go to Harbin, where there was an extensive Jewish colony, seemed to be a good idea. It was a curious thing: I had come so far that I trusted my life to the hands of the Jews more than to my own people. I broached the subject with my wife and children; they agreed with me, and we began to prepare for the move.

They knew we could not ship many of our belongings, for at that point in the war cargo had a way of disappearing, either through thievery or submarine warfare. We decided to sell most of our furniture and other surplus goods for whatever price anyone would pay. We loaded what possessions we had kept for ourselves into eight four-hundred-pound packing boxes. And on a rainy seventh of June, 1945, we left Kamakura. We felt a strong need to flee, and the words of the angels to Lot were with us: "'Get up,' they said. 'Take your wife and your two daughters here, or you will be swept away amid the city's sin.'"

I wondered about the sense of this conclusion. Were my fears ridiculous? I subsequently learned that my name was on the list of those to be assassinated by the Kempeitai and that my friend Professor Miki, not so fortunate as I, had been brutally murdered. My decision to leave Kamakura had been the right one.

Chapter Twelve

I learned that Japan had lost the war on our trip to Harbin. The atomic bomb and the surrender were still two months away, but the people were defeated. Like defeated people, they did not travel, they fled.

From Kamakura we went to Tokyo's Ueno Railroad Station. We had managed, through connections, to get second-class train tickets, but the station was jammed with people desperate to get out of Tokyo and willing to fight their way to the ticket counter if necessary. When the gate was opened, the mob poured through, sweeping my little family along with it. It was a nightmare. We each carried two suitcases, plus a rucksack on our backs. Stumbling along under this weight, with the mob of half-crazed people surging around us like thunderous ocean waves, we struggled desperately to keep our footing lest we be trampled underfoot. My daughters were pulled away from us. I couldn't reach them; but luckily, they were able to push themselves along until we all finally met on the train. Their faces and hands were scratched and bleeding, and when I saw those marks, I knew that the people of Japan had given up; it was each man for himself.

It took the train twelve hours to reach Niigata, a large port city on the Sea of Japan. The aisle was packed tight with people. It was impossible to sit down, even more impossible to walk to the lavatory. For twelve hours we stood, unable to move.

From Niigata we took a boat across to Rashin in North Korea. As the boat moved toward the dock at Rashin, I suddenly had a vision of thousands of Russian soldiers pouring down the red-colored hills to the east like an avalanche. The vision quickly passed; but two months later the Russians did indeed pour into Rashin, the first point they attacked on their march into Manchuria. From Rashin we took the train north to Harbin. The journey took twenty long, hard days, and when we finally reached the International Hotel in Harbin, we were completely exhausted.

Harbin, which was to be our home for almost a year and a half, had become a city of distress, misery, and poverty; of rapine, pillage, and death. A city of some three-quarters of a million people, it strongly reflected the international character of Manchuria. Five ethnic groups were officially recognized: Japanese, Manchurians, Russians, Koreans, and Mongolians, and of course there were small scatterings of other nationalities besides. The city was well governed. Each national group was to some extent responsible for maintaining its own order. Each group elected a leader, and those leaders who kept good order were commended by the Japanese authorities. Partly as a result of this orderly coexistence, Manchuria remained a relatively prosperous place up until the very last days of the war. Whereas Japan proper felt the shortage of nearly everything, in Manchuria only cigarettes were rationed. We bought almost anything we wanted, even meat and fish; and our health improved immediately with the change to a proper diet. My wife's good coloring came back, and the swelling in my face disappeared.

When we arrived in Manchuria, the Japanese forces were of course still in charge, although their days of power were numbered. They knew the end was coming, and they were nervous and high strung, suspecting spies and fifth-column agents to be lurking everywhere among the Chinese and Russian populations. (As it turned out, they were right to be suspicious.) Anyone who spoke English was doubly suspect, and I tried to speak only Japanese, especially in public. One time I was in the fur shop of a Jewish friend, David Goorevitch, who now lives in Migdal HaEmek, Israel. Goorevitch and I were having a conversation in English, and just as I was leaving, a Japanese policeman walked into the shop.

"Who is that man who just left?" he demanded of Goorevitch.

Goorevitch shrugged. "He's a customer. I don't know his name."

"Is he a friend of yours? Where does he live?"

Goorevitch shrugged again. "I've seen him around. You could call him an acquaintance if you want. But I don't know where he lives."

The policeman turned and raced out of the shop, looking for me, but fortunately I had gotten on a streetcar moments before and was gone.

Dr. Abraham Kaufman, the leader of the Jewish community, was involved in a similar situation. He was director of the Jewish Hospital and president of the Jewish Bank, and he had led the Far-East Jewish Conferences in the early days of the war. A person of considerable importance in Harbin, he was considered suspect by the Japanese police because he was well connected with people of the West.

One day, shortly after our arrival at the International Hotel, Kaufman's eighteen-year-old son Ted came to me, looking pale and shaken. The reputation I had made in my previous stay in Harbin as advisor to the South Manchuria Railway still lingered. Young Kaufman knew me as a man he might turn to in trouble.

"What happened?" I asked him.

"Yesterday a policeman came to our summer house looking for my father. He wasn't there, but he went down to the military mission this morning. They're claiming that he's a Russian sympathizer because he speaks Russian."

"I'll see what I can do," I told the worried boy. I knew that a month or so before, Dr. Kaufman had received an imperial gift: a picture of the palace in Tokyo in a special frame denoting it as a royal gift. The name of the Emperor still carried enormous weight among the average Japanese. I walked into the military mission, attempting to look casual. A grim-looking Kaufman was standing before the front desk, surrounded by a half-dozen officers, tough and determined.

I pretended to be surprised to see him and walked over, my hand extended. "Congratulations, Dr. Kaufman. I understand you've been honored with an imperial gift."

The policeman looked startled. Kaufman took my hand. "It's nice to see you, Dr. Kotsuji. Yes, it's the greatest honor I've ever received."

We chatted briefly, and then I left. The Emperor's name did its work, however. In order to save face, the Japanese military handed Kaufman over to the local police, who released him; but they dared not touch him, for he had the Emperor's blessing.

Kaufman's troubles were not over, however. Because of his difficulties he was ostracized by his community. Although they felt sorry for him, many of his friends would not visit him for fear of being suspected themselves. This attitude annoyed me, so on the Sunday following his arrest I went out to his summer house, located across the Sungari River from Harbin. He was there with his son, and he was delighted to see me. We spent the day eating and drinking and talking. It was bread cast upon the waters. When I left, he surprised me by giving me three thousand yen, enough to keep my family for many months.

July passed. The panic and sense of impending doom increased, and the Japanese authorities grew more tense and nervous. They had three armies to worry about: the Russian, the Chinese Communist, and the Chinese Nationalist forces of Chiang Kai-shek. On August 8 we were still living out of our suitcases in the hotel, for my eight huge packing cases had not yet arrived. That night at about midnight, my wife aroused me, filled with alarm. "Look," she cried, pointing out the window. "Something is burning."

The whole sky to the southwest was red. "Perhaps the American B-29s have dropped incendiary bombs on the city. But don't worry, they can never make the kind of air raid they made on Yokohama here. Go back to sleep." We slept. In the morning, we found out that incendiary bombs had indeed fallen, on the Asian Alcohol Factory – but the planes had been Russian. At the same time the Russians began a three-pronged drive on Manchuria, one fork of which reached Rashin two days later. The beginning of the end was at hand.

Harbin was now alerted and uneasy. My older daughter, Mary, had been going to a girls' school in Harbin. On the day of the Russian attack, all the girls at the school were taken to a military hospital located well out in the Harbin suburbs. There, the girls were compelled to act as nurses' aides. I was deeply worried about her, for in such tumultuous times, the threat of banditry was ever present. The incident had its comic overtones, however, for the schoolmaster ordered the girls to change their underwear every day, so that if they were murdered, they would not be ashamed.

On that first night when she came home for supper Mary asked me, "Father, is it painful to die?"

"No," I said gently. "Fear of death is more painful than death itself."

She smiled and nodded, but her eyes were grave, and it hurt me in my heart to think that a fifteen-year-old girl should have to face such a reality. Each day I saw her off was like a last farewell.

For four days Harbin remained in a state of suspension, waiting for what would come. Then, on the twelfth of August I received word that my packing cases had arrived at last. I went down to the Harbin station and discovered that they had come through absolutely untouched, one of the few instances of a cargo reaching Manchuria intact in those parlous days.

I began checking them through the usual red tape, expecting that I could hire one of the many Chinese draymen who hung around the station to carry the cases to my hotel in his wagon. But when I looked for one, I discovered that they had nearly all disappeared. Finally, I collared one and told him what I wanted. He quoted me three times the standard fee.

"What's this?" I demanded.

"Look around," he said. "The wagon drivers have all run off. The Soviet Army came into Harbin this morning."

"And Japanese money isn't worth anything anymore?"

He shrugged; just then I heard a distant patter of rifle shots coming from the south. It was no time for dickering. "All right," I said. "I'll pay. Let's go."

We loaded the cases and started for the International Hotel, when it suddenly occurred to me that the Japanese-run hotel would undoubtedly be searched. Instead, I ordered the driver to go to the Hotel Moderne, a handsome, Russian-owned hotel on Kitaiskaya Street, Harbin's Fifth Avenue. When we reached it, I immediately went to the manager, whom I knew to be a Jew named Pesner.

"Professor Kotsuji," he greeted me. "I haven't seen you since you addressed the Far-East Jewish Conference right here in this hotel. That was years ago."

"I need your help," I said. "It's urgent."

When I explained about my packing cases, he instantly arranged to keep them for me in a storage room in the hotel basement. *Barukh haShem!* "A man that hath friends must shew himself friendly; and there is a friend that sticketh closer than a brother" (Prov. 18:24).

That afternoon Mary came back from the hospital alone. The Japanese soldiers had disappeared, having pulled back from Harbin during the night. It frightened me to think that she had come into town by herself during a day of such danger, yet it was a relief that she would not have to leave again. (We learned later that the army had retreated to the southern mountains to make a last stand.)

By that afternoon nobody dared to go out. I returned safely to my own hotel and climbed up on the roof at about 2 p.m. There was the sound of sporadic rifle firing. It was not the Russians, however, but the local fifth column, which crept out of hiding to open the gates of the city. By evening the fifth columnists were everywhere, both Chinese and Russian. A few days later, when a Soviet captain arrived at the Japanese military mission to take it over, the secretaries who worked there were struck by the fact that the captain seemed somehow familiar. Several hours later they realized he had been a chauffeur for the military mission.

Manchuria was occupied first by the Russians, then by the Chinese Communists. The Russian occupation began in August and lasted for three months. The Russians' sole interest in the country was to loot it, and their plan was to hang onto it until it had been stripped. Later, they intended to turn it back to the Chinese.

For the Japanese living in the country, the Russian occupation was a period of hell. In theory, at least, Russian policy was to treat decently what they called "third nationals" – people who were neither victorious Russians nor defeated Japanese. The Japanese, however, were the enemy, and they were spared nothing. Hundreds of men were shipped as slave labor to Siberia, many of them dying before they got there. Women were raped, children beaten, and everybody robbed with impunity.

To survive, the Japanese had to keep their wits about them. The occupying Russian army had been recruited from the criminal classes. Dirty and ill-mannered, they were incredibly ignorant. They were so bad that even the Chinese coolies said, "*Solen pin push-in,*" meaning, "The Russian soldiers are bums." Barbarian and savage, they stole anything they could, even burglarizing the homes of their allies, the Chinese. A doctor told me a typical story. He was on a train, trying to reach Harbin from the small village in which he lived. Two Soviet soldiers came in to inspect the train. Their eyes fell on the doctor's stethoscope.

"What's this?" they demanded.

The doctor demonstrated by way of explanation. The soldiers didn't understand. They snatched it away from him and began pulling and twisting the apparatus to see what would happen. Finally, completely baffled, they gave up and returned the instrument to the doctor, who later used it on me.

They loved watches. They would steal any watch they saw. Some of them walked around with a dozen going all the way up their arms. They were so ignorant that they did not understand that watches needed winding. When a watch stopped ticking, the Russian soldiers took it to a watch repair man.

They took women as well as watches. They were absolutely shameless in this respect. Once a Russian soldier caught a woman from behind on Kitaiskaya, Harbin's main street, and tried to rape her in this posture in broad daylight. When the woman cried for help, a Russian military policeman appeared and ordered the soldier to desist. The soldier refused and began arguing with the policeman, who let him go on for a few minutes and then shot him dead in the street. There was a huge storehouse in the Nangan area of Harbin where such bodies were callously tossed. Life was incredibly cheap, and it was even worse in the villages outside the cities.

We lived in constant apprehension. The Russian soldiers indulged in "midnight visits." They would burst into a house shouting "*Davai,*" the Russian word for give, take whatever money and other valuables they could find, sometimes rape the women, and then go on their way. The Japanese ultimately learned to keep any valuables well hidden and to get the women out of the way when the Russians were around. Before they understood this, however, most of them had been robbed, and many of the women raped. Sometimes, in the aftermath, the women committed suicide. We escaped this disaster, but we were robbed of all the money Dr. Kaufman had given us. Ten times we were raided, and each time we hid in the mud under the floor, cowering in the dark among spider webs.

What saved me from almost certain shipment to Siberia was the kindness of my Jewish friends, who protected me as well as they could, and the fact that I do not have typical Japanese features. Most Japanese have round faces, flat in profile. My face is narrow and thin and sharp in profile; it is what is known as "a little high." I discovered that if I wore a Tartar's hat I was easily mistaken for a Tartar, and this piece of luck, coupled with the fact that I spoke both Russian and English, enabled me to walk around the city at small risk. I always dressed in my best suit and kept a high gloss on my shoes, and that helped to protect me, too, for the Russian soldiers assumed that a well-dressed man was an official of some sort, not a Japanese without a penny in his pockets.

But it was the kindness of the Jewish community that actually kept my family alive and safe. A Mr. Judkin, a man whom I had known in former times, arranged for me to have a house next to his in the Jewish quarter. I lived there for a year, and two of his friends, a certain Plotkin and Joseph Moiseeff, escorted my belongings to the new house so that they would not be stolen in transit. (Happily, I met both men again in Kfar Chabad on my trip to Israel in 1959.) Other kind people supplied us with small amounts of money or food from time to time. The names Klein, Malay Lehnenstein, and Birger stay in my memory. A man named Dagilaievsky, who owned a public bath, gave me a free pass.

Yet life for me was still risky. One day, as I was walking down Kitaiskaya Street, ignored by the soldiers, I was suddenly pounced upon by a ten-year-old boy. He caught my sleeve and clung to it in a determined manner, crying loudly, "Japanese, Japanese." I recognized him as a spotter for the Russian man-hunting squads, but unfortunately, in my first unthinking moment I answered instinctively in Japanese: "No, I'm not Japanese."

"Yes, yes, you spoke Japanese." The boy called out loudly that I was Japanese.

I tried to shake him off, but he hung onto my coat sleeve. Then Soviet soldiers began trotting up, waving their automatic rifles. I thought then that my end was near. A feeling of resignation passed over me, and I stared up at the calm blue of the sky. Then, as I looked down, I saw a military policeman's sentry box. Suddenly I decided, like the distressed bird, to fly into the bosom of the huntsman for protection. I dragged the wretched Russian boy toward the sentry box, and I snapped out in Russian, "Who speaks English?"

After a few minutes of confusion, a young lieutenant arrived; he spoke excellent English. "I am Professor Kotsuji," I insisted. "What is the meaning of this boy grabbing me like a common criminal?" I had once met the Soviet Consul Loginoff, and I decided to use his name. "I'm a professor, and I'm a friend of Consul Loginoff," I said boldly. The Russians have great respect for the word "professor" and the lieutenant relaxed his attitude toward me.

"Do you really know Consul Loginoff?" he asked. By this time several hundred Chinese civilians, drawn by the commotion, had gathered around.

"Of course. If you doubt me, call him up."

"When did you come to Manchuria?" he asked, still trying to feel me out.

"I have just come from Tokyo. I'm a historian, and someday I hope to have the chance to write about the good qualities of the Russian Occupation Army and not about its bad qualities."

This touched his pride. "All right, you can go."

I continued to act boldly and pushed through the crowd with my cane. I saw the Chinese staring at my face and heard them whisper, "What kind of Japanese is he?"

Without any leaders, the Japanese in Manchuria had become lost sheep. The army was gone, and the consul-general was in hiding. Finally, I decided that something had to be done to put a halt to the rape and robbery. Working through my friend Judkin, I managed to get an interview with Consul Loginoff. The meeting was considered by the Russian to be important, for it was attended not only by Consul Loginoff, but by Ivanoff, the Chief Staff Officer of the Red Army, along with an interpreter and two stenographers. I told them that I spoke for all the

Japanese in Harbin, but that I was speaking as a scholar, not a diplomat. I pointed out that the Soviets could not expect to rule entirely by force, that they needed the goodwill of the people, and that they couldn't expect to get it unless rape and pillaging stopped. I then suggested that one Japanese ought to be appointed to the board of the South Manchuria Railway to act as a kind of liaison between the government and the Japanese community.

The military staff man answered for the Soviets. "The bad behavior of the soldiers will cease in three days. As for the appointment to the South Manchuria Railway, that will have to be taken up with higher authorities."

The meeting changed nothing. I met twice again with the Russian officials, but nothing helped. Pillage was their program, and by the time they allowed the Chinese Communist Army in to take over the occupation, Manchuria was an empty house.

The arrival of the Chinese Communists was a great relief. They had suffered more at the hands of the Japanese than had the Russians, and they might have been expected to desire revenge. The reverse was true. Well-disciplined and of good moral conduct, they did not abuse the women or pillage to any large extent. It was true that there were occasional incidents about the countryside, where Chinese people avenged themselves on a specific person, but there was no general policy of vengeance. This is partly because as Asiatics they felt a closer kinship with the Japanese than the Russians had. Partly it was due to Chiang Kai-shek, who broadcast a message to all Chinese to return grace and kindness for the damages they had suffered. Finally, it was due to the simple fact that China has an ancient culture built on the ethical system of Confucianism.

It might have been otherwise had the Chinese Nationalist Army taken over Harbin. Beaten back from the city shortly after the Communists took it over, the Chinese Nationalist Army began there its long retreat down to South China and exile in Formosa. Despite Generalissimo Chiang Kai-shek, the morale of the Nationalist Army was low and its morals even lower; it was defeated in spirit before it began fighting the Communists. Later, when the Japanese were liberated from Manchuria and passed through Nationalist Chinese lines in the process, the Nationalists had to be bribed to keep the train moving. They also demanded ten Japanese women for the use of their troops; fortunately, the Japanese official in charge had been farsighted enough to bring with him ten prostitutes for this express purpose.

Even the Chinese Communists, though they controlled wholesale looting and rape, were not in a mood to be especially kind to the Japanese. Landowners – and those who owned businesses – in Manchuria were liable to be tried by so-called People's Courts and executed. No Japanese was allowed to operate a trade in a building: they had to work as street peddlers. Frequently enough, when a man grew slightly prosperous, the conquerors came and kicked his merchandise into the gutters. Once, when I was courageous enough to ask an official why he did such a thing, I was told that the defeated Japanese ought to look sorrowful and humble.

Not even in death did they show the Japanese any kindness. Japanese were dying by the hundreds from disease – mainly typhus. Due to a shortage of coffins, the bodies were simply wrapped in thin kimonos, carried on a baggage cart to a huge pit, and flung in. Down in the pit stood a Chinese coolie, who then stole the kimono and broke the gold teeth out of the dead man's mouth. One Japanese mother found the kimono of her dead child being sold by a street merchant. In this respect we were lucky again. My daughter Julie fell ill with typhus and lay sick with a fever of 104 degrees for almost two weeks. I was able to get a doctor to come only twice during this period. He showed me how to reduce her temperature with ice packs, and how to give her regular injections of camphor and digitalis. The child did not speak for a week; but her resistance was strong, and after twelve days her temperature began to drop.

During the first period of the occupation, I managed to keep my family alive through the kindness of the people in the Jewish quarters and by selling my suits, each of which brought me two bushels of potatoes. Later, I worked with a man named Jinnaka, a professor of applied chemistry, who had invented a tasty synthetic whisky which he bottled as Scotch and exported to Russia. Disguised as a Tartar, I traded the whisky and was able to make a little money.

For all Japanese in Manchuria, true hope was repatriation. We wanted to go home, for life under American occupation forces was far better than under the Chinese. We had, however, no grasp of what was actually going on in Japan. News from home was sketchy and, more often than not, inaccurate. We learned that the war was over through a brief radio message. We understood that the Emperor had killed himself. We knew about the atom bomb only months later, and we had no idea of its real significance or power. It was not until I actually set foot in Japan that I understood the monstrous extent of its destruction. Thus, when a Colonel Bell appeared in Harbin in July 1946, to negotiate repatriation for those of us still surviving in the Japanese colony, we were astonished but delighted.

Chapter Thirteen

According to the repatriation agreement worked out between the Americans and the Chinese Communists, each Japanese was assured of personal safety until he boarded ship at Kolotao. However, the Communists allowed the repatriated Japanese to take very little with them. One was permitted to carry only one extra set of clothes; no textile goods whatsoever except for a towel; no new shoes, writing paper, photographs, or jewelry; no gold, nor anything of value. Such was the stern directive handed down by the Communist authorities. What made it worse was the fact that the examinations, which took place at Harbin's railway station, were in the hands of teenage Chinese girls and their male supervisors. These girls were chosen from comparatively low classes. They were greedy and severe. They stole baked bread which the Japanese had prepared for their children. They also stole shoes and pretty kimonos. No Japanese dared to object to such treatment because objection might end in indefinite detention. The attitude of the United States Army of Occupation was generous by comparison.

My wife had suffered from chronic hemorrhoids and was very pale. One of the girls who examined us assumed she was a bad woman because she did not have a lively face. The girl cross-examined her sharply. I began to explain to the girl what was wrong with my wife. I showed her a special certificate which I had obtained beforehand from one of the Communist officials who had once studied at the Kyoto Imperial University. I also showed her my card which bore my Doctor of Divinity title. I did everything to explain that our family had served humanity steadfastly. The following conversation took place:

> "What is theology?" she asked.
>
> "Theology is the study of God."
>
> "What is your god? War? Trade?"
>
> "Neither. My God is the all-governing God of the universe. God is benevolent like your parents, and His goodness is perfect. When you were a feeble baby, God watched over you, and so you grew up to be a nice girl. Will you be kind as our God of loving-kindness is?"

During this conversation I gazed deeply into her eyes. She looked bored, half-understanding, half-puzzled. She said, "Can't help, all right." My spirit had won her over to our side.

We were required to walk part of the way, and most of the time we slept on the ground or on plain wooden floors. I had served as Colonel Bell's interpreter during the negotiations, and I had hoped that my elder daughter Mary, who had an American birth certificate, would be allowed to fly immediately to Japan, but there were no planes. Transportation of any kind was in short supply; we could carry very little, and most of our possessions were simply left behind in the hands of friends.

Fortunately, we had a helper. He was a young Japanese soldier who had been captured by the Chinese Communists at the end of the war and put into a labor battalion. Along with a group of fellow Japanese he had escaped, walking for days through the Manchurian wilderness to Harbin. He was, of course, a fugitive, and I had taken him into my house as a member of my family. Out of gratitude, he served as a guard and helper on the repatriation journey. He not only carried most of our baggage for us but volunteered to do the task work levied on me by the Chinese. We left Harbin in September and traveled by train and by foot for a month.

For all that time we had neither blankets nor mats, and we ate bad food of which there was very little. By the grace of Almighty God, we arrived a month later in Hakata, on the Japanese island of Kyushu, alive and transported with joy to be home again after a year and a half of exile.

We immediately went to my eldest brother Genjiro's house in Nishinomiya, a town near Kobe. Here we learned that an old prophecy had been fulfilled. My mother had died in my absence. Just as she had always believed, her youngest son was not at her deathbed. She was seventy-eight years old. She had not been eating for months, and she was suffering from malnutrition. When she heard of the mass murder of so many Japanese in Manchuria, she feared that I had died also, and she could not stand the shock. She died calling my name, "Setschan."

I am a reasonable and not a superstitious man. Yet curiously, I now found that as my mother lay dying in my brother's house, in Manchuria I had been overwhelmed by sudden, longing thoughts of her, poignant to the point of pain. It had been some time before I could shake the feeling off.

From Nishinomiya we went to Tokyo, with no idea whatsoever of what we were going to do, where we were going to sleep. Postwar Japan was a mass of confusion. Change was everywhere, some of it simply due to defeat, some of it brought in by the Americanization of the country under occupation. Unemployment was high, housing was short. Landlords did not always charge rent, since the feeling prevailed that you could not have people living in the streets just because they could not get work; for that reason, we were able to get rooms for nothing. I found a job with the American Red Cross and began the long, arduous task of remaking my life.

The most impressive part of that time was the peaceful and magnanimous American administration of Japan in the postwar period, especially to one who had seen how horrible an occupation army can be. Japan was extraordinarily fortunate in its conquerors. The dignity and goodness of General Douglas MacArthur captured the minds of the Japanese, pervading the whole country, even the smallest hamlets. To display one of those two qualities is easy; to possess them both is something only a rare personality can manage. MacArthur's dismissal by President Truman was a grave shock to the Japanese. I understood Truman's position better than most Japanese could, due to my familiarity with American constitutional procedures, but even so I was astonished. Truman's action cost the United States much prestige in Japanese eyes.

However, despite the admirable work of the American administration, my own position remained poor. There is still considerable unemployment in Japan, and of course there was far more immediately after the war. Furthermore, it is extremely difficult for older men to get work in Japan at any time. It is expected that a man work his way up; joblessness among the intellectuals, whose careers were broken by the war, is still acute.

My English was of course useful, and I was able, finally, to get a job with an import-export firm, where I worked from 1947 to 1950. Then I worked briefly as an advisor to the United States Navy in Tokyo, until I became ill with pleurisy and had to resign. The disease plagued me off and on for seven years, and after 1950 I did not hold a regular job, but worked part-time in export-import trade. I did various kinds of writing on the side. I wanted to teach, but there were times when there was no demand in Japan for Hebrew courses.

Yet throughout this time my Hebrew studies were my deepest concern. Everything that had gone before, reaching deep into my childhood, seemed to point toward a conversion to Judaism. Such an act, it seemed to me, was the natural culmination of a long sequence of events, beginning with my discovery of the Old Testament, intensified through my work with the Jews in Manchuria and the help I had given the Jewish refugees in Kobe, and climaxed by the life-saving assistance the Jews of Harbin had given me in return. My life had become bound up with this people; conversion seemed inevitable.

Some of my Jewish friends questioned my decision. Why adopt a religion which is so likely to bring troubles and sorrow? My response was that I would come to Judaism with joy and pride. From my suffering for the Jewish cause, my attachment to Judaism had grown and grown, and with it had grown my affection for the Jewish people. My unshaken belief in One God lived together in my heart with the love of His people. It seemed only natural for me to become one of them.

Yet formidable obstacles stood in my way. For one thing, there was the question whether the Jewish people would receive me. Jews are divided on the question of converts. Secondly, there was the problem of getting to Jerusalem, where I wanted to make a pilgrimage. In the years after the war passports were very difficult for Japanese to get. Then again, I was not in a financial position to make such a trip. I was beginning to feel discouraged. I was in my mid-fifties, and I was worried that I might not live long enough to find my religious home. Abraham was circumcised at ninety-nine. I was considerably younger, but my health was not as good as Abraham's.

Then one day I received a letter from Dr. Israel Ben-Zeev, president of the *Aguda Lemaan Gerei Tzedek* – the World Union for the Propagation of Judaism. It was dated March 20, 1957, and it said simply that if I wished to come to Jerusalem for my conversion, they would extend every assistance.

I began to work on my passport problem vigorously, and late in 1957 I received my passport. Two obstacles had been overcome, but my financial troubles continued. I simply did not have the money to finance a long trip. A year passed, and then another, and suddenly I became sixty. I recalled the proverb: Larks do not fall ready-roasted into the mouth. *Aguda Lemaan Gerei Tzedek* was eager to facilitate my conversion. The rest was up to me.

It was my wife who suggested I mortgage our house. "Life is short," she said. "When you want something, you should have it, regardless of the criticism of friends." So I mortgaged the house. I did not know what would happen later. I did not calculate like an accountant, but I placed my faith in God and went ahead with my plans. Without my wife's encouragement, perhaps I would not have done it. If she had opposed me, I would have been troubled in my heart; but she knew that conversion was my destiny, and she was my support. Thus, on August 8, 1959, without telling anyone but my family, I went out to Haneda Airport in Tokyo and boarded a plane for Israel. I felt, suddenly, as the plane flew down the runway, that I had embarked upon a brand new life.

As I had no particular desire to visit any of the places along the way in the midst of the summer heat – cities such as New Delhi and Tehran – I flew direct, nonstop, over the great Thar Desert, over the ocean, finally over the Mediterranean Sea. At dusk on August 9 the plane touched down at Lydda Airport outside Jerusalem. Friends met and drove me up the winding Shefela highway to the Holy City. Without sleep for thirty-six hours, I dozed off in the car. I dreamed I was climbing up a silver ladder; my friends awoke me and said, "Look, Jerusalem." There on the mountaintop across a valley were the lights of the city shining in the dark. I was in the land of Isaiah.

My friends took me to the Hotel Ron. When I awoke in the morning the sky above the Holy City was absolutely cloudless, absolutely blue, and the sunshine was dazzling. I went out and walked the streets where Isaiah had walked. The morning was so clear, so quiet; I saw the city through the eyes of love.[1]

That morning, too, I heard two women conversing in Hebrew. I was thrilled by the sound: It was the first time I had heard the living language spoken and of course I could not understand it. Modern Hebrew is much different from the biblical tongue.

Later that first day my friends took me sightseeing and then to meet Rabbi Yaakov Moshe Toledano, Minister of Religious Affairs. I had not expected to meet anyone, and I was wearing a blue aloha sport shirt, for which I apologized.

"Don't worry about it," Toledano said. "After all, man was born naked." His kindness was typical of the people of Israel.

My friends had arranged for me to stay in the private house of Mr. Mouyon instead of a hotel, which was a great blessing. How long I would stay I did not know. In the end, I remained there for four months. I had two major tasks to accomplish. One was to prepare myself for the rigorous examination I would have to undergo before I could be converted. The second was to learn to speak modern Hebrew. I daily attended Ulpan Etzion, a Hebrew school, for this purpose. I tried to practice conversation as much as possible.

Here the children were a blessing and a delight. To watch them at play in the evening was a charming sight. A scene so reminiscent of biblical illustrations that I was cast into the past. It was from the children that I

---

1. Later in my stay, as fall began to come, the sky began to fill with clouds a little more each day, and I understood for the first time the line from Isaiah 18:4, "...on the harvest heat a cloud of dew." It is impossible to have a complete understanding of some of the biblical verses until you have seen the land where they were written. Isaiah especially is filled with the weather of Jerusalem.

got the real sense of the language. Their speech was fresh, idiomatic, and enthusiastic, without the stiff formality sometimes found in adult talk. Moreover, they were the friendliest children in the world, showing no rudeness about my foreign appearance. Once I made a visit to Dr. Zorach Warhaftig, former Deputy Minister of Religious Affairs and now a full minister, a man who had been among the Kobe refugees as one of the leaders. For fun, I taught his son and daughter to count to ten in Japanese – *ichi, ni, san* being one, two, three. A week or so later I happened to meet a group of schoolchildren on King George Street. One of them saw me and raising her hand shouted, *"Ichi, ni, san."* Instantly, the others fell in with her, reciting the numbers in unison. There was nothing jeering about it; it was a salute, a welcome.

Another time, when I was strolling along the beach in Tel Aviv, I fell in with a group of young men and children who were curious about Japan. They asked me many questions, which I encouraged for the practice it gave my Hebrew. Finally, one of the boys said to me, "Sir, perhaps you did not know that there is a famous scholar from Japan now visiting in Jerusalem."

"Is that so?" I said. "I will certainly see him without fail."

"I saw his picture in the paper," the boy continued. "He looks like you."

"Is that so?" I asked soberly. "Isn't it surprising?"

Children are the flowers of the culture of the home, society, or state. By its flowers the health of the tree can be judged. For this reason, I tried to have as much contact with the children as I could, and from those little teachers I learned much. From them I felt the real pulse of the country and got the real sense of the language.

Another of the great pleasures abounding for me in Israel was the renewal of old friendships, some of them going back twenty years to my days with the South Manchuria Railway. There is, in the suburbs of Tel Aviv, a settlement called *Shikum Yotzei Sin* composed of Jews who have lived in China and Manchuria. I was asked to attend the dedication of their new synagogue, at which Rabbi Toledano spoke. I found so many old friends there that I was dazed with joy. When Rabbi Toledano finished speaking, I joined in the ovation, and then suddenly I heard somebody saying, "And now Dr. Kotsuji will say a few words."

I was embarrassed. My modern Hebrew was very shaky and I would have liked to refuse, but with the eyes of so many friends upon me I could not. So I stood and managed a few halting words about the relationship between Japan and Israel and ended by saying that I would be the tie which binds them both. I was so excited, I barely remember my own words, but considering the ovation I received, apparently I did well enough.

I met another old friend, David Goorevitch, the fur dealer from Harbin who had helped me in so many ways. He was living in Migdal HaEmek, and when he heard I was in Jerusalem, he traveled fifty miles to see me and fulfill an old obligation. In Harbin I had asked him to hide a classic woven picture of some value. He kept it in a trunk, but later, when I left Harbin, he couldn't find it. It had since turned up, and now he brought it to me. I took it, for the sake of his warm friendship, but I gave him another picture as a token of appreciation.

Although seeing so many old friends again was a thrilling experience, my real business in Israel was my conversion. And on September 9, 1959, I went to the *beit din*, the rabbinate court, to be examined. The examination took place in a rather nondescript office on Jaffa Road in Jerusalem. The three examining rabbis were formal and austere in their manner and conducted the questioning with utmost seriousness.

Why, they asked me, did I choose to believe in Judaism?

"My entire past life answers that question," I said. "When there is no God but one, what could I believe otherwise than that the Lord our God is that One?"

They were also concerned about the reaction of my wife. How did she feel about my conversion? "In Japan," I explained, "what the husband decides, the wife follows."

The questioning took about thirty minutes, and then I was asked to wait outside for another half hour while they deliberated. When I reentered the room the austerity and gravity were gone. They were smiling and cheerful, and they said they were happy to accept me into Judaism. Ten days later I went to the Shaare Zedek Hospital, where Dr. Nahum Cook performed the circumcision under the blessing of a number of high officials. There, on September 20, 1959, by the name of Abraham

Ben Abraham I was embraced into the fold of *benei Avraham*. Forty-seven years of wandering in search of my religious home were over.

Chapter Fourteen

Since that momentous day in September 1959, I have been asked many times why I became a Jew. I was not converted by one single event, but by many years of acquaintance with this great religion. The sum of my studies, of the events of my life, of all my contacts with the Old Testament culture brought me to Judaism. The prophetic spirit inspired me; faith and reverence led me to my spiritual home.

After my conversion, I spent three months in Israel, lecturing all over the country. Then, on December 8, I flew via El Al Airlines to the United States, my heart full of boundless gratitude toward my friends in Israel, especially Dr. Ben-Zeev, who did so much to further my cause. The Jewish Information Society had just been founded in the United States. They wanted me to speak at the inaugural meeting, and after that, tour throughout America under the auspices of the Jewish Center Lecture Bureau. For eight months I traveled up and down the country – and even into Mexico. I was always warmly received, not because I was a famous man, but because of the great interest among American Jews in the question of conversion.

Then, in the summer of 1960, after a year of separation, I returned to my homeland and my family, a new man. The next year I established the Institute of Hebrew Culture in Japan, which, while I was on another speaking tour of America in 1962 and 1963, was incorporated under American laws. The institute is the medium through which I hope to disseminate the Jewish faith in Japan. My task, I now believe, is to inaugurate a new branch in the stream of Jewish history. I shall try to establish a source in Japan from which a new river of Judaism may one day flow.

I have often been asked by many Jewish friends throughout the world which of the three versions of Judaism – Orthodox, Conservative, or Reform – I intend to espouse in Japan. To that I answer, none of them. I do not like schism, and I am convinced that the difference between the three is the matter of *minhagim,* the observing practice. Because I was converted in Jerusalem, the Orthodox customs are natural to me, but the Judaism I introduce will not be described as any of the three: It will be a genuine, living Judaism, which will take into consideration the special nature of the Japanese mind.

My Jewish friends also query me about my approach to missionary work. Orthodox Jews are inclined to oppose missions, and if they are thinking of the coercive type of missionary work practiced by some Christians, I fully agree. However, we Jewish people should not neglect to glorify the Great Name of the Lord among other peoples. What I plan to do, then, is simply to spread knowledge of Judaism throughout Japan. My program is tripartite. First, I will develop a Jewish library in Tokyo. Since so many educated Japanese already know English, we will be able to avoid having to translate vast amounts of work. I have been promised books by some publishers already. Second, I intend to publish in Japanese as much and as often as I can on the subject of Judaism and Jewish history. Third, I expect to lecture continually. Thus will I serve to glorify God. I believe in the power of truth to convince. So it will be with Judaism. I don't expect to convert vast numbers of Japanese. I am not going to urge Judaism on my countrymen. I will simply give them truth; and perhaps in a century's time, that truth will spread itself.

My act of homage to Jerusalem, the Holy City, has determined my life, not only since my conversion but during the many years before. I am conscious today of a single radiant fact – that I am an avowed Jew. This little seed of a faith that I am in Japan has a great power to live, for where grass withers and flowers fade, the word of our God abides. May the divine history of the Lord Almighty in the land of Japan be now declared; may the Holy One bless this enterprise, and may the herald proclaim:

For out of Zion shall go forth the Torah,
and the word of the Lord from Jerusalem

Sanctuary Secured:
The Man Who Extended the "Visas for Life"

Jundai Yamada

TRANSLATED BY
Doreen Jackson

My fate is your fate. Your lives are my life.

Kotsuji Setsuzo
Speaking to the Mirrer Yeshiva
Jerusalem, 1959

Introduction

A life of deprivation, constant dread of hard labor, torture, unspeakable human experiments, and gas chambers referred to as "shower rooms" awaited Jews transported to concentration camps by the Nazis.

About six million were slaughtered during the Holocaust, the most abhorrent event in human history. It is a sobering thought when one considers that the equivalent of about half the population of present-day Tokyo was killed in the span of just a few years, solely because they were Jews.

Viktor E. Frankl, a psychologist who miraculously survived several Nazi concentration camps, described his own experience of the Holocaust in detail in his book *Man's Search for Meaning*. The following is an excerpt from an eyewitness account written in April 1945 by Kurt Gerstein, an SS officer who was present at mass gassings.

> Behind the little windows closed with barbed wire were children, women, and men, yellow filled with fear. They were driven out of the train cars with leather whips. They were instructed to remove

> all clothing and forced to turn in all valuables and all money. The women and girls had their hairs cut off. Then the march began [to the gas chamber]...led by a girl of singular beauty. They passed us completely naked, the men, the women, the girls, the children, the babies. A strong SS-man told the unfortunates in a pastoral voice: "Nothing will happen to you...." [But] the majority knew everything, the stench indicates their fate....Brothers, mothers nursing their children on their breasts, naked, many children of all ages, naked. They hesitate, but they enter the death chamber, the majority without saying a word pushed by others behind them who are kept moving by the whips of the SS. Many pray.... The doors are being closed.... One can hear them cry.... After twenty-five minutes pass: Many it is true are dead.... After twenty-eight minutes a few are still alive. After thirty-two minutes at last, everything is dead.... The dead are standing like columns.... Even in death, one can recognize the families who are still clasping hands. It is difficult to separate them.

In 1940, Jewish refugees fleeing Nazi Germany flocked to the Japanese Consulate in Kaunas, Lithuania, seeking visas to Japan. Vice-Consul Sugihara Chiune issued transit visas on humanitarian grounds to the refugees, enabling them to flee to other countries from Japan. Thanks to Sugihara's bold decision, many Jewish refugees escaped the Holocaust by heading for Japan.

Beginning about one year before Japan plunged into the Pacific War, Jewish refugees were thus arriving in droves in Kobe, Yokohama, and Tokyo. It is believed that the number may have ultimately reached six thousand. These Jewish refugees had listed Curacao, a Dutch colony in the Caribbean, as the final destination on their transit visas. However, they actually hoped to gain entry to the United States, Palestine, or Canada. Once in Japan, swift passage to these desired destinations was limited to the few wealthy people who already had entry visas for those host countries.

Meanwhile, the many refugees who did not have an entry visa for a specific destination after Japan had no choice but to wait in Kobe. The visas that Sugihara issued only allowed transit through Japan, and refugees were permitted to stay in Japan for at most ten days.

It was impossible to negotiate with the destination country and secure transportation by ship in just ten days. The Jewish refugees begged for extensions of their visas, but these pleas were denied. If the visas were not extended, the refugees would be deported back to their countries of origin. This meant certain death for them.

One Japanese man came to the rescue of the Jewish refugees in this excruciating predicament. His name was Kotsuji Setsuzo.

Kotsuji Setsuzo became the point of contact for the Jewish refugees who managed to arrive in Kobe, and negotiated with the Japanese government in a variety of ways. In the end he was able to successfully extend their visas.

And that is not all. He helped Jews who were stranded at sea, unable to enter Japan because they did not have visas. These refugees were waiting to be rescued aboard a ship in the Sea of Japan. He made every effort to ensure that Jewish refugees in Kobe could live in Japan with peace of mind. He negotiated with shipping companies to secure their sea travel to final destinations. Thanks to Kotsuji's efforts, most Jewish refugees left Japan before the outbreak of the Pacific War and were able to continue their flight to safety.

What kind of person was Kotsuji Setsuzo? In writing this book, I interviewed Mr. Ishida Kunio, former director of the Diplomatic Archives of the Ministry of Foreign Affairs of Japan. He shared this article.

> When we talk about Japanese saving Jewish refugees, Sugihara Chiune, who was vice-consul in Kaunas, Lithuania, is known for his great undertaking to help Jewish refugees. The visas he issued were transit visas. It turns out that Jewish refugees ended up staying in Japan for quite an extended period of time. During that time, they found their final destination to take refuge [and emigrate] and departed Japan.
>
> Some questions that come to mind in revisiting this history: How were the Jewish refugees able to remain in Japan for such a long period of time? If Sugihara in Lithuania was the sender

allowing passage, who was receiving and helping the Jewish refugees in Japan? These questions have long been neglected and unanswered. There are two Japanese names that always come up as benefactors from the Jews who survived. One is Sugihara Chiune of Lithuania. The other is Dr. Kotsuji Setsuzo of Kamakura. He was known among Jews as an expert in Jewish studies. When Dr. Kotsuji received a request for cooperation from the Kobe Jewish community, he took on the role of intermediary in negotiations with the government.

He scrambled on behalf of the refugees who arrived in Japan so that they could stay in Japan until they were able to find a country that would accept them. It was said that toward the end of the war, his life was in danger a number of times because of these actions.

If Dr. Kotsuji had not been in Japan, the circumstances of the Jews who arrived with Sugihara's visas would have been very different. Sugihara and Kotsuji had a common quality: They each had a clear understanding of the adversities that the Jewish refugees encountered in Europe from their own perspectives. Dr. Kotsuji, in particular, was well versed in Jewish language and culture as a scholar. Consequently, from a sense of moral duty he decided that he needed to help the Jewish refugees. Their determination to take action to save the Jews came from a strong sense of justice. Another commonality between these two men was that their actions changed their own destinies.

By telling Kotsuji Setsuzo's story, we are able to see the full picture of a pair of folding screens telling the story of the Jewish refugees who fled from the distant land of Europe.

At the time the Jewish refugees were flooding into Japan, Nazi Germany stationed SS leadership in Japan and were planning to persecute the refugees. If Jewish refugees had remained in Japan after the Pacific War broke out, it is very likely they would have ended up in these Nazis' hands.

Although Japan allied with Germany and joined World War II, there is no historical evidence that it was directly involved in the genocide of the Jews. This notwithstanding, however, had it not been for Kotsuji it is certain that thousands of Jews who made their way to Japan would have faced forced repatriation and as a result been handed over to the Nazis. The result would surely have been to add a bloody Holocaust page to Japan's history.

Many people may find my interest in Kotsuji Setsuzo and the Jewish refugees rather curious and wonder how it came about. I had lived in the United States as an exchange student starting in my early teens and was quite comfortable closely interacting with people of all races. But even with this background I knew very little about Jews. My knowledge was limited to basic information we learned in school, that Jews are an ethnic group that suffered persecution by Nazi Germany during World War II. But I was aware that there were many famous people who were Jewish, such as Albert Einstein, Nobel laureate in physics; Mark Zuckerberg, founder of Facebook; and, my favorite in the world of movies, Steven Spielberg stands out among many Jewish directors.

In 1993, Spielberg's movie *Schindler's List* was released in the United States. This movie, based on Thomas Keneally's book of the same title, is a grueling depiction of the Holocaust. Schindler, a businessman and member of the Nazi Party, struggled with love and justice amidst the horrors of the Holocaust as his humanitarian spirit was awakened. He hired Jews to work in his own factory and saved their lives.

At the time I was studying at an American university and deeply moved. The Holocaust, which resulted in unimaginably more than six million victims, was shocking to me. At the same time, I was impressed by the hero who doggedly persisted in his humanitarian efforts with wisdom and courage while surrounded by turmoil. It was at this same time that I learned of a similar Japanese person, Sugihara Chiune, who came to be known as the "Japanese Schindler." I admired this diplomat who issued "visas for life" and remember thinking that there were incredible Japanese heroes too.

I first became aware of Kotsuji's existence when I read a book about Sugihara's visas for life. At that time, I had three questions. First, how did the Jewish refugees get from Lithuania to Japan with these visas? Second, where in Japan were the six thousand Jews and what kind of lives had they led there? And third, how did they manage to gain entry to their final destinations when they were permitted only a ten-day stay in Japan?

When I did some research, I found the following about the route to Japan. The Jewish refugees who escaped from Lithuania, with only the clothes they were wearing, used the Trans-Siberian Railway to travel across the continent. Then from Vladivostok, they boarded a ship and arrived in Japan. Their visas were valid for ten days to two weeks. Some were only good for three days. Some didn't have visas at all.

How were the refugees able to arrange their next destination in such a short period of time? They needed to submit an application to the host country and be granted passage. Even in today's internet society, international communications can be complicated and time-consuming. In pre-war Japan, it would have been a next-to-impossible undertaking to try to determine one's next destination in such a short span. Moreover, the Japanese language and customs were completely different from what the refugees knew. How did they get food? Where did they stay? How did they arrange transportation to their final destination? It must have seemed like nothing but hurdles for the Jewish refugees who didn't know right from left in this new place.

And for Japan, on the receiving end of the six thousand refugees arriving in droves, this must have been an urgent situation. Almost all of these people made their way to Kobe. While Kobe at the time was the only Japanese city to have a Jewish community, it was comprised of only a few dozen households, and it would have been impossible for them to accommodate so many refugees. And yet, none of the Jewish refugees were deported and in time were able to flee to safety, away from the Nazis' reach. How on earth was this possible?

I concluded the only possible explanation was that someone was working on their behalf in Japan. But who could this person have been?

It took a long time for me to find the answer. I searched through any books or materials that I could get my hands on that dealt with Jewish refugees. And then I finally discovered the answer I was looking for: There was indeed an individual who helped the Jewish refugees rushing into Japan. That person was Kotsuji Setsuzo (1899–1973). From what I was able to learn, Kotsuji had a doctorate in Hebrew studies. He converted to Judaism nearly fifteen years after the war ended in 1959, when he was sixty years old, but no further details were provided. I began my research into Kotsuji and soon came across a surprising fact. He was buried in Israel.

When Kotsuji died in October 1973, Israel was in turmoil. The Yom Kippur War raged from October 6 to October 25 of that year; it was no time for flights from Japan to land. Even so, Kotsuji's body was airlifted to Israel. Upon arrival, it was met at the airfield by the Minister of Religion and other dignitaries. They had all been refugees who had fled the Nazis to Japan, and who credited Kotsuji with saving them. Even amidst the great tumult of war, the radio reported that Kotsuji's body was buried in a cemetery in Jerusalem, and my research found that many Israelis soon went to the cemetery to pay their respects to Kotsuji. In Israel, the Jews whose lives were saved by Kotsuji had not forgotten him. They remembered the man from Kobe, and his name has been passed on in stories to their descendants.

What kind of person was Kotsuji? I found few written accounts of him and no photographs at first. I searched desperately to find out what Kotsuji was like and learned that he published his autobiography in 1964. The autobiography was written in English and published by an American publisher. A revised edition was issued in 1975, but both editions were out of print. I thought a Japanese translation might have been published and made inquiries, but I could not locate it. His autobiography had not been published in Japan.

Questions swirled in my mind: Why did Kotsuji, a Japanese man, write in English and publish his autobiography overseas? Why was it not published in Japan? I had to get hold of this book by any means I could and read it as soon as possible, so I asked a friend in the United States to look for it on my behalf.

In the spring of 2010, Kotsuji's autobiography arrived in the mail. Even though it had been published almost fifty years before, the book was in much better shape than I expected. On the orange cover was an illustration of someone who looked like Kotsuji undergoing a Jewish ritual, under the title "From Tokyo to Jerusalem" written on it. On the back of the dust jacket was a large profile photo of Kotsuji holding a Bible.

I thought, "So this is Kotsuji Setsuzo, the individual who saved thousands of Jewish refugees who fled to Japan from unspeakable horrors with Sugihara Chiune's 'visas for life'" He looked rather serious, and he had a well-defined, dignified profile.

Opening the book, I found a *Newsweek* magazine article clipping inserted between the pages. It said that Kotsuji had converted to Judaism at the age of sixty. The fact that this was reported in *Newsweek* tells just how important a person Kotsuji was at that time, not only to people in Israel, but also for Jews in the United States. The previous owner of the book must have clipped it and saved it in these pages. It was a short article, but to me it seemed like a gift from Kotsuji himself.

Jacket cover of Kotsuji Setsuzo's autobiography, *From Tokyo to Jerusalem*

I read Kotsuji's autobiography with a full heart. He wrote in great detail of his life from childhood until the age of sixty, when he was circumcised and converted to Judaism. It also recounts how he helped and saved Jewish refugees, communications with the military, and fascinating untold stories of interactions with government dignitaries. The book recounts how Kotsuji himself was tortured by the military police because he helped Jewish refugees, and how his life was in danger. Japan's alliance with Nazi Germany guaranteed that certain elements of the military saw

Kotsuji as a threat to the status quo. The autobiography ended at his conversion to Judaism. I was left still not knowing what kind of life Kotsuji had led thereafter, and how he came to be buried in Israel.

I thought that R. Marvin Tokayer, a friend of Kotsuji's who wrote the commentary in the revised edition of the autobiography, must know what had happened to him. Judging from the commentary, R. Tokayer seemed to have had considerable interactions with Kotsuji in his later years. If that was the case, I might be able to learn more details about Kotsuji's involvement and relationship with the Jewish refugees.

Marvin Tokayer was born in New York in 1936. He was a rabbi (a religious leader and scholar in Judaism) and a former headmaster of a Jewish school. He came to Japan for the first time in 1962, and in 1968 he became the rabbi of the Jewish Community of Japan, based at a Jewish synagogue in Shibuya.

He lived in Japan for a total of eleven years. He wrote many books on Judaism and Japan. He praised Kotsuji in his writings as a Jewish benefactor. But I had no idea how to contact R. Tokayer. I was stumped. One day, while talking to a friend from my university days in America, I casually mentioned his name.

"Do you mean R. Tokayer?"

"Yeah, I hear he's in New York."

"Okay. I'll see if I can get hold of him." My friend said it perfectly casually.

"What? What did you just say?"

"I'll try contacting R. Tokayer."

"How would you have Tokayer's contact information?"

"Because R. Tokayer is an old friend of my father."

It was pure coincidence. My friend's father had been a good friend of R. Tokayer. I wondered, how could there be such a coincidence? Or was it inevitable? I felt as if a powerful force was trying to lead me to Kotsuji.

In November 2010, I went to New York to see R. Tokayer. We met in front of the train station in Great Neck, a small town on the outskirts of New York. Great Neck has a population of about ten thousand. It is a town from which many people commute to New York City. When I got off at the station, R. Tokayer had come to meet me in his car. He wore a small black Jewish cap on his head known as a *kippa*.

"I'm Yamada. Are you R. Tokayer?"

In response to my greeting in English, R. Tokayer lowered the car window, poked his head out, and suddenly spoke Japanese: "Are you that weird Japanese person?" (He was playing on words often used by Japanese to describe unique foreigners!) He continued in Japanese as I stood there bewildered: "It's very strange, you know, for you to come all the way from Japan to New York to hear about Kotsuji! But it's wonderful! You've come to the right place. Because all those who know as much as I do about Kotsuji are no longer living."

As he said this, R. Tokayer cheerfully laughed. He is a very humorous person and known for using this "Weird Japanese" greeting.

"Sugihara's 'visas for life' are famous. But I've been desperate to find out what happened to the Jews who arrived in Japan with these visas and how they managed to leave the country to a safer place."

When I said that, R. Tokayer said with pride: "It was all because of Kotsuji. He's our hero."

Author with Rabbi Marvin Tokayer

R. Tokayer recounted how the Jewish refugees in Kobe asked Kotsuji for help anytime one of them had a problem, and he offered many examples. He said that Kotsuji went around solving all kinds of problems big and small, not only helping with visa extensions but also challenges that arose from differences in lifestyles and daily customs.

R. Tokayer continued. "During the war, Japan was an ally of Nazi Germany. Even so, Kotsuji wrote a book[1] calling for the defense of Jews, he spoke out against Nazism, and gave lectures throughout Japan. Don't you think that was insane? It was during the war. An individual acting in that way was surely putting his life in danger."

"That's why Kotsuji was tortured by the military police," I said.

R. Tokayer nodded. "What Kotsuji did was incredible, something no one could have done. If it weren't for Kotsuji, I don't know what would have happened to the Jews in Kobe. No matter what the problem, Kotsuji took on any issue facing the Jews. But he didn't receive a penny, not one penny, mind you. He completed a mission you see, something that was of no benefit to him. That is what real courage is."

"Unfortunately, most people in Japan don't know about Mr. Kotsuji."

R. Tokayer laughed and said, "Then you should write a book about him."

I replied that, unfortunately, I was an actor, not a writer.

The time I spent with him passed quickly.

"If you want to know more about Kotsuji, you should meet his daughters."

R. Tokayer told me that Kotsuji's two daughters lived in Kamakura. Thinking that if I talked to the daughters, I would certainly be able to get a clearer picture of Kotsuji, I asked him for their contact information and decided to reach out right away.

Back at my hotel, holding the note with the phone number that R. Tokayer gave me, I hesitated. Perhaps I should at least wait to call until after I returned to Japan. And yet, this was a precious connection that R. Tokayer had given me. I felt a sense of urgency, that if I waited even a short time the connection might be lost. When I picked up the phone I

1. *Yudaya Nanmin no Sugata* [The True Character of the Jewish Nation].

was hit by a wave of nervousness that I had never felt before, but I made the call to Kamakura.

"Hello...?" The voice I heard was refined.

"Uh.... My name is Yamada."

After introducing myself, I explained how I was moved by reading Mr. Kotsuji's autobiography and that I wanted to learn more about his life. I asked if I could meet her in person.

"Thank you for reading my father's book," she replied politely. "But we don't want to be interviewed or talk about my father. I'm sorry. Thank you."

The tone in her voice had an air of *please leave us alone.*

"I see.... Can I call you again?" was all I could manage to say, but the phone disconnected, leaving me without an answer to my question.

I was disappointed, because I had thought for a moment that I was getting closer to Kotsuji. I had moved too fast. I was sure that I had surprised Kotsuji's daughter by calling her out of the blue. When I returned to Tokyo, I consulted Toru Hironaka, an attorney whom I regularly work with. His advice was, "People will understand your intentions if you speak sincerely from your heart. Wait a little while."

Hironaka understood my feelings and promised to contact the daughters on my behalf. Two months later, thanks to Hironaka taking his time as he gently persuaded them, Kotsuji's two daughters agreed to meet with me.

In January 2011, I went to Kamakura. Hironaka brought Teruko, Kotsuji's second daughter, and Yuriko, Kotsuji's third daughter, to a coffee shop to meet. They were both petite, very elegant women.

"You've come a long way to meet us, but there's not much to share about our father." Teruko and Yuriko were reticent.

"It can be about anything. Won't you tell me about him? It doesn't matter what you talk about."

The two of them looked at each other doubtfully. "Even if we talk about our father, you probably wouldn't understand."

They told me about how in the past when they spoke to writers or reporters about their father, they churned out amusing articles to satisfy readers' curiosity, and some even rudely insinuated that he must have gotten a lot of money in return for helping Jews. I saw that the family had

Author with Kotsuji Yuriko (Left) and Kotsuji Teruko (Right)

been hurt as a result of talking about Kotsuji. I was wondering if they would choose not to share any information with me. While considering this real possibility, I took Kotsuji's autobiography out of my bag. I opened the book and started to flip through the pages, earnestly pointing out which parts deeply moved me.

"My heart ached when I read this passage where he was held by the military police. To try to save the Jews without regard to the risk to his own life, that's not something most people could do."

In addition to the events that saved the Jewish people, there were many other things I wanted to talk to them about. I listed each part of Kotsuji's autobiography that had touched me and expressed how they made me feel. Nodding, they said, "You've really read it thoroughly," and smiled. That was the moment.

"You've said that you admire my father, and it seems you have done a lot of research." As she spoke Teruko reached into her bag, took several photos out and placed them in front of me.

The photographs were taken in 1959, when Kotsuji visited Israel for his conversion. The photographs were from a thank-you party hosted by the Jews whom he had saved. It was my first time seeing a photo of Kotsuji together with Jews. Kotsuji had a small mustache and was wearing a hat, and he was surrounded by men with thick beards. There was also a photograph of Kotsuji with children wearing playful expressions. On the back of each photo, in his own handwriting, were the following annotations:

> *1959 in Jerusalem, "Thank-you party hosted by R. Shmulevitz, Director of the Talmudic Academy of Jerusalem"*
>
> *"Scolded by parents, [children] forced to be in a picture. They were just on their way out."*
>
> *"On the right, Dr. Israel Ben-Zeev, Doctor of Philosophy from a prestigious German family sent to concentration camp and who suffered from psychological trauma"*
>
> *"They are all people who fled to Kobe when they were young. Now they are respected teachers, gathered around me."*

The photographs reflected how they regarded Kotsuji with respect and gratitude for his actions. With my own eyes I could see that after nearly twenty years, such a large group of people gathered for a reunion with Kotsuji. Kotsuji, likely worried about what happened to the refugees who left Kobe, must have been overjoyed with the reunion. Those who had been children in Kobe had matured into fine adults. Kotsuji certainly must have been moved to see them living good lives.

Both Teruko and Yuriko looked proud as they pointed out their father in the photographs. I felt that they truly loved and respected him. This made me want to ask more and more questions. However, I could sense that the two of them were still uncertain about me. I couldn't help but feel like they wanted to ask me, "What do you intend to do with what you learn about our father?"

As we parted, one of them murmured: "Just before he died, our father said, 'Maybe in a hundred years, someone who truly understands me will appear.'"

Those words struck a chord in my heart. In the car on the way home, I suddenly remembered R. Tokayer's words when I met him in New York. "You should write a book about Kotsuji."

Children join in a picture with Kotsuji, at a party hosted for him by R. Shmulevitz, Director of the Talmudic Academy of Jerusalem, 1959

Kotsuji is second from left, with Dr. Israel Ben Zeev on the far right

Kotsuji (third from left) with now-eminent scholars at the party, who had gathered to thank him

Kotsuji Setsuzo was the man who bridged the "visas for life" to unknown futures for thousands of Jewish refugees in Japan. However, few Japanese knew about his brave actions. Without him, six thousand

Jews may have been handed over to Nazi Germany and slaughtered. And we Japanese would have been complicit in it.

I wanted more people to know about Kotsuji, this man who has been buried and lost to history. I started by translating his autobiography into Japanese, since it was only published in English overseas. Kotsuji's writings are full of unique metaphorical expressions, and I feared that an ordinary translation would fail to convey his true intentions. He also quoted from many religious writings as well as the Bible, and even though I had lived in the United States for many years this translation was not easy for me. The work was extremely difficult. I wrote for two weeks straight with little sleep. Many times I felt like giving up, but Kotsuji's words, "Maybe in a hundred years, someone who truly understands me will appear," encouraged me to persevere.

Oddly enough, Kotsuji passed away in 1973, the same year I was born into this world. It seemed to me that this was not a coincidence, and my mission must be to let as many people as possible know about Kotsuji.

Chapter One

As a Child and Young Man

Kotsuji was born on February 3, 1899, the youngest of five siblings, into a long line of Shinto priests in Kyoto, Japan's capital from 794 to 1868. His father's name was Kisaburo and his mother's name was Fukuko. Shinto taught by his father and *Bushido* teachings at school both had a significant influence on him as a boy. Don't be cowardly. Refine your character. Cultivate virtue. Kotsuji wrote of this in his autobiography.

> Like knightly chivalry, *Bushido* is a code of behavior, stressing the virtues of courage in battle and serenity in the face of death.... [T]he true samurai possessed gentler qualities: courtesy, honor, and fidelity.

Around that time, during a field trip a friend became too tired to walk on a steep climb uphill, and Kotsuji carried his friend on his back up the mountain. He did not tell anyone about this, but unexpectedly one month later Kotsuji was praised by his teacher, who had just heard of this feat. Kotsuji felt as if he had been rewarded.

"There is never a need to hide good behavior. But boasting about it may be a step toward hypocrisy."

The spirit that Kotsuji learned when he was young remained in his heart until his death. In his later years, when Kotsuji helped Jewish refugees, he said the aphorism "It is cowardly to see what is right and not do it" was his code of conduct. This was rooted in the spirit of *Bushido* cultivated in his childhood.

When Kotsuji turned thirteen, Emperor Meiji died, followed by General Maresuke Nogi's ritual suicide. These events had a profound impact on him. Many Japanese praised General Nogi's loyalty, because sacrificing oneself upon the death of one's leader is an act at the heart of *Bushido*. At first, Kotsuji also accepted it as expected behavior. At the same time, he soon started asking himself this question again and again: "What is the meaning of life? What is life? Should people take their own lives?" He pondered these questions as he wandered the streets, stopping at a second-hand bookstore. He picked up an old book.

That book was the Bible. This fateful encounter with the Bible would come to define his later life. The book mesmerized the young boy, and he suddenly came to a realization. Although he was born into a family steeped in Shinto, the Bible fascinated him. There is no way that this would be seen as acceptable behavior. Isn't it an act of betrayal toward my family? What in the world should I do?

Kotsuji was deeply troubled, and after agonizing over his feelings he went to his parents to openly share these conflicted thoughts with them. Much to his surprise, his parents accepted his spiritual conflict, which at the time he thought was nearly miraculous. With both parents' understanding, Kotsuji began attending a Christian church. He soon discovered a desire to study theology at university. This was going too far, and his father was fiercely opposed. Kotsuji's feelings, however, did not change, and, assuming he would be virtually disowned, he decided to study at the theology department at Meiji University in Tokyo.

Kotsuji received a scholarship, and in addition to theology studied languages such as English, Latin, German, and Greek. His grades were always excellent, but gradually he began to see inconsistencies within Christian doctrine. Despite being monotheistic, Jesus may be said to be the "God inside God." If so, doesn't this mean that there are two

Gods, God and Jesus? But no one could answer this question. Even as he brooded over these doubts about doctrine, he had no other path than to become a pastor. He accepted a position as head pastor of a church in Asahikawa, Hokkaido.

This proved to be a fortuitous choice. In 1923, twenty-four-year-old Kotsuji found a very suitable partner in Asahikawa. His wife's name was Mineko. She was the daughter of a family that ran a large ranch in nearby Hidaka, Hokkaido. Shortly after getting married, the couple were transferred to Gifu, where their eldest daughter, Aiko, was born. They lived a happy married life there.

One cold winter night, there was a weak knock at the Kotsuji home's door. Assuming a member of the congregation had come, Kotsuji opened his door to see a man standing in front of him. When Kotsuji saw him, he hesitated to invite him into his home, for he showed symptoms of Hansen's disease, leprosy. Instead, Kotsuji gave him some clothes and enough money to get by for a few weeks, but immediately after closing the door, Kotsuji was overwhelmed with shame.

> I was supposed to be a religious leader, and yet what could I do for this poor man? I could not take him into my bed. I could not take him into my house. I wanted only to send him on his way. For what else could I do? What use was my religion?

He could not even help someone who had sought him out. Kotsuji was tormented by an intense sense of helplessness. He wanted to be a true leader. How could he accomplish this? Kotsuji was deeply troubled. He could not find an answer in Christianity. But Kotsuji thought perhaps he could find the answer in the Old Testament, which had once so fascinated him. So Kotsuji decided to go to America, to relearn the Bible.

On July 23, 1927, the Kotsuji family used all their assets for travel and expenses for his studies in the United States. They boarded a ship at the port of Yokohama and departed Japan.

At a university in Auburn, a small town in upstate New York, Kotsuji started learning Hebrew so that he could read the Old Testament in its original text. If one studies the Old Testament, one naturally ends up learning about Judaism. He was eager to learn Jewish law, the

Talmud, which is based on the Old Testament, and he began taking private lessons.

In search of deeper knowledge, Kotsuji eventually decided to attend the Pacific School of Religion in Berkeley, California. He had a strong desire to be taught by Professor William Frederick Badè, who was on the faculty. Professor Badè was a renowned archaeologist and linguist at the time. His wish came true, and Kotsuji was able to study under him. Professor Badè spared no effort for Kotsuji, who had come all the way from Japan. Kotsuji was struggling to support his family financially, so at times Professor Badè helped find him part-time jobs. He went out of his way to tutor him for free and otherwise looked after his outstanding student. Kotsuji in turn admired Professor Badè and studied hard to meet his expectations. Kotsuji learned from the professor how to archaeologically examine and interpret the Bible. Being taught archaeology by Professor Badè at this time in his life would become a lifelong asset to Kotsuji.

It was during this time that Kotsuji first set foot in a synagogue, Congregation Emanu-El in San Francisco. The people of the synagogue were curious about this Japanese man who fluently read from the prayer books in Hebrew and warmly welcomed Kotsuji.

In September 1931, just when Kotsuji had finished his life as an exchange student in Berkeley, an armed conflict flared up between Japan and China, known as the Manchurian Incident. The Imperial Japanese Army advanced into northeastern China, and by the following year the last emperor of the Qing dynasty was installed in a puppet regime. The state of Manchuria was formed, with Japan assuming de facto control over Manchuria.

Around the same time the Manchurian Incident was taking place, Kotsuji was on a ship heading back to Japan. He had no way of anticipating that in a few years he would be swept into the same vortex of historic events. He traveled with his wife Mineko and daughters Aiko and Teruko, having received his doctorate from the Pacific School of Religion after completing long and arduous work on his dissertation, "The Origin and Transformation of Semitic Literature."

Kotsuji's heart was full as he returned to his home country with his beloved family and bearing a hard-earned doctorate as his prize. At thirty-two years of age, he dreamed of becoming a teacher and scholar of Hebrew and religious studies in Japan. Kotsuji set foot on Japanese soil again for the first time in over four years.

His parents in Kyoto were delighted that their youngest son had earned a doctorate degree. They invited relatives to a dinner party and celebrated Kotsuji. Kotsuji, who left home assuming he would be disowned, was overjoyed to see his parents happy after causing them so much worry. It was a successful return to his hometown.

Kotsuji's joy did not end there. As he had hoped, he found work as a teacher at the prestigious Aoyama Gakuin University in Tokyo. On July 3, 1932, his third daughter Yuriko was born, and the Kotsujis were content in their new life. Those peaceful days were not to last.

The following year, the winds of misfortune began to shake the Kotsuji household. In October, his oldest daughter, seven-year-old Aiko, died suddenly of dysentery. In addition, Kotsuji contracted typhoid fever, which was designated an infectious disease requiring official reporting, causing him to lose his job. Kotsuji narrowly escaped death, but then his wife Mineko came down with pleurisy. He managed his own chronic appendicitis with medication, while taking care of little Teruko and Yuriko and tending to his wife.

Even as he was buffeted by tragedy, Kotsuji never lost his passion for learning. One year later, when the whole family had regained their health, Kotsuji looked for work, but he was not able to find a job at a university. At that point, he decided to start his own school. On October 1, 1934, he opened the Institute of Biblical Research on the eighth floor of the Seishokan Building in Ginza and began teaching Hebrew and the Old Testament.

I listened to a recording of Kotsuji teaching, and it was obvious that he was happily engaged in the class, reciting and at times chanting his favorite Hebrew psalms. Monthly tuition was quite inexpensive, about two thousand yen at today's prices (thirteen dollars). He apparently wasn't interested in making a great profit. It seems that Kotsuji's desire was to teach the Hebrew language he loved so much to his heart's content. Perhaps because he had a fair amount of free time, Kotsuji often took his daughters to the zoo and other places, walking hand in hand. Teruko and Yuriko say they remember these times as a period of great happiness.

Perhaps Kotsuji's enthusiasm was infectious, because many students from top universities in the city started to gather at the Institute of Biblical Research. Some professors from other universities and religious leaders frowned upon this and began to harass Kotsuji. The building management succumbed to this pressure, changing the lock on the door to the classroom. Kotsuji was shut out. His Bibles and textbooks, all his precious books, were thrown in the trash. He wept bitter tears. This was the first time Kotsuji had experienced such humiliation. Despite his deep sorrow, he resolved to reopen the Institute. Unfortunately, his efforts were in vain. Three years after its opening his school was forced to close.

But this was only the beginning. Kotsuji was just thirty-eight years old, and he would soon be overtaken by turmoil.

Chapter Two

Nazi Persecution of the Jews

With his Institute of Biblical Research forced to shut down after just three years, Kotsuji was in the doldrums. He had pursued his theological ideals, and the time spent deepening his knowledge of the Old Testament, Judaism, and Hebrew had been sheer bliss for him. His sense of loss was immeasurable.

In addition, it must have greatly pained him knowing that it was pressure from other religious groups that forced the closure of the institute. As he retrieved the dust-covered Bibles from a trash bin at the Seishokan Building, and facing oppression of his religion and studies, Kotsuji no doubt felt deep sorrow and anger. On the world stage, however, unimaginable persecution of Jews, not even remotely close to what Kotsuji was experiencing, had been set in motion.

In 1933, Adolf Hitler took the helm of the German government. In 1935, he promulgated the Nuremberg Laws to protect German blood and honor. These laws expelled Jews from public office, banned them from corporate management, and stripped them of their civil rights. Once this law came into force, the persecution of Jews in the private sector intensified. Retail shops posted signs that read "Jews forbidden," and restaurants created segregated sections exclusively for Jews. Jewish physicians were banned from seeing non-Jewish patients, and Jewish attorneys were banned from performing any work. Widespread discrimination and oppression of the Jews had begun.

In November 1938, a young Polish Jew shot and killed a German Embassy official in Paris to protest the Nazis' inhumane treatment of Jews. This set off anti-Jewish riots and the destruction of Jewish businesses and synagogues all over Germany. Many Jews were killed in what came to be known as *Kristallnacht* (German for "Crystal Night"), the night when shattered glass glittered like crystal in the moonlight.

Following this, the persecution of the Jews in Nazi Germany spread across Europe. From 1939, when the German military invaded Poland, until the end of World War II in 1945 six million Jews were massacred in the Holocaust.

Until I was touched by the life of Kotsuji, I thought the persecution of the Jews was a European saga, far removed from me, like a fire on a distant shore. I knew about the transit visas, the "visas for life," issued by Sugihara Chiune, the vice-consul in Lithuania, but that was something that seemed to lack a direct connection to us in Japan.

When I read Kotsuji's autobiography, however, I learned that Nazi Germany sent people to Japan to spread anti-Jewish propaganda. In 1935, the Nazis established an organization called the International Political-Economic Association. One day the chairman of this organization visited Kotsuji and told him, "Japan is facing a Jewish problem. Won't you help us with this?" Kotsuji accepted, believing that he could be of use to Jewish people, and he attended meetings and translated articles written in English.

Kotsuji soon realized that this group's aim was to disseminate Nazi propaganda and left the organization. He describes this group in his memoir.

> [A]lthough the association never seemed to put any money in the bank, it was always able to draw out as much as it needed. [Also,] the organization was violently anti-Semitic. It published

> a journal called "Research into the Secret World Power," which was essentially a vehicle for translations of anti-Jewish pamphlets. They were full of the ancient notion that there was a conspiracy of Jews to take over the world, stated in the usual hysterical accusations....
>
> I withdrew; the organization continued, to startling effect. Japanese officials first laughed at it, but... some of the officials grew convinced of the justice of the charge.

"Research into the Secret World Power" was published in October 1936 by the International Political-Economic Association. It refers to this "secret world power" in its preface.

> This secret power skillfully uses its secret societies that span an international network as well as affiliated groups for its hidden purpose, or to promote socialism and Communism, or to incite liberals and internationalists. It is nothing but a hidden purpose. By provoking internal destruction and international wars, its ultimate objective is to destroy existing nation states through a global revolution, thereby creating a world for its own purpose.

It also described Italian fascists and German Nazis as sensible people who did not tolerate international secret powers. Furthermore, it included an article entitled "Reexamining the Jewish Problem," asserting that the Jewish problem was an important issue in international affairs, which needed to be addressed in Japan as well.

According to Kotsuji, Dr. Pausch, a member of the Nazi Central Committee for Germans Abroad, was sent to Japan in 1938, and toured the country giving anti-Semitic lectures. In these speeches he said that Jews were hatching multiple plots to conquer not just Japan but the entire world. We can glean from the activities of the International Political-Economic Association that the Nazis were actively seeking to spread their anti-Jewish ideology in Japan as well.

The Japanese, however, did not adopt an anti-Jewish stance. I believe there are four reasons why this was the case. The first is that while there were small communities of Jews in Kobe and Yokohama, they were few in number and most citizens did not have much, if any, direct contact with Jews, nor did politicians or military personnel. Thus, everyday Japanese people were not personally familiar with Jews. Therefore, I think they had no reason to overreact to the Nazis' anti-Jewish ideology.

Second, Japan was advocating a principle of racial equality to the world. At the League of Nations Paris Peace Conference in 1919, Japan had proposed that the League of Nations Covenant include the elimination of all racial discrimination and state that "all races should be equal." This proposal may have been aimed at racial disparities in the US, where Japanese immigrants faced discrimination. The proposal was defeated due to pressure from the US, but the principle of racial equality subsequently became an important pillar of Japan's foreign policy. It is possible that this position also contributed to Japan's decision not to participate in the persecution of the Jews.

Third, many Japanese government officials remembered the Russo-Japanese War, which had occurred just three decades earlier, and the crucial financial backing Japan had received from the Jewish American banker Jacob Schiff.

Finally, Kotsuji's writings during the war years about Jewish culture and history presented a fact-based portrayal of the Jews. Some influential Japanese were even beginning to consider how getting closer with Jews could actually help Japan's national interests.

Chapter Three

The Fugu Plan

While most Japanese had no knowledge about or interest in Jewish people, there were those in government, military, and business circles who dealt with Jewish issues out of necessity. When Hitler took power in 1933, he immediately initiated a boycott of Jewish companies and ordered that Jews be expelled from government as well as cultural and educational institutions. In response, many Jews began leaving Germany.

In 1934, Aikawa Yoshisuke, founder of the Nissan Group, published a paper titled "Plan to Resettle 50,000 German Jews in Manchuria." The aim of this plan was to bring development to Manchuria by taking in fifty thousand Jews escaping Germany, which would then attract investment by American Jews. The plan, it was believed, had a fair chance of success. During the Russo-Japanese War thirty years earlier, Jacob Schiff, of German Jewish ancestry, provided $200 million to the Japanese Army, which was struggling in the war and had little money. It has been said that the Japanese military was able to defeat the Imperial Russian military thanks to this aid. One reason Schiff supported Japan may have been to avenge Imperial Russia's persecution of Jews.

The thinking was that if Jews fleeing Hitler were taken in and given autonomy, then American Jews were sure to support them. This could help improve the strained US-Japan relationship and avoid a war. It would also serve to restrain the Soviet Union and act as a buffer. The unlikely plan was crafted with the secret participation of military officials, such as Navy Captain Inuzuka Koreshige and Army Colonel Yasue Norihiro, who were said to be experts on Jews.

While it would be beneficial for Japan to admit Jews, a single misstep could be fatal, considering its alliance with Germany. Captain Inuzuka likened it to eating puffer fish, or *fugu*, which combined a delicately sweet taste with a potentially deadly toxin, and so it was called the Fugu Plan.

Prime Minister Konoe Fumimaro, Foreign Minister Arita Hachiro, Army Minister Itagaki Seishiro, Naval Minister Yonai Mitsumasa, and Ikeda Shigeaki, who was serving as both Minister of Finance and Minister of Commerce and Industry, discussed this plan on December 5, 1938. With the advance of the Nazis in Europe, many Jewish refugees had already fled to Manchuria. Japanese people had little to no interactions with Jews. Some were of the view that they should be left to the Germans or Soviets, while others believed that if Japan followed the German example and persecuted the Jews, it would lead to a significant loss in trade with the US. The debate continued late into the night. The Jewish problem had become an issue that Japan could not avoid.

The outcome of the five ministers' meeting was a highly ambivalent, contradictory conclusion stating, "Our diplomatic ties with Germany and Italy require that we avoid publicly embracing the Jewish people"; however, "we should not reject them as they [our allies] do... in light of our desire not to alienate America." The Fugu Plan was not scrapped. Inuzuka, Yasue, and the others would next have to consider specific plans to take in Jews, although not openly, and devise strategies to attract American Jews' involvement. In July 1939, a confidential document titled "The Study and Analysis of Introducing Jewish Capital" was submitted to the government. It is unclear whether this plan was formally approved by the government. I visited the Diplomatic Archives of the Ministry of Foreign Affairs of Japan to seek information, but there was no record of the plan there.

Ultimately, the Fugu Plan was not implemented. There are several theories as to why, but a prevailing view is that American Jews reacted too negatively to the plan as it was advanced. R. Tokayer, whom I met in New York when I was researching Kotsuji, described the Fugu Plan as being based on a fundamental misconception.

> Japanese officials were never able to comprehend... that the American Jewish community considered its ties to its political family, America, at least as strong as its ties to its religious family in Europe.

In other words, American Jews chose to side with the US government. It was also unthinkable that the US would team up with Japan, which was part of the Tripartite Pact with Italy and Germany. This theory assumed that the plan to attract American Jewish money to Manchuria failed because American Jews' aversion to working with an Axis power outweighed their desire to aid European Jews.

Another theory is the Tripartite Pact, signed in 1940 under the leadership of Foreign Minister Matsuoka Yosuke, led to the sinking of the Fugu Plan. If this plan had been implemented, a Jewish autonomous zone would have been created in Manchuria. What would have happened to the relationship between Japan and Nazi Germany? Would the Tripartite Pact even have been signed? Would Japan's relationship with the US have improved? Could war actually have been avoided?

In the book *The Fugu Plan* by Marvin Tokayer and Mary Swartz, it is stated that if the plan had succeeded, "it could have saved a million Jews from Hitler's Holocaust and even halted the war between Japan and the United States before it began."

So how much did Kotsuji know about the persecution of the Jews in Europe by Nazi Germany, the Fugu Plan, and how the Japanese government was pressured to adopt anti-Jewish policies? In his autobiography, he wrote about his memories of 1936.

> The matter of most importance to me was the Nazi persecution of the Jews. I knew nothing about the details until much later, but the little I knew began to touch my life before that time.

From reading this passage, it seems the Nazis' anti-Jewish activities in Japan were becoming more extreme due to the International Political-Economic Association and publications like the "Research into the Secret World Power." Notwithstanding the relative paucity of information, Kotsuji had some awareness of Jewish persecution taking place in Nazi Germany. In his autobiography, however, he does not mention the government or military policies toward Jews, and whether he had any involvement in how they developed. Most likely, Kotsuji was immersed in his academic pursuits at this time and did not have the opportunity to be exposed to Japan's policies on Jews.

Then a turning point occurred in 1938 that would change Kotsuji's life. He received an invitation from the president of the South Manchuria Railway: "I would like you to work for the South Manchuria Railway as my adviser." Kotsuji was perplexed by the request.

The South Manchuria Railway, shortened to Mantetsu in Japanese, was a Japanese government-controlled company operating not just the railway business, but also coal mining, oil refining, and ports. It managed urban infrastructure (roads, bridges, etc.), health care facilities (hospitals and research laboratories), educational institutions such as schools and libraries, and social services (public halls, welfare, etc.). Much more than a railway company, it fulfilled the role of a government agency.

Why would the president of Mantetsu need him as an adviser? Kotsuji could not understand his intentions.

The president had read some of the books that Kotsuji had published and sought his assistance in handling the Manchurian Jewish issue. At that time, Kotsuji had finally managed to recover from his despair over the forced closure of his Bible institute and was spending his time researching and studying the Bible. Kotsuji was satisfied with his life.

The thinking of that time held that a scholar who went into the world of commerce was a sell-out, and Kotsuji himself looked askance at "selling his scholarship for money." He flatly refused the offer.

According to his autobiography, the railway president did not give up and raised the original monthly salary offer from three hundred yen to three hundred and fifty yen. Kotsuji refused again, and again the offer was raised. This back-and-forth continued for almost half a year. Eventually, Kotsuji's thinking started to change. Was he really doing the right thing by continuing to reject the offer? There were likely to be many Jews in Manchuria who had fled persecution in Nazi Germany and Russia. If he could be of service to Jews, wouldn't that time be now? Was the learning he had accumulated "merely a matter of cold knowledge"? Kotsuji debated with himself. Then he decided to accept the president's offer and go to Manchuria.

The monthly salary offered by the president was now five hundred yen. This sum in those days was the equivalent to that of a top-level executive at a large company; in fact, it was so high that the Mantetsu personnel department rejected it. But it apparently was pushed through as a top-down decision by the president, reflecting just how much he felt he needed Kotsuji.

This railway president, Matsuoka Yosuke, later became Japan's foreign minister and a central player in the signing of the Tripartite Pact among Japan, Germany, and Italy.

In *Matsuoka Yosuke: Sono Hito to Shogai* (Matsuoka Yosuke: The Person and Life), a biography authored by the Matsuoka Yosuke Biography Publication Society, Kotsuji wrote about the relationship he had with Matsuoka at that time:

> Mr. Matsuoka, president of Mantetsu at the time, took a half-year to persuade me to leave academia, and I went to Dalian to work in his office. I believed that working in the corporate world was taking a spiritual step down from academia, and I hesitated for about six months before making my decision. When I visited Mr. Matsuoka in his office on October 14, 1938, he explained the state of the world to me over the course of two hours. He warned that "if even one thing goes wrong, Japan will be kicked off the continent." At the end, he said, "Kotsuji, you have a great mission so I want you to make full use of Mantetsu's resources and conduct your research deliberately."

This was the moment when Kotsuji, until then a mere scholar, was first thrust into the maelstrom of history.

Chapter Four

To Manchuria

In October 1938, Kotsuji arrived in Dalian, Manchuria, with his family.[1] His objective was to put his language skills and knowledge to good use for the Jews there. He never imagined that this decision would eventually lead to his destiny of saving the lives of many Jews, and that his own life would in turn be saved by Jews.

Kotsuji was assigned to the public relations department at Mantetsu, and he worked as an adviser to President Matsuoka. His job was to serve as a liaison between Mantetsu and the Jews in Manchuria. He was to research what the Jews were seeking and then report that back to Matsuoka.

The Otpor Incident occurred in March of that year. The Otpor train station was on the Soviet side of the border with Manchuria, and it was overflowing with Jewish refugees fleeing Europe on the Siberian railway. They did not have official visas and could not enter Manchuria. With nowhere to stay, they slept outdoors, enduring the cold and hunger as

1. Author's note: Kotsuji's autobiography states that it was 1939, but his family's testimony confirmed that it was 1938.

they waited for permission to enter Manchuria. They would either die of hunger or cold or be deported back to Germany. There was not a moment to waste.

When Major General Higuchi Kiichiro, head of the Kwantung Army's Special Service Agency in Harbin, learned of the situation in Otpor, he persuaded Manchukuo (the Japanese-controlled puppet state) to issue entry visas on humanitarian grounds. Matsuoka took charge of the nine-hundred-kilometer transport from the Manzhouli train station on the Manchurian side of the border to Harbin, and mobilized trains for the rescue effort. It is said that he ordered that no fare be charged to the passengers.

The number of Jewish refugees who arrived in Harbin from Otpor was thought to be around twenty thousand. Russian Jews had flowed into Harbin since early in the century, so there was already a Jewish community. The Harbin Jews rejoiced at the rescue and helped take care of the new arrivals. After what happened at Otpor, their numbers continued to increase. At the same time, the Fugu Plan was being meticulously crafted in Japan. For Captain Inuzuka and Colonel Yasue, the plan's principal architects, the treatment of Jews in Manchuria was an important matter.

Kotsuji wrote about his time at Mantetsu:

> The most enjoyable aspect of my life in Dalian, and the most valuable to me, was the many friends I made. Later, these friendships were to become a matter of life-and-death importance to me; but during those South Manchurian Railway months it was a happy matter of getting to know a large number of Jewish people.

At a restaurant called the Victoria, run by a Russian Jew, Kotsuji would interact with many Jewish people and learn about their circumstances. In particular, the reality of Nazi persecution that Jews were enduring now became clear. Until that point, he had only been exposed to limited information.

Karl Rosenzweig, who had worked in a senior position in a coal industry company in Vienna, told Kotsuji the story of going to work a few days after the Nazis invaded that city. A young man who had been his secretary was sitting at his desk, and he announced, "I'm the director now." This man had been a Nazi spy all along. Rosenzweig said he was forced out of the company, fleeing for his life to Manchuria.

A Jew named Weinberg was rounded up by Nazis in Vienna, one of 67,000 Jews taken to a concentration camp. But for some reason, he was set free. It seemed like a miracle. However, a camp guard who was annoyed about his release shot Weinberg in the arm without warning. He ran and managed to escape, eventually reaching Dalian.

Kotsuji was able to learn about the situation in Europe from stories told to him like this, and he continued to report what he heard to Matsuoka. Kotsuji wrote in his autobiography, "I began to develop a hatred for the Nazis and began to find myself thinking and feeling more and more like a Jew."

Kotsuji's daughters, Teruko and Yuriko, remember those days well. When he came home from work, Kotsuji always seemed to be agonizing over something. His brow was usually furrowed and his face was grim, so the sisters tried dancing to try to make him laugh. Kotsuji's expression though remained dark. The persecution of the Jews by the Nazis was much worse than he had imagined, and Kotsuji undoubtedly felt the weight of this reality.

Kotsuji deepened his relationships with not only Jewish people but with Japanese as well. Shirahama Yoshinori, a military police officer, was one of them. Shirahama extended a helping hand to Kotsuji and the Jews in a variety of ways. He assisted Kotsuji with a Jew who was about to be arrested for smuggling, and someone who was being unfairly taxed. At one point, he helped Kotsuji bring a Jew who needed surgery to the hospital. Kotsuji described Shirahama in his autobiography as "the best of men" and a kind man. During Kotsuji's time at Mantetsu, he and Shirahama were like family. Shirahama and Kotsuji were to subsequently have a fateful reunion in Japan.

One of Kotsuji's work responsibilities related to Shanghai policies. At the time, Shanghai had a great deal of European capital, primarily from Britain. In the latter half of the nineteenth century, it was a prosperous city to which much capital flowed from Japan, France, and other nations. Beginning in the 1920s until the 1930s, it was China's largest city and enjoyed significant economic growth. Shanghai was traditionally open to Jews, and David Sassoon & Co., a Bombay-based trading and banking company, was the first Jewish business there when it arrived in 1840. Subsequently, many Jews from the Middle East found success in Shanghai.

A large number of European Jews arrived in the early twentieth century, primarily fleeing persecution by Imperial Russia. Many of the European Jews who migrated in this early period were middle-class and successful business owners in Shanghai, enjoying stability in the Jewish settlement. It is thought to have been home to between four thousand and seven thousand Jews.

By 1937, the number of European Jews who had escaped Nazi Germany swelled to over twenty thousand in Japanese-occupied Shanghai. It was difficult for the Shanghai International Settlement to house them all, and many of the Jewish refugees had no choice but to live in tents or barracks.

Kotsuji went to Shanghai in May 1940 with Navy Captain Inuzuka, Army Colonel Yasue, and Consul-General of Shanghai Ishiguro Shiro to investigate the situation. Kotsuji wrote about what he saw.

> When our party walked through the community kitchen in one of the camps, which was guarded by a high wire fence, young men and women outside stood staring hungrily at the huge pots bubbling on the stoves. I asked one of the girls how old she was. "Sixteen," she said.
>
> "How are conditions here?"
>
> "I'm hungry," she said, and glanced again at the cooking pots. "I want to get out of here, to find work as a housemaid. Please, take me to your house. Please help me."
>
> I was deeply touched by this hungry girl. When we left, I told a high Japanese official about her, and he was able to find a place for her. To my regret, we left to return to Dalian before she was released, and I lost track of her.

Originally, Kotsuji told his family that he would be in Shanghai for a few days, but ultimately his work in Shanghai took about one month. It is likely that he extended his stay in order to listen to the stories of the

Jewish refugees. Mineko was very worried about him when his expected return date came and he had not appeared.

I found Kotsuji's trip to Shanghai to be a very interesting episode. His travel mates, Captain Inuzuka, Colonel Yasue, and Ishiguro of the Foreign Ministry were the team that worked on the Fugu Plan created in 1938.

In addition to seeking to avoid a war with America, the plan would, it was thought, serve as a check on the Soviet Union. Tokyo had a strained relationship with Moscow, and Manchuria could be a buffer between the Soviet Union and Japan. Matsuoka, who had lived in the US as an exchange student, did not believe that Japan could win a war against the US, and must have been determined to implement this initiative. Inuzuka, Yasue, and Ishiguro continued to work on the plan to attract American Jewish money.

Nevertheless, there was almost no reaction from Washington. Inuzuka's team turned its attention to the Jewish community in Shanghai and decided to try to mobilize them, hoping that might stimulate Jewish investment from the US. The first part of this strategy was a success, as it became possible to freely meet with the privileged Middle-Eastern Jews. This had previously been forbidden. Captain Inuzuka began a new position in Japan's military office in Shanghai in April 1939. The nexus for the Fugu Plan shifted from Manchuria to Shanghai.

Kotsuji chronicled his visit to Shanghai with these three Fugu Plan implementation team members in his autobiography. It seems implausible that the only reason Kotsuji was sent with the team was to conduct a study. Considering this background as context, it would have been absolutely necessary to negotiate with Middle-Eastern Jews in order to carry out the plan. It is conceivable that they viewed Kotsuji, the preeminent scholar of Jews, as an essential participant. We also cannot forget that his boss, Matsuoka Yosuke, president of the Mantetsu Railway, had ordered him to go to Shanghai.

The situation is described in Tokayer and Swartz's *The Fugu Plan*:

> By mid-1939, Inuzuka had been successful in converting good faith into cash: the Pacific Trading Company was formed with an initial capitalization from Japanese, Chinese, Ashkenazic [European

> Jews], and Sephardic [Middle-Eastern Jews] sources.... [I]t was a well-publicized demonstration that Japanese and Jews could work together for a common goal. At about the same time that the Pacific Trading Company got off the ground, Inuzuka achieved another long-sought goal: the elusive Sir Victor Sassoon [known as the "J. P. Morgan of the Orient"] afforded him the social and personal honor of accepting one of his dinner invitations.
>
> Yasue... also was stepping up his activities. Plans were proceeding for the third [Far-East Jewish] Conference. More important, Yosuke Matsuoka had hired into his public relations department the only Hebrew-speaking Japanese in the world... Kotsuji. Kotsuji's particular field, the Bible, had led him to become proficient in classical Hebrew. He had, in fact, written a Hebrew grammar [book] in Japanese... [which] did qualify Kotsuji as a first-rate suitor to woo the Manchurian Jews.

The Far-East Jewish Conference was a summit of sorts for Jews and Japanese in Manchuria, hosted by the Kwantung Army. It seems the intentions of the Kwantung Army were to win over the Jews of Manchuria. Jews seeking autonomy were aligned, resulting in this summit. The first conference took place in 1937 and the second in 1938, in Harbin. Kotsuji attended the second conference. When the third conference was held in December 1939, Kotsuji gave a speech on behalf of the Mantetsu Railway. This speech would lead to his later being caught up in even more turbulent events.

When Kotsuji began his speech, the Jewish audience gasped. In front of an audience of more than one thousand people, Kotsuji was speaking in Hebrew. Moreover, he spoke in classical Hebrew that even many Jews found hard to understand. The Jews listened dumbfounded but soon began to gaze at him with respect, as Kotsuji, a man of a different ethnicity, fluently spoke. At the end of the speech, they gave him a standing ovation.

Word that there was a Japanese scholar in the Far East who was fluent in Hebrew spread quickly around the world, and a newspaper in Jerusalem featured Kotsuji in its pages. As a result, he gained the Jews' trust and was able to deepen his interactions. In his autobiography, Kotsuji wrote that his work was made easier thanks to the speech. But he did not elaborate on the content of his speech.

I had a keen desire to know what kind of message Kotsuji had delivered to the Jews. Then, as if in answer to my wishes, I was able to get a copy of the speech from his daughters Teruko and Yuriko, who had carefully kept it in storage. The document was a Japanese translation of the Hebrew speech done by Kotsuji himself.

> *A Congratulatory Message to the Far-East Jewish Conference*
>
> *Chairman Kaufman, wise representatives of the Far-East Jews, ladies and gentlemen in this full house!*
>
> *To attend the Far-East Jewish Conference, and to give a speech in Hebrew, the language of your forefathers with its rich history, is a great joy to me as a scholar.*
>
> *In a world filled with turmoil, the fact that this conference is being held in this peaceful climate suggests something very significant not only to you, but to Jews around the world.*
>
> *Of course, this one conference will not immediately resolve the complex Jewish issues. However, at this time, I would like to offer you comfort by quoting from the prophet Isaiah: "For darkness may cover the earth, and clouds shroud nations, but over you, the Lord will be shining, His glory manifest over you" (Isaiah 60:2).*
>
> *"For Zion's sake I cannot be silent, for Jerusalem's I cannot be still until righteousness bursts forth shining, and rescue burns like a brand" (Isaiah 62:1).*
>
> *I hope you will remember the old proverb, "Without vision, people perish," and do not despair of the current circumstances in the world. I want to say to you, "Strengthen your heart with courage." We will look to the Jewish issue now with great sympathy. My hope is that you will prosper through purposeful action and can become a righteous community in the Far East.*

The Jewish audience members likely applauded Kotsuji's speech because they admired him, a Japanese person, for speaking in very challenging classical Hebrew. But when I read the text of the speech, I did not think that was the only reason they were impressed. They had left their homeland and traveled to the Far East, not knowing if they might fall into the hands of Nazis again, and he sought to encourage them and give them courage. His short speech is full of his feelings of friendship and respect for the Jewish people. I am sure that is why they stood and applauded.

As a side note, at the opening of his speech, Kotsuji mentioned Chairman Abraham Kaufman, the most influential Jewish leader at that time, and later they would become lifelong friends. After Kaufman passed away, I heard that his son Ted, who was acquainted with Kotsuji, was in Israel. I was so looking forward to hearing from him about his father's friendship with Kotsuji. Unfortunately, however, one month before my trip to Israel, Ted fell ill and passed away. I was terribly disappointed and saddened.

Chapter Five

Matsuoka Yosuke

Kotsuji's friendship with Matsuoka Yosuke would prove to be a most extraordinary and fateful relationship. Kotsuji wrote about him in his memoir.

> President Matsuoka Yosuke...the man to whom I was directly responsible, was a badly misunderstood man. Short and stocky, he wore a heavy mustache and projected an attitude of self-importance, but he nonetheless was basically a good-hearted man.

Matsuoka played a major role when Japan and Germany signed the Anti-Comintern Pact in November 1936, yet his attitude toward Jews was clearly positive. Also, because he spent part of his boyhood in the US, and studied at the University of Oregon, he had favorable views toward America. He was opposed to war with the US until the end. This was because he understood that Japan could not win.

Matsuoka is known for announcing Japan's withdrawal from the League of Nations in 1933, after rejecting a declaration the League of Nations had adopted calling on Japanese troops to withdraw from

Manchuria. After he became foreign minister, he worked on concluding the Tripartite Pact with Germany and Italy and had an image as a capable and powerful politician who promoted the war. Kotsuji, however, described him as kind. And although Matsuoka did sign the pact with Nazi Germany, Kotsuji wrote that Matsuoka's attitude toward Jews was "correct." Kotsuji once asked him why Japan signed agreements with the Communist Soviet Union and Nazi Germany (the Soviet-Japan Neutrality Treaty and the Japan-Germany Anti-Comintern Pact, respectively), even though these countries had very different ideologies from Japan.

Matsuoka explained it in terms of the Soviet "bear" and the German "leopard." Bear cubs that are fed vegetables and nuts grow up tame, but once they taste meat, they will start biting and even attack people. The Soviet Union is like the bear that has learned the taste of meat; it is no longer a tame bear. That is why the Neutrality Treaty was necessary.

On the other hand, the leopard will bite no matter what it is fed; it was the nature of the beast. But one could avoid being bitten by keeping a safe distance, and that was what the Anti-Comintern Pact achieved. Matsuoka said that he personally did not like leopards, but they had to get along with them.

Kotsuji took this opportunity to ask him about his thinking regarding Jews. Matsuoka replied: "It's very simple. I support the anti-Communist agreement, not anti-Semitism. These are quite different things, and Japan must be clear minded on this point."

Matsuoka crossed the Pacific in a cargo ship when he was thirteen years. He lived with a family and did housework for them while attending school. He went to high school in Oakland, California, and did odd jobs for a local newspaper. After graduation, he returned to Oregon and attended evening classes at the University of Oregon and worked as an interpreter at a Japanese-owned employment company during the day. He was a good example of a "starving student."

He graduated from the University of Oregon with excellent grades and returned to Japan, where he enrolled in the institution now known as Meiji University. Having lived in the US for nearly ten years, I would have expected him to become a liberal thinker, but he actually became the opposite, a nationalist, after returning to Japan.

Foreign Minister Matsuoka Yosuke

In the US at that time, there were frightening acts of anti-Japanese violence by white Americans. I have no doubt Matsuoka faced severe discrimination as a young person living in America. It would not be surprising if his experience opened him to feelings of sympathy for Jews, who endured discrimination and persecution wherever they went. I myself went to the US when I was twelve and experienced anti-Japanese bias several times, so I understand if Matsuoka identified with Jews.

As if to dispel the humiliation he suffered in the US, upon returning to Japan Matsuoka devoted himself to Japan's much older culture and traditions, placed his faith in the emperor system, and delved deeply into nationalism. And yet, at the same time, he still loved America and did not hesitate to say that it was his "second home." Matsuoka was perpetually going back and forth between these contradictory notions.

In his final days before death, Matsuoka was baptized as a Catholic. His Christian name was Joseph. The Dunbars, with whom he had lived as a boy in Oregon, were a devout Christian family. The house where Matsuoka had washed dishes and chopped firewood was near the Church of St. Paul, with its eighty-four-foot bell tower. Matsuoka would have heard the sound of the bell and looked up at the tower every day.

Isabelle Dunbar Beveridge treated this boy who had come to live with her family from a distant country with kindness, and Matsuoka respected her greatly. It is possible that Matsuoka's conversion to Catholicism in his final days was due to her influence. Perhaps the motherly love he felt from her as a youth was rekindled as he lay on his deathbed.

Matsuoka had professed himself as a "Japanist," but in the end he turned away from the emperor system he had worshipped and embraced Christianity. It might be said he chose America over Japan. Matsuoka could be seen as a man swept along on a great wave of history as he carried these conflicting values within himself.

Matsuoka left his position as president of the Mantetsu Railway in 1939 and returned to Japan. The following year he was appointed foreign minister in the second Konoe Cabinet. Shortly thereafter, Kotsuji also resigned from Mantetsu and returned to Japan. He undoubtedly had much unfinished work in Manchuria, but Kotsuji felt that since Matsuoka, who had hired him to be his adviser, had departed, it was appropriate that he resign as a sign of loyalty.

> The two years in Manchuria had affected me considerably. For one thing, I had experienced the world outside the ivory tower, and I had participated in large events. For another, I had finally come to be familiar with the Jewish people, to make friends with them, to understand their ways. I was closer than ever to Judaism.

This is how Kotsuji summarized his time in Manchuria. And these two years would have a significant impact on the rest of his life, which he seemed to anticipate:

> ... I began ... feeling more and more like a Jew, as if there was a Jew living inside me. There was, it seems to me now, a prophetic spirit residing in me.

The Kotsuji family rented a summer home in Karuizawa after returning to Japan and began their life there. He had received twenty months' salary as a retirement allowance from the South Manchuria Railway and did not have to worry about making ends meet. Kotsuji began to work on revising his book on Hebrew grammar. He was able to focus on scholarly endeavors for the first time in a long while. Looking back, he realized that he had not had time for himself in Manchuria. The gentle breeze of the Karuizawa mountains eased his fatigue.

In the autumn, the family moved to Kamakura. There was a sandy beach just across the road, and they could see the Miura Peninsula from their windows. At night the light from a lighthouse would flash into their rooms, and Kotsuji enjoyed looking at the distant cape as he drank his tea.

"That time in Kamakura was our happiest as a family," according to Teruko and Yuriko.

Chapter Six

Sugihara Chiune's Visas for Life

Around the time that Kotsuji was living these idyllic days, history was being made in the small European country of Lithuania. On July 19, 1940, Jewish refugees fleeing the Nazis from Poland crowded outside the gates of the Japanese Consulate in Kaunas. They were seeking to obtain visas to Japan. Vice-Consul Sugihara Chiune sought permission to issue visas. The government of Japan did not allow it. Sugihara knew if nothing was done, the refugees would be captured by Nazis, taken to concentration camps, and killed.

Seeing the surge of refugees at his doorstep, Sugihara made the decision to go ahead and issue transit visas on humanitarian grounds. Approximately six thousand refugees received these visas as a result of Sugihara's courage to defy his superiors and were saved. These came to be called the "visas for life."

Kotsuji had no way of knowing about Sugihara's heroic act. No one in Japan knew. Kotsuji wrote in his autobiography that Sugihara later disappeared and could have been assassinated by the Nazis.[1]

In 1960, when he wrote his autobiography, Kotsuji was living in the US and likely unaware of Sugihara's fate following the war. What did Kotsuji think of Sugihara? Later, in May 1973, Kotsuji wrote to Marvin Tokayer in a letter about Sugihara: "I think the reason my life and Sugihara's life were saved was thanks to our prior jobs." Both had held important positions, Sugihara as vice-consul, Kotsuji as an adviser with Mantetsu. The next line in the letter warmed my heart: "I wish to meet him." Kotsuji passed away five months after writing this letter. The meeting never took place.

According to the materials I researched, among the Jews who obtained visas for life issued by Sugihara in 1940 were 350 students and teachers of the Mirrer Yeshiva, a Jewish seminary, as well as Zorach Warhaftig, who would later become Israel's Minister of Religion and who delivered a eulogy when Kotsuji was buried in Jerusalem.

The students of yeshivas were an elite group who studied Jewish religion and philosophy and would become leaders of the next generation of Jewish society. After the Nazis invaded Poland, they dismantled many yeshivas and burned Torah scrolls and other religious materials. The students were sent to concentration camps. Almost all theological institutions were destroyed in the genocide of the Jewish people.

The Mirrer Yeshiva was located in the town of Mir in northern Poland. When the Germans invaded, they fled, managing to escape certain death. For all 350 students and teachers to have survived and for their school to endure was truly a miracle. This was in fact the only yeshiva in Poland whose students and teachers all would survive.

Most of the Jewish refugees crossed the continent on the Trans-Siberian Railway to Vladivostok. At stations along the way, there were frequent interrogations, including by the Soviet secret police, the NKVD. Tragically some refugees were arrested and sent to prison camps in Siberia.

It was not only the NKVD that the refugees feared. They were also anxious about what kind of treatment awaited them in Japan. For one

1. Sugihara died in 1986 in Japan at the age of eighty-six.

thing, they had very little knowledge about Japan and Japanese people. They wondered whether they would be permitted to enter the country with the visas granted by Sugihara. And if they were, would the government guarantee their safety? Clutching the visas and battling their fears, they rode the train in complete uncertainty.

Eleven days after starting their journey, the Jewish refugees arrived in Vladivostok. From here, they would board a ship to the Port of Tsuruga, in Japan's Fukui Prefecture. Just as they had suspected, trouble lay ahead. By the time they arrived, the Ministry of Foreign Affairs in Japan had issued instructions to the consulate in Vladivostok not to allow the refugees with visas from Sugihara to board ships bound for Japan. This meant the refugees who had risked everything to cross the continent could go no further, and that they would be deported back to Nazi Germany to face certain death. They must have felt bottomless despair.

As fate would have it, there was a Japanese person who understood Sugihara's actions. Nei Saburo was vice-consul in Vladivostok, and he was in a position to take the next step to extend the visas for life. He defied the Foreign Ministry's instructions:[2]

> Japan's prestige is at stake in the visas issued by Imperial consulates. Japan will lose international credibility if they are invalidated. Accordingly, I shall not follow the instructions.

Nei did not stop Jews from boarding the ship, instead issuing travel documents to those without visas and helping them get to Japan. Thanks to his humanitarian actions, the ship carrying Jewish refugees sailed across the Sea of Japan toward the Port of Tsuruga. Huge, dark waves, however, lashed the ship, appearing as mountains that might swallow the refugees. The passengers were frightened and seasick. That is when someone started to sing.

> *As long as the Jewish spirit is yearning deep in the heart,*
> *With eyes turned toward the East, looking toward Zion,*
> *Then our hope – the two-thousand-year-old hope – will not be lost:*

2. Excerpt from *Jindo no Minato Tsuruga* (The Humanitarian Port).

To be a free people in our land,
The land of Zion and Jerusalem.

Then it was a whole chorus of voices singing the anthem, "*HaTikva*," meaning "The Hope." Once they arrived in Japan their long journey of escape would end, with no more fear of living under the boot heel of the Nazis. This is what the refugees believed, and they sang with all their strength, placing their hopes on this new place, Tsuruga. When Israel was founded, *HaTikva* became its national anthem.

Chapter Seven

Jewish Refugees Arrive in Japan

The city of Tsuruga materialized in front of the Jewish refugees. It was the first time any of them had set eyes on Japan. Standing on the deck, they commented on the scene: "What a beautiful city." "It's so green!" "The houses are small... so this is where the Japanese people live." They managed to forget for a moment their worries of what difficulties might lie ahead as they gazed at the scene.

One of the refugees standing on deck was Zorach Warhaftig, who described his impressions of their arrival in Japan in his book *Refugee and Survivor: Rescue Efforts During the Holocaust.*

> When we disembarked from the boat in Tsuruga, we found ourselves in a strange, exotic land. The people were well disciplined, diligent, and seemingly placid, but introverted and suspicious as well.
>
> Japan is a densely populated and closely settled country, with no wide-open spaces: it is only the ubiquitous sea that lends the

> sense of endless distance. The port was packed with fisherman who set out on their daily hunt early and returned at dusk laden down with their bulging nets. The countryside was a patchwork of rice fields, worked by masses of men and women wading knee-deep in the mud. One could not but marvel at the dexterity with which the locals applied their chopsticks to the finished product, the staple Japanese diet – rice. Work in the factories and workshops was carried out zealously and punctiliously. The aesthetic sensitivity that could produce a perfect miniature portrait was now applied to crafts and industry. There was no Sabbath. Only government offices and major enterprises closed on Sunday. Little houses – scrupulously clean, lightweight wooden structures – dotted both the urban and rural horizons.

In this unfamiliar country of Japan, everything the Jewish refugees saw and heard surprised and bewildered them. Even Warhaftig, who was a leader for the refugees, had, as one can see from his writing, no prior knowledge of Japan.

Although they had been allowed to board the ship, this country was an ally of Nazi Germany. Would they really be accepted? The refugees' fears fed on their doubt as they disembarked. But no one was arrested, and they were able to go ashore. As was apparent from the ship, the city of Tsuruga had many rows of small houses. They walked through neighborhoods filled with these homes made of paper and wood and started to believe that they were now safe. According to *Jiyu e no Toso* (Flight to Freedom),[1] one of the refugees proclaimed when they were granted permission to disembark, "The city of Tsuruga seemed like heaven."

At their lodgings, the laughter of relieved Jews could be heard from outside the rooms. It makes one wonder how long it had been since they had laughed in this way. They probably felt they had at last escaped the horrors of the Holocaust.

The Jewish refugees were to travel to Kobe and Yokohama by rail from Tsuruga. However, the station and streets were overflowing with Jews who were unable to board the packed trains. What did the people

---

1. Edited by *Chunichi Shimbun* Shakaibu/Features section.

of Tsuruga think of the large number of Jews descending on their town, seemingly from out of the blue?

The Jews who arrived in Tsuruga were surprised at how clean the Japanese were. One refugee looked at the line his compatriots formed as they walked the streets, and he noticed for the first time that their faces were dirty, their clothes ragged and foul-smelling. They had not had the chance to properly wash their faces during their long journey by train and ship. The people of Tsuruga could be forgiven if they did not want to get close to the Jewish refugees.

And yet they treated the refugees with kindness. The owner of a public bath closed it for a day to let them bathe. Children brought apples to hungry Jews. One woman had given birth on the ship as it crossed the Sea of Japan, and local doctors and nurses gave her and the baby lifesaving treatment. Why did the people of Tsuruga not ostracize the Jews, and instead accept them so warmly?

Tsuruga had long been a gateway to the Asian continent as a port city. Its railroad network was well developed, and trains traveled between Tokyo and Tsuruga. Since Japan opened to Europe in the Meiji Era beginning in the 1860s, many Westerners freely came and went. Tsuruga was a city full of foreign influence. This history may have created a tolerant environment in which Jewish refugees were not regarded with suspicion or discriminated against. Whatever the reason, it is undeniable that countless, nameless people in this city continued the effort to help the refugees that had begun with Sugihara's visas for life.

Many of the Jews who arrived in Tsuruga traveled on to Kobe. Kobe was home to Japan's only Jewish community. Some of the Jews in Kobe were merchants from Iran and Iraq who had lived there since before World War I, as well as Russian Jews forced to move from Yokohama after the Great Kanto Earthquake in 1923. The community numbered only about fifty households, and they were quickly overwhelmed by the sheer number of refugees who now came one after another seeking help.

Kobe was overflowing with Jewish refugees with nowhere to go. The local Jews scrambled to secure housing and act as intermediaries with the Japanese. Most distressing was the limited number of days the refugees with Sugihara's visas were permitted to stay in Japan. For most of them, it was just ten days. In that brief amount of time, they had to arrange for their destination country. That destination was supposed to have been Curaçao, a Dutch territory in the Caribbean, where at the time there were no customs or visa requirements. The majority of them, however, wished to go to the United States. But it was impossible to find a guarantor and a place to settle in merely ten days. If they exceeded ten days, the refugees would be deported. The people whose lives were saved by Sugihara and the goodwill of other Japanese people along their journey had finally reached Kobe. It was unthinkable that their stories would end here, with the chain broken by deportation.

Representatives of the Jewish community tried to persuade the government to extend the refugees' stay, but this request was refused. They were at a loss. Then one of them remembered a Japanese scholar who had spoken at the third Far-East Jewish Conference. He told his colleagues the only person who could save the Jews from the predicament they were now facing was the Japanese man who gave that moving speech in Hebrew. When he learned this man had returned to Japan from Manchuria and was now living in Kamakura, he immediately wrote him a letter. Everything started from this single correspondence.

Kotsuji had finished his work in Manchuria and was spending his time studying the Hebrew language that he loved so much. Life in Kamakura was peaceful. He passed his days reading books while drinking his favorite tea. But he had not forgotten about the Jews he had met in Manchuria, and the stories he had heard from Europe still disturbed him. He felt though that he was just a scholar without the means to help Jews who were suffering so far away. So he kept these troubling thoughts locked up as he went about his life in Kamakura.

One day, upon returning home from a walk on the beach, he found a letter that had been delivered. It was from the representative of the Jewish community in Kobe, and its contents would change the course of Kotsuji's life.[2]

> Dear Professor Kotsuji,
>
> My apologies for this sudden communication, but since you have previously shown interest in all matters relating to the

2. Letter translated from Japanese by Kotsuji.

Jewish people, with this in mind, I am making this request of you. At this time, I would like to respectfully ask for your assistance with our plan.

As you already know, several thousand Jewish refugees who fled European countries are in transit in Japan as they seek to go to their destinations, and we in the Jewish Community of Kobe have been interceding on their behalf. This is a very serious problem, and a positive solution would save the lives of at least several hundred unfortunate refugees. We in the refugee relief committee would like to send two representatives to Tokyo to petition the Minister of Foreign Affairs, A. Ponevejsky and B. Sidline.

We are aware of your interest in international Jewish issues, and if you do not mind, the representatives above would like to visit you and seek your assistance. After all, "without facilitation, a mission is a mere wish," but in any case, these representatives will provide you with a detailed explanation of our mission. These representatives would like the honor of meeting with you so they may request your good offices. Further, when you receive this letter, I would be grateful if you could send a telegram regarding a date for this visit. These representatives will depart on November 17th, and arrive there in the morning on Monday, the 18th.

For now, I shall await your kind reply.

November 12, 1940
A. Ponevejsky, Deputy Director
Jewish Community of Kobe, Ashkenazim Sect

Kotsuji did not hesitate for a moment. He immediately sent a telegram to the Jewish Community of Kobe promising to meet with their representatives. On the appointed day, the two representatives and Kotsuji met in Tokyo. "Every day our compatriots are flooding into Kobe from Tsuruga. There is nothing we can do. Won't you please help us?"

The two representatives explained the plight of the refugees who had managed to reach Kobe. He instantly grasped the situation and knew he had to appeal to the government for assistance. He jumped on a train to Kobe and arrived there twelve hours later.

At that time, there were a few hundred Jewish refugees who had reached Kobe. When Kotsuji arrived at the Jewish community center, people were sleeping on coats on the floor and there was hardly any place to walk. With not much to do and nowhere to go, during the day many gathered near the road in front of the community center.

There were three basic problems. First, extending their visas: ten days was not enough time. Second, many refugees did not have transit visas. The travel documents issued by Vice-Consul Nei Saburo in Vladivostok only allowed the refugees to board the ship, not to enter Japan. Those refugees remained on the ship and were traveling back and forth between Vladivostok and Tsuruga. They were in a dire situation with many suffering from seasickness and physically weak from exhaustion, but they were enduring, waiting anxiously for the chance to enter Japan. Something had to be done to enable these stranded refugees to enter Japan. Third, they had to deal with practical, day-to-day difficulties of life in a completely foreign land and culture. The refugees were perplexing to Japanese people, with different lifestyles, religion, and values, and this resulted in a variety of problems. Solutions were urgently needed.

The Kobe Jewish Community likely asked for Kotsuji's help in addressing these three issues. R. Tokayer recounted that the attitude of Kobe residents at the time was generally positive toward the Jews, but there were problems. For example, one day several Jews were walking in the town of Sannomiya. They encountered a funeral procession for a Japanese soldier who had died in battle, and they watched the procession proceed without removing their hats. A police officer stopped them, ordering them to take off their hats, but they showed no sign of complying. According to Jewish custom, it is proper etiquette to keep one's hat on in this situation. The police officer arrested them for ignoring his order.

Kotsuji immediately went to the police station and explained this to the officer: "You don't understand much about the Jews. When paying respect, they don't remove their hats. On the other hand, they remove their hats when they are being disrespectful." With Kotsuji's explanation, the police officer understood the refugees' behavior and freed them from detention. The freed Jews thanked Kotsuji for his help.

There were many other incidents. The Mirrer Yeshiva students enjoyed the rooftop of the Daimaru department store in the Motomachi part of town. There weren't any department stores where they had lived, and they passed the time there playing games with local children and enjoying the view of the city.

One morning, a student was praying with a *tefillin* (a small leather box with a long strap made for this purpose) on his forehead on the rooftop of the store. An elevator operator who saw this mistakenly believed the student was a spy sending information to an enemy country and called the police. He thought the strap was an antenna and the box was a transmitter. The student was arrested by a police officer who had rushed over and was jailed on suspicion of spying. Kotsuji immediately went to the police station and explained that the Jewish boy had been praying, thus resolving the misunderstanding.

These kinds of occurrences happened on a daily basis. Each time, Kotsuji would go to the police station or the municipal office and explain Jewish customs and habits.

It was the first and second of the three problems, however, that proved the most challenging: extending the refugees' visas and rescuing the refugees trapped aboard the ship at sea. R. Pinchas Hirschprung was one of those refugees, and he wrote about their dire circumstances at that time in his book *The Vale of Tears*.

> On our ship there had been seventy-two refugees who did not have visas for Curaçao in the Dutch West Indies, and the Japanese authorities sent them back to Vladivostok. The Yevkom [Jewish Community of Kobe] asked Professor Kotsuji to intercede on behalf of these refugees.

"It is cowardice not to do, seeing one ought." This old Japanese proverb crossed Kotsuji's mind. He should not run away from problems. That would go against the *Bushido* spirit he had learned as a child. So he headed to Tokyo to try to solve the problem.

Sugihara's visas had been sustained in relay form by Vice-Consul Nei Saburo in Vladivostok, and by the people of Tsuruga and Kobe. Now the baton had been passed to Kotsuji. From that day forward, Kotsuji's days were spent going back and forth between Kamakura and Tokyo. He visited various offices of the Foreign Ministry seeking visa extensions as well as entry permits for the refugees who were drifting between Vladivostok and Tsuruga. Even though Kotsuji was getting the runaround, he persevered as he traversed the Ministry's halls.

After some time, the refugees aboard the ship were finally allowed to disembark and go ashore at Tsuruga. R. Hirschprung wrote, "Kotsuji advocated for them and managed to get permission from the government for them to enter the country." Several interventions likely led to this outcome, but it seems safe to conclude that Kotsuji's actions greatly contributed to the resolution of the crisis.

While that took care of the problem of the refugees stranded on the ship, the most difficult problem remained, getting the visas for the refugees in Japan extended. One Foreign Ministry official refused to listen to anything Kotsuji had to say. Even worse, he summoned Kotsuji and tried to intimidate him, telling him he was forbidden to make any move on visa extensions. Kotsuji's hands were tied. He had reached a dead end. Meanwhile more and more Jewish refugees fleeing the Nazis were flooding into Kobe from Tsuruga. Then a possible way forward occurred to him. Foreign Minister Matsuoka Yosuke might at least be willing to consider the problem.

Surely if he could make Matsuoka, his former boss in Manchuria, aware of the issue there was a chance he could be swayed. Kotsuji made an appointment and visited him in his office at the Foreign Ministry. It was their first meeting since 1939, when they had parted ways in Manchuria. Matsuoka signed the Tripartite Pact in September 1940 and was now concentrating on tensions between Japan and the Soviet Union. He had only limited time. After happily but hurriedly catching up with Matsuoka, Kotsuji jumped straight to the issue at hand.

"I'm desperate to awaken Japan's conscience, but I've been powerless to do it." Matsuoka listened to Kotsuji and murmured, "It's such a shame but . . . ." Kotsuji gazed with despair at Matsuoka. "I came here to consult with you, the Foreign Minister, in distress, as a last resort." Matsuoka was silent for a few moments. Then he responded, "Dr. Kotsuji, I must talk as your friend, not as foreign minister. So we cannot talk here. Let's go outside."

In those days, the military held overwhelming power, and it applied pressure on politicians in different ways. Even the foreign minister had to gauge the attitude of the military before making any move. The Jewish refugees were an issue that required cautious handling by Japan, now an ally of Germany. Matsuoka took Kotsuji outside and walked near the Imperial Palace to a quiet restaurant.

Kotsuji describes the dialogue in his autobiography. Matsuoka listened intently to Kotsuji's explanation and then responded, "Further pleas by you or the Jewish committees will be useless. The ministry has set its policy, and the pressure is on us to keep it unchanged. But there is something that can be done. It is possible that you can get the local prefectural government in the Kobe area to extend the refugees' visas. If you can, I promise you that the ministry will look the other way. The central government in Tokyo simply will ignore whatever action the local government takes."

The advice that Matsuoka thus imparted to Kotsuji on resolving the problem was very clear. Kotsuji wrote about this when he contributed a story entitled "The Suggestion That Saved the Jewish Refugees" to Matsuoka's biography.

> My request to Matsuoka, the foreign minister, was made after six thousand Eastern European Jewish refugees fled the Nazis and arrived in Japan. They only had transit visas good for ten days. I had visited the Ministry of Foreign Affairs a hundred times to no avail. And after much consideration, I decided to go to Mr. Matsuoka himself to seek his help directly. After he explained the difficulties of the situation, he suggested a certain approach. This was truly a godsend. This was how six thousand Jews were saved, but I kept this welcome advice from Mr. Matsuoka safely in my heart.

Matsuoka's position was precarious and complicated. Openly rescuing Jewish refugees would invite the wrath of Japan's ally Germany, as well as from Japan's own military, which was influenced by Germany. This explains Matsuoka's desire to speak as a private citizen, and why he limited himself to merely offering a suggestion as to how Kotsuji could help the Jewish refugees. A doubt that I had long harbored was now resolved. This goes back to when the visas for life were issued by Sugihara. At that time, Sugihara sought permission from the Foreign Ministry to provide visas to the refugees. The Japanese government's response, however, was "No." The person who refused this request was Foreign Minister Matsuoka. Why did Matsuoka, who was involved in the Fugu Plan, who sent trains to Otpor station to rescue stranded refugees, reject Sugihara's humanitarian proposal? That question had stuck with me like a thorn in my heart.

"I wish to maintain good relations with Germany and avoid war with the United States." The perspective that Matsuoka expressed to Kotsuji revealed the truth about his position. If Matsuoka had unconditionally permitted visas to be issued to Jewish refugees in Lithuania, Nazi Germany would not have stood by quietly. He wanted to avoid jeopardizing the relationship with Germany as much as possible. If Japan had taken actions that were openly favorable to Jews, alliance with Germany would have been difficult. Japan's priority was forming this alliance, and provoking Germany was therefore unwise. This reasoning probably led him to refrain from unconditionally extending a helping hand to the refugees in Lithuania.

Nazi Germany was an important trump card for Matsuoka in his US policy. If Japan were allied with Germany, and with the Nazis probably heading for control of all of Europe, then the US would regard Japan as a greater threat. Matsuoka believed this would prevent Washington from adopting hardline policy positions against Japan. As he told Kotsuji when he was head of Mantetsu, Matsuoka thought Japan should avoid war with the US at all costs. Matsuoka had lived in America as a student, and he knew it would be impossible for Japan to win. He first needed to fulfill his responsibility as foreign minister to protect Japan, before he could allow his pro-Jewish feelings to affect his policy decisions. I had come to a greater understanding of Matsuoka's perspective.

A second significant question I had harbored for some time was also answered in "The Suggestion That Saved the Jewish Refugees."

> Mr. Matsuoka entrusted me with a mission for the future. Even if I were to tell people about our secret agreement, most of them

> would probably not believe it. This great scheme relating to the Jews was intended to save our homeland from crisis. But it was too great a burden for the young person I was then (forty years old). To reveal it to the public would invite ridicule from those with ill intentions so I will keep this close to my heart.

What was the mission that Matsuoka entrusted to Kotsuji? And what was his great scheme to save Japan?

It had to be the Fugu Plan. The goal was to avoid war with the US by allowing the Jews to have an autonomous zone. Additionally, allying with Nazi Germany would keep the US in check and prevent the outbreak of war. By taking these contradictory actions, one pro-Jewish and the other pro-Nazi, Matsuoka thought he could avoid a Pacific conflict. He had likely revealed this to Kotsuji during their time together at Mantetsu. Kotsuji remained loyal to his friend. He kept the plan that Matsuoka revealed to him a secret close to his heart for his entire life.

Chapter Eight

The Secret Plan to Extend the Visas

With Matsuoka's advice in hand, Kotsuji struggled to come up with a way to persuade the Kobe government to extend the visas. There was no immigration agency, and visas for foreigners were handled by individual local governments. The police department was responsible for actually issuing residence permits, and the most expedient way to get the police to do what one wanted was money. Handing the official in charge an appropriate sum could, for example, make it possible to obtain visa extensions. Kotsuji did not choose that approach, probably because as a religious man he had a strong sense of ethics. He also knew he would be denied if he directly asked for visa extensions. He decided instead to become "friends" with the officials. Handing them cash would be bribery, but if he became friendly with them, and then they granted his request, that would be different. It was an idea very much suited to Kotsuji and his *Bushido* ideals.

He needed money to become friendly with the officials, and he considered how he could raise these funds. The straightforward approach would probably be to contact Jewish associations in the US and ask for money to help the refugees. That, however, meant the plan could become public. Because he needed to keep his interactions with the police secret and behind the scenes, Kotsuji gave up this idea.

Kotsuji repeated one passage from the New Testament to himself many times: "When giving alms, do not let your left hand know what the right hand is doing" (Matthew 6:3). Kotsuji was living a life of relative ease with the money he had earned from Mantetsu, but he was not wealthy. There was one person, though, whom he could turn to for money. According to his daughters' recollection, this person was Mr. Meshii, who lived in Osaka and was the husband of Kotsuji's sister, Hisako. Mr. Meshii inherited a large fortune from his parents and was a businessman in Osaka. He always said that people had to make their own way in life, and that if you paid attention to your appearance your fortunes would increase. When Kotsuji was young, he asked why dressing well would bring good things. "Because when people look at you, they care about dignity and prestige. You should wear good-quality clothes so you don't lose face," Mr. Meshii replied with great confidence. He was on friendly terms with Kotsuji, and he often passed expensive clothes on to him.

So, Kotsuji went to visit him in Osaka. Mr. Meshii welcomed the unexpected visit from his brother-in-law. After exchanging pleasantries, Kotsuji went straight to the point.

"My brother, I would like to save some very dear friends."

"Friends?"

"They need my help right now. I don't want to let them down."

Kotsuji proceeded to tell him the story of the Jewish refugees' plight in Kobe in a single rush of words. Hearing this tale for the first time, Mr. Meshii was taken aback. Kotsuji told him, "You've always said we should wear good-quality clothes so we don't lose face. But right now, I can't save face with just good clothes."

"Do you need money?"

"Yes."

"Is this very important to you at this moment?"

Kotsuji looked straight into his eyes and replied, "This money is not for me. It's for the lives of human beings." Mr. Meshii was silent for a time.

He was a wealthy man, but he was careful with his money. He responded, "Let me think about it for one night."

The next morning, Mr. Meshii placed before Kotsuji what must have seemed a huge sum of money, 300,000 yen. That would be roughly eleven million yen today. He said, "This is the money to use to save lives," handing the cash to him. Kotsuji gave his brother-in-law heartfelt thanks, filled his pockets, and headed back to the waiting refugees.

When he arrived back in Kobe, Kotsuji immediately went to see the senior police officials at their headquarters to become "friends" with them. He introduced himself as someone interested in Jewish issues and wanting to have in-depth talks with police officials about what could be done. He said he would like to have this discussion over a leisurely dinner and invited them to the finest restaurant in Kobe. Kotsuji described the scene in his autobiography.

> Five or six people came that evening. I took them out to the best restaurant in Kobe and fed them a luxurious Japanese dinner: shellfish soup, lobster in soy sauce, seaweed with vinegar, and bean jelly, and plenty of sake along with it all. We had a *geisha* girl with us to play the guitar-like *shamisen* and to sing to us.

It was probably the most extravagant business dinner in Kobe at that time. Kotsuji did not speak a word about the Jewish refugees' visas that evening. They just drank, ate, and sang.

Two days later, Kotsuji once again invited the police officials to dinner and again shared an expensive meal with them. He did not bring up the Jewish refugees. Several days later, he invited his "friends" to dinner for a third time, where he carefully broached his real topic of interest.

"Actually, I would like to ask you for a favor," he began. Kotsuji earnestly spoke to them of the plight of the Jewish refugees who had fled to Japan, and he bowed his head low several times as he pleaded that they be given visa extensions so that could stay in Japan longer.

Now that they had established a relationship, the police officials were comfortable talking with Kotsuji, and they acceded to his request. They issued permits extending the ten-day visas for an additional fifteen days at a time. The refugees could stay in Japan for a longer period by extending their visas several times, as needed. Kotsuji's strategy proved a grand success.

Kotsuji traveled to Kobe almost every week for several months to sustain this relationship of trust he had developed, and he earnestly shared his thoughts and feelings with his police friends. By the same token, they were moved by Kotsuji's humanitarian passion and started showing more understanding toward the Jewish community. Eventually they became supportive enough to approve the opening of a Jewish school.

The refugees were deeply grateful to Kotsuji, and yet Kotsuji never talked of his own actions to others. He summarized what had happened.

> Though the hospitality of Japan toward the suffering Jews was nothing to boast about . . . the country at least tolerated their presence until they could find a way to move on safely.

Kotsuji said that the Jews were saved not because of his actions, but because of the goodwill of the Japanese people. There is no question, however, that if Kotsuji had not obtained these visa extensions many of the Jewish refugees would have had nowhere to go and been forced back to Europe.

Among the refugees were people who would become important figures in Israel, Jewish life, and world affairs, including Israel's Minister of Religion, the Chief Rabbi of Montreal, the Chairman of the Chicago Mercantile Exchange, and the Chief Rabbi of Mexico and Latin America.

Chapter Nine

A Gift from an Ancient Past

As I pursued Kotsuji's life, there was something that always puzzled me. I wasn't able to understand how Kotsuji, who valued the spirit of *Bushido* and scholarship and had a rather stern image, nonetheless entertained Kobe police officials so skillfully with *geisha,* music, and sumptuous meals, and in so doing persuaded them to grant visa extensions for Jewish refugees. How was he able to so easily slip into this most unique, private world of pleasure?

In his autobiography, Kotsuji wrote that his family had been Shinto priests at a shrine in Kyoto until his grandfather's generation. It was not clear to me how his father, Kisaburo, had made his living, however. I wondered what kind of environment Kotsuji had grown up in.

Kyoto has five *Kagai* ("flower districts"), neighborhoods where *geisha* and *maiko* (apprentice *geisha*) live, train, and work. Gion and Ponto-Cho are very well known and lively, in the center of Kyoto. Kamishichiken, on the other hand, steps from the fabled shrine Kitano Tenmangu, is believed to be the oldest *Kagai,* dating back to 1444.

The Kaburenjo is a theater in this district, built in the 1890s, where *geisha* and *maiko* hone their singing, dancing, and musical skills, and where they perform in front of audiences. The Kaburenjo is open to the public in the summer for a limited time as a beer garden, where people can chat with *geisha* and *maiko* in a less formal atmosphere. In an amazing twist of fate, I spent a great deal of time here in my adult life. I always looked forward to visiting this magical place.

After my book was published in Japan in 2013, I received a copy of the Kotsuji family registry from Kotsuji's daughters. The registry included Kotsuji's birthplace, and I was startled to see that the address listed was this very beer garden, the Kaburenjo Theater in Kamishichiken!

I visited the office at the Kaburenjo to find out more and learned that Kotsuji's father had been one of the representatives of the tea house guild that was involved in the construction of the theater.

The property at the address listed as Kotsuji's birthplace includes not only the theater but also several other buildings. It is not possible to know for certain if he was born in the Kaburenjo itself. However, he was indeed born at this location in February 1899, and that is where he lived until he went to college in Tokyo.

In 1902, Kisaburo built the Futamiya tea house just behind the Kaburenjo. This was when Kotsuji was around three years old. The Kotsuji

Kotsuji grew up in Kyoto's Kamishichiken, the ancient capital's oldest *Kagai*, and steps away from the venerable Kitano Tenmangu Shrine.

Kitano Tenmangu Shrine, with a history spanning more than one thousand years

The entrance to the Kaburenjo Theater in Kamishichiken

family moved into the newly built tea house, and lived there with the *geisha*, *maiko*, and the staff as they ran the tea house business.

This building has been designated as a cultural treasure and is still used as a residence to this day. I could not hide my surprise at these newly discovered facts. And just as I had been led to write a book about Kotsuji all those years ago, I had unknowingly been visiting the place where he was born for most of my adult life. I couldn't help but feel a deep connection to him once again.

As I pondered this amazing coincidence, a scene emerged in my head:

> Candles flickering.
> Beautiful, richly colored kimonos.
> Inside a *tatami* room, lovely music played by a *geisha* on her instrument.
> Floating in the candlelight's glow, elegant *geisha* and *maiko* appear, wearing crimson lipstick.
> The guests drink sake as they watch the performers sing and dance, and then enjoy conversations with them.
> A young boy wants to take in the scene. He cracks open a sliding door very carefully with one finger, just a tiny bit.
> He peeks into the room, and the scene becomes indelibly etched in his memory.
> This is young Setschan (Kotsuji's nickname as a child).
> I realized: So this is how it was!

Kotsuji grew up surrounded by *geisha* and *maiko, shamisen* and *taiko* drums, and was raised in the heart of Kyoto's performing arts world. He learned as a small child how to entertain guests, how to make them happy. It was part of him. He used that knowledge to the fullest when he was in Kobe so many years later, successfully assisting the refugees in extending their stay in Japan.

A place where time is measured in centuries and eras, ancient Kyoto, and a world within that world, Kamishichiken, would come to be forever connected by Kotsuji to the fate of thousands of Jews. Now I understood.

Chapter Ten

The Encroaching Shadow of the Nazis

The visas were extended, but Kotsuji had little time to catch his breath. The refugees now needed safe passage to their final destinations, and this became his next mission. Most wanted to go to the United States. Kotsuji visited the ports of Kobe and Yokohama almost every day to try to arrange their onward journeys.

In the spring of 1941, the refugees began departing Japan a few at a time. Those with visas went to the US and Canada, those without went to Shanghai, which did not require them. Still, over 1,500 refugees remained in Kobe with nowhere to go.

The Jews who stayed believed it was safest for them to remain in Japan as long as they could continue renewing their visas. However, their safety in Japan was no longer assured. Kotsuji and the refugees were unaware that Josef Albert Meisinger, notoriously known as the Butcher of Warsaw, was now stationed in Tokyo.

Meisinger, a Gestapo and SS officer, had been chief of the secret police in Warsaw, Poland, from 1939 to 1941. He was widely feared, having been responsible for the slaughter of an estimated 100,000 Jews there. Now he was based in the German Embassy in Tokyo as a liaison for the SS intelligence section.

Meisinger was posted in Japan on the orders of Heinrich Himmler, the leader of the SS and a close aide to Adolf Hitler. He stated that his job was to work with Japan's Special Higher Police and the Military Police (Kempeitai) to expose Jews and anti-Nazi elements in Japan. In reality, Meisinger's ruthless tactics were too much even for Himmler, and it was said that Himmler was planning to try and execute him. One theory was that Himmler's close aide Reinhold Heydrich stepped in and had Meisinger sent to distant Japan to keep him from this fate. For his part, Meisinger, who had been demoted, was likely eager to prove himself to Hitler and return to Germany, having burnished his reputation by eliminating as many Jews as possible in Japan.

Meisinger was exasperated by Japan's lack of cooperation with Nazi Germany's policy toward Jews. After the outbreak of the Pacific War, he went to Shanghai, which was then under Japanese occupation, and announced his plan to kill the twenty thousand Jews there, pressing the Japanese government to carry it out. The plan was meticulous and specific. On the Jewish holiday of Rosh HaShana in September, Jews would gather at their synagogues, where they were to be rounded up. Meisinger said the Japanese could decide on how best to kill them. He proposed three options, each brutal and terrifying: put the Jews on derelict ships and set them adrift on the East China Sea; after they had starved to death, the ship would be sunk by the Japanese Navy; or, take the Jews to the salt mines on the outskirts of Shanghai and force them to work until they died; or, build a concentration camp on an island at the mouth of the Yangtze River and use the Jews for human experiments until they perished.

Meisinger recommended the third method. There were apparently some Japanese military officers in Shanghai who supported this extreme plan. They respected Hitler and admired Nazi Germany. Japan rejected Meisinger's plan and stood by its position that its alliance with Germany and the expulsion of Jews were separate issues.

Japan's refusal did not, however, stop Meisinger in his relentless pursuit. He worked closely with the Special Police and the Military

Police to apply pressure on the Jews in Japan. He had his aides set up an office in the German Consulate in Kobe to monitor Jewish refugees there. Records show that Meisinger himself frequently went to Kobe. As fearsome as he was, Japan never allowed him to lay a finger on a single Jew.

According to German historian Heinz E. Maul's book, *Nihon wa Naze Yudayajin wo Hakugai Shinakattaka* (Why Japan Did Not Persecute Jews), among the 2,600 Germans in Japan at the time 116 were Jews. They included a professor at the Tokyo Academy of Music (now the Tokyo University of the Arts), Leonid Kreutzer, who was also a world-renowned pianist; pianist and conductor Leo Sirota; conductors Josef Rosenstock and Klaus Pringsheim Sr.; philosopher Karl Löwith; economist Kurt Singer; and physical chemist Louis Hugo Frank.

The German Embassy called on the Japanese government to dismiss all German Jews in Japan from their jobs. It is believed that Meisinger was behind this request. When it was ignored, Meisinger grew more frustrated and began using Japan's Special Police and Military Police to persecute Jews.

Professor Louis Hugo Frank arrived in Japan in 1913 and taught at the Otaru School of Higher Learning (now the Otaru University of Commerce). From 1926 he was a lecturer at Yamanashi Technical College (now University of Yamanashi Faculty of Engineering). In recognition of his achievements after many years in education, he was awarded the Order of the Sacred Treasure 5th Class in 1936. But in 1943 he was abruptly dismissed. His removal was thought to be due to pressure from Meisinger.

In 1944, his son Hugo Karl Frank was arrested in Yokohama by the Military Police on suspicion of spying. He endured harsh interrogations and died of illness at the Sugamo Prison, the result of Meisinger's collaboration with the Military Police.

Meisinger increased his pressure on artists as well, and anti-Semitic rhetoric in the music world intensified. Yamamoto Hisashi's book, *Nihon wo Aishita Leo Sirota,*[1] contains an interesting truth.

---

1. Leo Sirota: The Jewish Pianist Who Loved Japan, published by *Asahi Shimbun* in Japan.

> After listening to a performance of the Japan Symphony Orchestra conducted by the Jewish conductor Rosenstock, the music critic Yoshimoto Akimitsu denounced it: "Even as the Japanese and American navies fought the battle of Guadalcanal, and the US and Britain were annihilated in the Greater East Asia War, fighting in this war continues so we can crush the Jewish plot to pull the strings in the background. I struggled to understand the psychology of the three thousand spectators who so enthusiastically applauded this Jew, who left Germany to escape the Nazi cleansing, merely because he was musically gifted and had outstanding skills.[2]

While it was part of a hate-filled anti-Jewish campaign, this text demonstrates that even in wartime Japan many in the audience enthusiastically applauded a Jewish conductor. Jewish musicians were continuing to perform in Japan, despite the effect Germany's efforts were having on the environment there.

Nevertheless, in October 1943 the Tokyo Music and Culture Association sent a notice to all its Japanese members instructing them not perform with musicians who were not from the Axis nations (Japan's allies Italy and Germany). This meant that it would be impossible for Jewish musicians to perform.[3] Then in 1944 the Tokyo Academy of Music decided to expel its Jewish musicians, and world-class pianists Leo Sirota and Leonid Kreutzer were forced out.

Two years earlier, Meisinger was growing increasingly frustrated with Japan's stance toward the increasing numbers of Jewish refugees. According to R. Marvin Tokayer, he was applying more pressure on his Japanese interlocutors to stop providing safe haven for the Jews, and both within the government and certainly inside the military, officials were growing much more uneasy with the negative implications of so many Jews entering Japan for Tokyo's relations with Berlin.

2. As quoted in *Ongaku no Tomo*, Dec. 1942 issue.
3. See Leo Sirota: The Jewish Pianist Who Loved Japan.

The government was protecting the Jews, but the military was not necessarily aligned with the government's policy. Some officers were showing signs of sympathizing with Meisinger.

R. Tokayer's research shows that the number of Jews who arrived in Kobe in January totaled 236, in February 969, and in March 805. The numbers of those who departed Japan, on the other hand, came to 236 in January, 147 in February, and 182 in March.

Pressure on Japan from the Nazis to do something to stop the influx grew as the numbers of refugees continued to increase. Finally, the government relented. Officials had begun to realize that holding back Germany on this issue was no longer a viable option. They chose instead to do more to encourage the Jews to voluntarily leave Japan.

According to R. Tokayer and Mary Swartz's research and their book, *The Fugu Plan*, the Kobe Jewish Community received a summons from military authorities in early May 1941. "Send two representatives from among the refugees to Tokyo within three days for interrogation," the letter stated. It came from the Ministry of the Imperial Navy.

Tensions now ran high in the Jewish community in Kobe. The word "interrogation" in the letter created a sense of anxiety. Depending on their answers to the interrogation, they feared they might be deported. And what awaited them would be forced labor or gas chambers. But having been summoned, they could not flee. They had no choice but to immediately answer the invitation to the interrogation.

Following much discussion, two representatives were chosen from among the rabbis, Shimon Kalisch, the Amshinover Rebbe, known as a witty and eloquent leader, and Moshe Shatzkes, a preeminent talmudic scholar.. Ultimately, a third rabbi, Shlomo Shapiro, would also join them. The fate of the Jewish refugees was now in the hands of these three rabbis. A member of the Kobe Jewish Community accompanied them, and the four boarded a night train to Tokyo. As the trip was made on such short notice, they had not been able to get a sleeper car. They sat for the twelve-hour journey.

The rabbis' distinctive robes and caps, as well as their long beards, made them stand out on the train. The other passengers were kind and some even shared food with them. There was no way Nazis would overlook such a conspicuous group. Several German soldiers in the next car noticed the four travelers and approached them. As they shouted, "You animals!" "Pigs!" "We will eradicate your whole race from the face of the earth!" the soldiers kicked the rabbis' legs, pulled their beards, and spat in their faces. But the four Jews endured the attack with no resistance. It was nothing compared to the humiliation they had suffered in Poland.

The Germans soon returned to their car, deflated by the lack of resistance. Nearby Japanese passengers had been holding their breath in shocked silence. The Jews, however, wiped their faces and went back to talking as if nothing had happened. The truth is that the rabbis probably felt they could not afford to respond in anger to the assault by the German soldiers. They were certainly already preoccupied with the interrogation that awaited them in Tokyo and wondering what the Japanese military was planning to do with them. Facing such circumstances, I am certain they did not sleep a wink.

When the train arrived at Tokyo Station, the rabbis found Kotsuji waiting for them. He had come to accompany them to the Imperial Navy headquarters. Kotsuji insisted on being their interpreter to ensure clear communication, and the four visitors were glad to have their benefactor by their side.

According to Tokayer and Swartz's findings, and as described in *The Fugu Plan,* and David Mandelbaum, in his book *From Lublin to Shanghai,* the interrogation by Japanese officers at a Navy facility in Tokyo appears to have unfolded in a dramatic way.

"What is the evil of your people that the Germans hate you so much?"

The rabbis looked at each other. How were they to answer such an ignorant and arrogant question? The Amshinover Rebbe spoke.

"It's because we are an Asian people like you ... perhaps someone who has not lived in the midst of their hatred can understand it. I have lived with the great hatred the Nazis have for other races. Read what the Nazis write in the original German. You will learn that the gypsies, the blacks, the Slavs, and the Japanese also are on their list of inferior peoples."

"Japanese are considered an inferior race?"

"That's ridiculous!"

The Rebbe addressed the angry officers. "In Berlin, not many years ago, a young German woman fell in love with a man who worked at the

Japanese Embassy. They were not permitted to marry. Such a marriage with people of other races was forbidden by law to protect the purity of the Germans."

The Amshinover Rebbe met the stares of the four Navy officers and continued to speak slowly.

"You haven't realized this yet? The Nazis don't accept the existence of any race except Germans. After the Nazis eliminate Jews from the earth, next they'll try to eliminate you, the Japanese. Why don't you realize that? Dr. Kotsuji, please tell them exactly what I said."

Encouraged by the Rebbe's determination, Kotsuji interpreted his words verbatim. The officers were silent. Then they said they needed some time to think and would resume the meeting in two hours. They left the room. After two hours, the four Jews and Kotsuji were shown to a different room, one that was much brighter than the first interrogation room.

After a while, Foreign Minister Matsuoka entered the room. He had just returned from a trip abroad meeting with Hitler and Stalin. Matsuoka explained Japan's position to the rabbis and concluded with these words: "The Japanese people wish to maintain good relations with Jews, and I pray that the Jewish people will have a good impression of the Japanese." In the end, the specific reasons why this meeting ended well

Kotsuji (second from left) with the Jewish representatives summoned to Tokyo for a penultimate meeting with Japanese military authorities in May 1941. Shimon Kalisch, the Amshinover Rebbe, is third from the left.

for the Jews remain unclear. Did the authorities change their mind after hearing the Rebbe's argument? Did Matsuoka himself decide? Or was it a combination of both?

One thing seems certain; Kotsuji's friendship with Matsuoka had once again impacted the Jews' fate. He must have been deeply thankful that the foreign minister, despite his extremely busy official schedule, came to see the delegation himself and assured their safety.

Now that the refugees' safety had been secured, the next task for Kotsuji was to send them to safe destinations. He had a mountain of issues to deal with, including raising funds for their journeys and securing transportation. The person who took on these tasks on the refugees' side was Zorach Warhaftig. As mentioned earlier, in 1973 after Kotsuji died, Warhaftig met Kotsuji's body at the airport in Israel as the Minister of Religion and spoke at his burial in Jerusalem. Warhaftig was a legal scholar and one of the leaders of the refugees. Being fellow academics, he and Kotsuji had quickly become friends and kindred spirits. Later, Warhaftig wrote about their bond in his book *Refugee and Survivor: Rescue Efforts During the Holocaust*:

> We became friends and he would come to see me occasionally from the holiday resort of Kamakura, where he lived. We would take long walks together and converse in either English or Hebrew on religion and philosophy, on Jewish and Japanese history. My own command of English at the time was rather limited, and Kotsuji's Hebrew was biblical and halting, although he knew several psalms by heart. Our talks therefore proceeded at a slow pace and were interrupted by long silences that gave us time for reflection. There was a distinct ceremonial element to the procedure.

As we can tell from this passage, their friendship matured over time. Subsequently when Kotsuji decided to convert to Judaism he sought Warhaftig's guidance. Kotsuji also visited his home in Israel many times, and this enduring friendship included their families.

Warhaftig had begun negotiations with the shipping company Nippon Yusen (NYK) to transport the refugees to their destinations. He also contacted the leadership of the World Jewish Congress to gain their cooperation in securing funding for the refugees' journeys. In addition, he sent out urgent appeals for assistance to Jewish organizations around the world. Although there were many twists and turns in the process, thanks to Warhaftig's diligent efforts, by the fall of 1941 the majority of the remaining Jewish refugees had departed for the US, Canada, Shanghai, and other countries.

There are no records to indicate how Kotsuji worked with Warhaftig on this endeavor. According to R. Tokayer, Kotsuji went to Yokohama almost daily during this time to negotiate with the shipping agent. He also likely served as an interpreter in meetings.

Once Warhaftig was satisfied that most of the Jewish refugees had indeed departed Japan, he himself set off for the US. Later, as a key member of the World Jewish Congress he published his research on Jewish refugee issues and the Nazis, contributed to Israel's independence in 1948, and signed its Declaration of Independence. He served as Minister of Religion until 1974.

Chapter Eleven

The Jews Who Remained in Kobe

Most of the Jews had departed Japan by the autumn of 1941. On December 7th of that year, Japan plunged into the Pacific War with its attack on Pearl Harbor. I cannot help but wonder what would have happened had the Jews not been able to leave before Japan entered the war. After conditions during the war deteriorated, would the Japanese have accepted the Jews as warmly as they had before the war? During wartime chaos, their safety probably would not have been guaranteed. Moreover, the SS and Meisinger surely would not have sat back and done nothing. Because most of the refugees had left Japan before the Pacific War began, the Holocaust does not stain the pages of Japan's history books. It seems clear that Kotsuji contributed greatly to this result.

What did the Jews think of their lives in Japan? After landing in Tsuruga, Japanese people were kind to them in Kobe, they had plenty of food, and they were safe. Were there any refugees who wished to stay on in Japan? I started wondering about this as I did my research on the Jews in Kobe.

I found an article[1] from the newspaper *Kobe Shimbun* at the time in Martin Kaneko's book *Kobe Yudayajin Nanmin 1940–1941* (Kobe Jewish Refugees 1940–1941).

> Do the Jews like Kobe? They fret – we don't want to go to Shanghai, we want to stay in Kobe forever. The Jews who fled war in Europe and came to Kobe, at one time reaching three thousand in number, were living charmed lives in exile in the port city, but the external affairs office of Hyogo Prefecture, adhering to its hardline policy, was forcing more and more of them out, and on the 28th 350 were to be sent to Shanghai to begin removing all Jews from Kobe. But these people strongly opposed going to Shanghai, and on the afternoon of the 26th a group of forty representatives, led by a young beautiful woman, barged into the prefecture's external affairs office and pleaded to be allowed to live in Kobe.

Unfortunately, their pleas were ignored and the Jews were sent to Shanghai, excluding the Jews who were originally in Japan. The story shows, however, that they loved Japan and their lives there, and appreciated the Japanese people.

The same book quotes a news article[2] about Jews who were still in Kobe after the start of the Pacific War and offers a sense of the lives of Jews who remained there.

> There are just over ninety Jews in Kobe, wanderers with no homeland, harbored in the heart of Japan, leader of Greater Asia, and they were living in gratitude for the kindness of the citizens of the port city. They felt the greatness of the latent power of Japan in the continued news of the Imperial Military's victories in the war with the United States and United Kingdom, and the more

1. "The Jews Like Kobe: A Beautiful Woman Leads in Tactic to Persuade Using Tears," *Kobe Shimbun*, August 27, 1941.
2. "Jews Among the Pump Handlers in Civil Defense Unit, Donations and Blessings in Gratitude to Japan," *Kobe Shimbun*, December 18, 1941.

> than ninety Jews in Kobe were discussing returning this favor of Imperial Japan this autumn. In the international city of Kobe, in the most cosmopolitan area of 2-chome, Yamamoto-dori, Oliver Evans, chairman of the Kobe Jewish community, went to the neighborhood association to apologize for that fact that even as the neighborhood's civil defense group is protecting the home front, the Jews, while living in the same town, are standing by doing nothing. He asked that the Jews be allowed to join the civil defense unit, and the neighborhood association warmly accepted this beautiful request, which resulted in Sidline, Carlton, and Ezra being placed on the No. 1 pump team, and Ponevejsky and Guterman were assigned to the No. 2 pump team. "We as citizens of Greater East Asia, we are intent on doing this for Japan."

The article also reported that the Jewish community donated one thousand yen each to the Army and Navy, conducted a prayer ceremony at the Jewish community center for Imperial Japan to win the war, and offered three cheers of "*Banzai*" for the Great Japan Empire and the Imperial Army and Navy.

I do not know how much allegiance the Jews truly felt to the Japanese military. It might have been a wise move for them, with their long history of persecution, to seek to ensure their survival. At the same time, positive communications during wartime between the Jews and the Japanese are interesting and heartening as historical fact.

Chapter Twelve

The Battle Against Anti-Semitism

With the departure of Jewish refugees for their respective destinations, Kotsuji was finally able to spend quiet days at his home in Kamakura with his family. This peaceful time only lasted two months, however, with the beginning of the Pacific War.

During the war years, Kotsuji devoted himself to fighting anti-Semitism. Meisinger used the outbreak of war as an opportunity to demand more forcefully the persecution of Jews. As previously described, he sought to kill the twenty thousand Jews in Shanghai and increase monitoring of Jews in Japan. He also spread Nazi propaganda in Japan to promote anti-Semitic ideology.

Kotsuji was appointed by the Ministry of Foreign Affairs to a committee formed to work on foreign policy issues. He was probably sought out for his views on Jewish policies. According to his autobiography, legal scholar Tanaka Kotaro and philosopher Miki Kiyoshi were also members of this committee. After the war, Tanaka served as Minister of Education and Chief Justice of the Supreme Court. Miki was detained in 1945 pursuant to the Peace Preservation Law as an influential philosopher and later died in prison due to the poor sanitary conditions. Kotsuji mentions his own remarks to the committee in his memoir.

> I was among the speakers; and I took advantage of the opportunity to counter some of the anti-Semitic propaganda so prevalent in government circles. I began by pointing out that the Nazi notion of *Rassenschande* – racial shame – was absurd.... I pointed out why Hitler was so interested in promoting anti-Semitism in Japan....

It was courageous of him to speak this way during strict wartime restrictions on speech. One man who heard about this statement became interested in Kotsuji. His name was Ishibashi Tanzan.

Ishibashi was the president of Toyo Keizai Shimposha, a publishing and media company, and after the war he was elected to serve in the House of Representatives. In 1956 he would become prime minister. Ishibashi had sounded the alarm when the Tripartite Pact among Japan, Italy, and Germany was concluded, and he wrote an editorial in his own newspaper against starting a war with the US. Ishibashi was a proponent of liberalism and democratic principles, and was critical of Nazi Germany.

Kotsuji was invited to Ishibashi's office at Toyo Keizai Shimposha, and the two spoke primarily about the Jewish issue. "What do you think about traveling around Japan to share your thoughts about the Jewish people?" Ishibashi asked Kotsuji. Toyo Keizai Shimposha had branch offices at chamber of commerce sites in thirty-five cities around the country, and Ishibashi conducted lectures once a month at each location. He wanted Kotsuji to speak at these events.

Ishibashi asked Kotsuji, "Do you know Shiratori Toshio?"

"Just the name," he answered, as Ishibashi continued.

Shiratori was thought to be an expert on Jewish issues, so Ishibashi hired him as a speaker at these events. Shiratori was a former diplomat with the Foreign Ministry, and in 1938 had been appointed ambassador to Italy. He played a key role in the signing of the Tripartite Pact. However, Shiratori was not actually an expert on Jewish issues, and as he lectured around Japan, he praised Nazi Germany and Hitler while slandering Jews. When Ishibashi realized this, he fired Shiratori.

"But it seems Shiratori is still going around Japan spreading Nazi propaganda. He's apparently saying the Jews are planning to overthrow Japan."

Hearing this, Kotsuji readily accepted the lecturing assignment. He began traveling across the country and explained the truth behind anti-Semitic ideology and offered his accurate knowledge about the Jewish people. He was always accompanied by bodyguards who stayed close to him while he traveled. Of course, they were most likely provided by Ishibashi.

The content of Kotsuji's lectures was preserved in the Toyo Keizai Shimposha's lecture archives, within the National Diet Library. They describe the history, religion, and characteristics of the Jewish people, while explaining the situation Jews were facing around the world at that time. His summary of the situation in his closing remarks is most striking.

> Now, I've talked at length about the nature of the Jewish problem, and I'd like to close with my personal perspective. First is the traditional antagonism because of religion. Judaism and Christianity have been at odds since they split, and in this age where scientific thought should be able to dispel religious animosity, it is not easily done once these emotions of two thousand years have been awakened. It is critical to understand that the Jewish problem in the West has an emotional charge that we Japanese simply cannot understand. Add economic issues to these emotions, then pile on political issues, and make the Jews the scapegoat whenever you hit a roadblock. This tactic of taking society's complaints and steering popular sentiment in this direction could easily happen in any country. With respect to these issues in Europe and the US, it is important that we look at them more objectively from the perspective of a third party, and deal with matters in a way that upholds our unique situation of having a clean slate, where we have not once persecuted Jews nor have they harbored any resentments toward the Japanese.

Kotsuji gently urged his audience to think objectively about the Jewish issue without being misled by the Nazis' anti-Semitic ideology, but there were times when he spoke passionately in his lectures.

His lecture schedule was written at the end of his lecture notes: July 2 in Tokyo, July 6 in Kansai and Kyoto, July 7 in Chubu and Hamamatsu, July 16 in Kagoshima, July 17 in Binan Fukuyama, and July 18 in Okayama.

In light of what transportation was like in 1943, this was a physically and mentally demanding schedule. It is clear from this record that Kotsuji put both his mind and body on the line, racing around Japan to battle anti-Semitism.

This nationwide mission continued for several months, but as wartime conditions deteriorated, restrictions on travel by private citizens made it impossible to continue the lectures. And yet, Kotsuji still believed there was more he could do to stem the spread of anti-Semitism. He wanted Japanese people to understand the true nature of Jewish people. Kotsuji's faith never wavered. He shut himself in his study in Kamakura and devoted all his effort to writing.

Eventually, he visited a publisher in Tokyo to whom he had been introduced by an acquaintance and showed him his manuscript. The title was *Yudaya Minzoku no Sugata* (The True Character of the Jewish Nation). It explained Jewish history and religion and offered an analytical critique of Hitler's anti-Jewish ideas. Kotsuji must have known it was a dangerous book. If it was seen by the Special Higher Police or Military Police, not only could publication be prohibited, but he could very well have been arrested. Even so, Kotsuji enthusiastically explained his thoughts on the book to an editor. The publisher was moved by Kotsuji's passion and agreed to publish it. It seemed that the book was on track to being published.

However, starting around this time, Meisinger's suppression of pro-Jewish thinking was gaining momentum. Kotsuji received a summons from the director of the central government's Intelligence Bureau, who had received a copy of the manuscript submitted by the publisher. The Intelligence Bureau handled censorship.

"Dr. Kotsuji, do you intend to publish this book as it stands?"

"Yes, of course," Kotsuji replied, steeling himself. The director began to talk gently, as if to persuade Kotsuji.

"I don't want to stop publication of this book. It is the first solid, well-balanced history of the Jews offered in Japan. However, there are sections where you criticize Hitler and the Nazis outright, and Italy as well. You have criticized both of Japan's allies. Isn't that so?"

"Yes, that's right," Kotsuji answered calmly.

"The military police will probably arrest you if I let them see the book. I don't have to tell you any of this. But I respect you, and I wanted to ask you to make the cuts."

Kotsuji was persuaded by the director's sincere request, and he decided to delete passages that directly criticized Germany and Italy. The first printing of five thousand copies of the book sold out before they even hit bookstores. The publisher was praised by many readers and began preparations for a second edition. But by then paper was being rationed, and then its offices were hit by an air strike, destroying the original printing plates. They were forced to give up on the second edition.

Shortly after the book was published, Kotsuji was visited by two Special Police officers. The Special Higher Police were known for extracting confessions with violence and torture. It was said to be so terrifying that even a crying child would go silent. They looked at Kotsuji suspiciously and asked, "We understand that the Jews of Kobe are extremely grateful to you?"

"Is that so?"

"You must have made a lot of money from the book."

"Yes, I made some money."

"Who paid you that money?"

"The publisher, of course."

"Don't lie. It was the Jews, right?"

Kotsuji dismissed this with a laugh and said, "If the Jews were paying me a lot of money, would I be living so simple and frugal a life?"

The police officers frowned at him and left. Kotsuji realized for the first time that the Special Police had been surveilling him for some time. It was not long after this that a listening device was discovered in Kotsuji's house.

To make matters worse, in the autumn of 1944 Kotsuji found a letter stuck in his front door upon returning home one day. It was a summons from the widely feared Kempeitai, the Military Police Headquarters, Finally, what he had been certain would happen had come to pass. He read through it word by word to confirm every detail. Normally, when the Military Police arrested people, they just showed up and took them away. So why was he summoned? Was it some expression of respect for him? Or maybe they did not intend to arrest him. His emotions were in turmoil.

The Nazis lurked like a shadow behind the Military Police. Thoughts swirled in his mind. Would he be arrested? Did they plan to torture or even kill him? In that moment, the presence of his wife and daughters seemed very distant. His heart raced and all color drained from his surroundings. Kotsuji wrote in his memoir that he stood there in shock for a moment.

Dinner was as it always was. His daughters, unaware of anything unusual, happily talked to their father about school and about when the autumn leaves on the trees at the nearby temple would reach full color. His wife Mineko warmly smiled as she listened to their conversation. It seemed like a normal dinner.

But for Kotsuji it was unlike any other evening meal. Tomorrow, if he went to the Military Police Headquarters, he might not be able to return home alive. Yes, this was his last dinner with his family. Even so, Kotsuji did not change his demeanor and behaved as he normally would.

Late that night, after he finished organizing his writings in his study, he gazed at his wife and daughters as they slept. In his heart he said goodbye to his family.

The next morning, Kotsuji did not tell Mineko about being summoned, saying instead that he had work in Tokyo. He departed his house in Kamakura. No doubt it would have been too painful to part in tears. Kotsuji wrote in his autobiography about his memory of that day.

> A great love welled up in my heart I said to them silently, "Goodbye forever." The hour train ride seemed to last only minutes, and those thirteen steps up to the Kempeitai Headquarters were a heavy climb.

Accepting that he would not be returning to his family alive, Kotsuji climbed the steep steps in front of him. He was led to a dim, windowless interrogation room. The questioning by a young executive officer of the Military Police began. What had he done for the Jewish underground? Who were they? What kind of organization was it? What were they planning? The questions flew at him like arrows.

Kotsuji denied the false accusations, but the officer did not listen. He even came up with an absurd Jewish conspiracy theory. Kotsuji denied this calmly as well. These exchanges were repeated over and over again as the hours went on.

How much time had passed? When Kotsuji started to fall asleep from exhaustion, the officer grabbed his hair and yanked him awake. This was the turning point. The interrogation turned to physical violence. The officer put a pencil between Kotsuji's fingers and squeezed hard. Kotsuji grimaced from the pain. But he was determined not to give in to the officer. He had to deny the slander against the Jews, even if it cost him his life. Otherwise, not only would Kotsuji's reputation suffer, but it would leave a stain on his own soul. He clenched his teeth and endured the pain.

He was given nothing to eat or drink and began to feel faint. The abuse continued. His head was pressed against the table and slammed onto it, over and over. A young cadet placed a basin of water filled to the brim in front of Kotsuji. The officer held Kotsuji's head close to the water, threatening water torture. Kotsuji's willpower had reached its limit. He was starting to lose consciousness.

Suddenly the door flew open, and he heard a man's voice. "What are you doing?" It was a voice that he had heard before. Kotsuji looked to see who it was. The face was also familiar. He wore the insignia of a colonel on his uniform.

"Mr. Kotsuji, what are you doing here?"

The fog started to clear, and Kotsuji searched his memory for this person's face.

"Mr. Shirahama."

The man was Shirahama Yoshinori, the friend who had socialized with Kotsuji and their families in Manchuria. He had helped Kotsuji rescue Jews in many ways. Kotsuji collapsed in relief.

Shirahama berated and shouted at the executive officer, then ordered him to leave this matter to him and kicked him out of the room. He also tore up the affidavit he had written. Tears were streaming from Shirahama's eyes.

"If only I'd known sooner.... I'm sorry."

Kotsuji gradually regained his composure and sat in the chair again. Shirahama sat down next to him and spoke to him softly.

"It's been a long time, old friend."

Could there be such a coincidence, for two friends from faraway Manchuria, one a military police officer, the other an adviser with Mantetsu, to meet again here in the interrogation room of the Military Police Headquarters? To Kotsuji, the presence of Shirahama beside him was like a dream.

Shirahama instructed Kotsuji to leave right away. "Grab a taxi if you can. I'll watch you from here until you're out of sight. Tomorrow I'll try to think of a way to protect you, but there is nothing I can do tonight. Good luck."

He escorted Kotsuji outside and a taxi took him to Tokyo Station. His body dragging from exhaustion and pain, he managed to catch a train back to Kamakura. He was grateful to Shirahama from the bottom of his heart for his friendship. Kotsuji described his arrival at home.

> When I arrived home all the houses were blacked out; there seemed to be no sign of the human world, just the myriad sparkling stars and the roaring of the waves sounding the beat of the eternal universe. I was hungry, exhausted, and disturbed; yet I had never seen the natural world so beautiful, nor felt so moved by the sight of it.
>
> I told my family very little about my harrowing experience, just enough to explain my lateness. I didn't want to distress my wife, nor cast a blackness on the innocent minds of my two children.

The interrogation he endured by the military police officer left lasting scars on his body and spirit. And yet his beliefs were unshaken. The persecution that Jews suffered for centuries had become viscerally real for Kotsuji.

On June 7, 1945, Kotsuji, his wife, and daughters left Kamakura and boarded a ship for Harbin in Manchuria. He believed he needed to leave Japan to protect himself and his family from the Nazis and the Japanese authorities. Later his name was discovered on a list of people targeted for assassination by the Military Police. If he had remained in Japan, Meisinger or the Military Police would surely have shown no mercy in killing him. It was even possible that his family would have been in danger as well.

So why did Kotsuji choose Harbin as his refuge? He explained it this way: "I had many Jewish friends in that country.... It was a curious thing: I had come so far that I trusted my life to the hands of Jews more than to my own people."

He must have now identified more with the Jewish refugees driven from their homeland and on the run in the Far East. So, he set his sights on Harbin, where the Jews were waiting. A Jewish spirit was beginning to dwell inside Kotsuji.

Chapter Thirteen

Return to Manchuria

In June 1945, Kotsuji and his family arrived in Harbin, Manchuria (now Harbin, Heilongjiang Province, China). Harbin was the third-largest city at the time after Xinjing, the capital of Manchukuo (now Changchun), and Mukden, where many military factories were located. It had a population of over 600,000, with residents from many different countries, including Japan, China, Russia, Korea, and Europe.

Kotsuji chose this city as his refuge because Harbin had the largest Jewish community in Manchuria. It was also a familiar place to him, because of his job at Mantetsu and also for being the host city for the Third Far-East Jewish Conference. The speech he had given in Hebrew served as the impetus for Kotsuji deepening his involvement with Jews. It also made an impression on Jews around the world.

Harbin was a nostalgic place for Kotsuji, and the cityscape was essentially the same as it had been. The political situation enveloping Harbin, however, had greatly changed.

From February to March of 1945, the biggest battle of the Pacific War had taken place on the island of Ioto (formerly known in English as Iwo Jima). After this crushing defeat, the tide of the war turned decisively against the Japanese military, and the prospect of defeat grew. Harbin was far from the southern front and was not directly affected by the fall of Ioto, but the movement of the Soviet Union to the border just four hundred kilometers from Harbin was alarming. Indeed, Harbin was no longer the peaceful city that Kotsuji had known.

After arriving, the Kotsuji family stayed in a hotel until their household goods could be delivered from Japan. But it took a long time for the shipment to arrive. In August, the Soviet military conducted an air strike on Harbin. The Japanese military that ruled Manchuria was intensively searching for Soviet spies in the city. There was even an incident where Kotsuji was pursued by police after they overheard him conversing in English with a Jewish fur dealer, David Goorevitch. It was around this time that the atomic bombs were dropped on Hiroshima on August 6 and on Nagasaki on August 9, which resulted in Japan's ultimate defeat.

On August 12, receiving word that their belongings had been delivered, Kotsuji went to the Harbin station to pick them up. But the station looked completely different and was in a state of tumult. The forwarding agent demanded three times the usual fee to haul the goods.

"The Soviets have invaded Harbin! All the couriers have fled!"

"Does Japanese money have any value?" Kotsuji asked. The agent shrugged and grimly smiled. They could hear gunfire from a distance. The Kwantung Army did not resist the Soviet invasion and would flee in the night, leaving behind the 78,000 Japanese residents of Harbin. Japan's rule of Manchuria had come to an end.

Because their hotel had closed, the Kotsuji family ended up staying at the home of the hotel's general manager. They were now living in a small room huddled together with the Japanese hotel employees. At night the Soviet soldiers came to loot. Kotsuji hid his wife and daughters in the basement and held his breath until the soldiers left. The family suffered no physical harm, but their watches and gloves were taken. Kotsuji could not tolerate these unjust acts and managed to secure a meeting with the Soviet consul-general, a man named Loginoff, to protest.

Kotsuji told him that he represented the Japanese people in Harbin, but that he was speaking as a scholar, not a diplomat. Kotsuji said that the Soviets could not expect to rule by force alone, that they needed the goodwill of the people for their support. Unless the raping and looting stopped, the Soviet army occupation of Harbin would not succeed.

Even though the Japanese were now under occupation, Kotsuji appealed to the consul-general as a Japanese person with dignity. His approach was reminiscent of the Amshinover Rebbe who asked Navy officers to protect the Jewish refugees in Japan from harm. The Amshinover Rebbe had faced the Japanese officers without flinching, with pride in his heart as a Jew.

Consul Loginoff was apparently persuaded by Kotsuji and promised that the soldiers' bad conduct would end in three days. But this promise was not kept. The looting continued, and Mineko and their daughters were said to have felt threatened several times.

Kotsuji frequently found himself nearly hauled off by Soviet soldiers. The soldiers hunted down the remnants of the Japanese troops as well as civilians who had worked for the Japanese military and took them into custody. They were usually sent to forced-labor prison camps in Siberia, where prisoners were said to have numbered from 570,000 to 700,000 at the time. Over ten percent of them never set foot in Japan again.

Kotsuji wrote in his autobiography about when he faced being hunted down by Soviet soldiers:

> What saved me from almost certain shipment to Siberia was the kindness of my Jewish friends, who protected me as well as they could, and the fact that I do not have typical Japanese features.

It was said that Kotsuji would often be mistaken for a Mongolian when he wore a Mongolian-style hat. Indeed, he had an angular, chiseled face and did not look very Japanese. This was how he managed to hide his origin when he walked the streets of Harbin. During the more than three months that the Soviets occupied Harbin, Kotsuji was on edge, hiding that he was Japanese and evading Soviet soldiers, much as the Jews had when they were seeking to escape the grasp of the Nazis.

Kotsuji recounted that he was aided by many Jews who helped protect him. Now Kotsuji, who had done so much to rescue Jewish refugees, was being helped by Jews.

On the day of the Soviet invasion, the manager of the hotel, a Mr. Pesner, took Kotsuji's household belongings that had been delivered from Japan and hid them away from the eyes of the soldiers. Mr. Pesner had heard Kotsuji's speech at the Third Far-East Jewish Conference, and as a Jew had never forgotten it.

Two Jewish men named Judkin and Plotkin negotiated a safe house for the Kotsuji family and took care of them. Thanks to their efforts, the Kotsujis were able to sleep at night without fear of being harassed by the Soviet soldiers. Plotkin and Joseph Moiseeff also helped move the family. If they loaded a horse-drawn carriage with luggage, not only would it catch the attention of soldiers, but it would also make them an easy target for looting. Kotsuji was worried that if the two Jews were discovered to be helping Japanese people, they could be harmed too.

After the two men loaded the carriage, they hoisted a long stick and attached a red flag to it. Kotsuji looked at the piece of cloth in surprise. It had a yellow hammer and sickle on it, the flag of the Soviet Union. Plotkin and Moiseeff grinned at him mischievously and urged the horse forward, heading for the safe house at a fast clip. Although they were Russian Jews, carriages that showed the Soviet flag were able to move around Harbin's major streets undisturbed by soldiers or anyone else.

With the help of his Jewish friends, Kotsuji's life in Harbin safely passed the one-year mark. The pillaging Soviet soldiers departed, and now the Communist Party of China ruled Manchuria. Kotsuji noted that, while they did not plunder as the Soviets did, the Chinese were not friendly toward the Japanese either, because they had long suffered under Japan's occupation. Japanese landowners and businesspeople were tried in the people's court, with execution a possible sentence in some cases.

The Japanese people were prohibited from conducting business inside buildings. If they ran a successful business outside on the side of a road, Chinese people would come and toss their wares into a ditch. Kotsuji asked a Chinese person, "Why do they do these things?" "Because the Japanese lost the war and should look weak and humble," was the answer.

Unable to return to Japan even a year after the war's end, Kotsuji and his family lived their lives quietly and anxiously in the face of persecution and humiliation.

In May 1946, a repatriation agreement was finally reached between the US and China, and the journey back to Japan began. The Jewish friends who had helped the Kotsuji family saw them off as they departed Harbin. On the day of their departure, Kotsuji gave his prized tapestry to the fur dealer David Goorevitch. Goorevitch knew that Kotsuji treasured it and refused to accept. Kotsuji pleaded with Goorevitch to take it because when they were repatriated, the Chinese government would seize most of their possessions.

"I understand, Professor Kotsuji. I will hold on to it until the next time I see you," Mr. Goorevitch said as he held the tapestry.

Would they really meet again? Repatriating to Japan was a risky journey. Would they even reach Japanese soil alive? Kotsuji was very uneasy.

Ships bound for Japan from Manchuria at that time set sail from Huludao. Huludao was a port city about four hundred kilometers southwest of Harbin. The trains did not run on a set schedule and were completely unreliable. If a train stopped along the way, passengers had no choice but to walk to the next station. Valuables were all confiscated, so the Kotsuji family embarked on their trip with just the clothes on their backs. They apportioned a small amount of food among them, and along the way Kotsuji traded his suit for some potatoes to feed his hungry family, not unlike the Jewish refugees on the Siberian railroad from Lithuania to Vladivostok.

Chapter Fourteen

The Fall of Nazi Germany

On April 30, 1945, Nazi Germany lost the battle of Berlin to the Soviet Army, and Hitler committed suicide in his underground bunker. Then on May 2, the Soviets took control of the German capital of Berlin. On May 8, Germany surrendered to the Allied forces, ending the bloody Nazi era. It meant the end of the slaughter of Jews, six million of whom had already been murdered. Dawn had broken after the long, dark night at last for the Jewish refugees who had fled Nazi Germany's persecution.

Viktor Frankl described his emotions when he was released from a concentration camp in his book *Man's Search for Meaning*:

> One day, a few days after the liberation, I walked through the country past flowering meadows, for miles and miles, toward the market town near the camp. Larks rose to the sky and I could [hear] their joyous song. There was no one to be seen for miles around; there was nothing but the wide earth and sky and the lark's jubilation and the freedom of space. I stopped, looked around, and up to the sky – and then I went down on my knees.

> ... How long I knelt there ... memory can no longer recall. But I know that on that day, in that hour, my new life started. Step for step I progressed, until I again became a human being.

Never in my life have I read such a joyous and moving passage. I can almost hear the Jews' relief and rejoicing after being released from the terror of death. Jewish refugees around the world must have looked up at the same sky Frankl described and sang the praises of their liberation.

Zorach Warhaftig, one of the leaders of the Jewish refugees in Japan, was in New York and reveling in the fall of the Nazis. Warhaftig had left the Port of Yokohama with his family on June 5, 1941, on the ship *Hikawa Maru.* Their destination was Vancouver, Canada. Warhaftig was to assist Jews as a member of the World Jewish Congress in New York. However, his wife was denied a visa by the United States so they had no choice but to go to Canada, where she and the children would live in Montreal.

Warhaftig traveled to New York alone, and as deputy director of the Institute of Jewish Affairs began researching refugee issues and the circumstances of the Jews' persecution under the Nazis. According to his book *Refugee and Survivor: Rescue Efforts During the Holocaust,* six months before Kotsuji's departure from Harbin, Warhaftig was standing on Polish soil, in Warsaw. It was his first time back in his hometown after being forced out seven years and four months before by the Nazis. The place where he had been born and raised had been turned into unrecognizable mounds of rubble. There was not a human being as far as the eye could see, only ruins. After walking aimlessly for three days, he found the graves of his ancestors. He slumped against the tombstones and wept.

Warhaftig spent the rest of his life seeking to understand what the Jews who escaped the Holocaust had experienced and endeavored to contribute to the recovery of the Jewish people. In 1947, as a member of the World Jewish Congress, he devoted himself to the creation of the State of Israel, and from 1962 he served as Minister of Religion for twelve years.

Shimon Kalisch, the Amshinover Rebbe who represented Jewish refugees in the interrogation session with the Japanese Navy, went to Shanghai from Kobe. Similarly, the students and teachers from the Mirrer Yeshiva in Poland who landed in Kobe also traveled to Shanghai. Life in the Japanese settlement in Shanghai was hard. Even so, they held on to hope as they lived their lives. Beginning around 1942, according to David Mandelbaum's research, they lost contact with family and friends who had remained in their home country. The letters they sent were returned. Finally, they learned that most of those who had remained behind in Poland had been lost in the Holocaust.

In David Mandelbaum's book *From Lublin to Shanghai*, he described the reaction of the yeshiva students when the terrible news eventually reached them: "[T]he cries and shrieks of the *talmidim* [disciples] rose to the heavens... [they] tore their clothing, overturned the benches, and sat on the floor for a short time, in keeping with the *halakha* [Jewish law] of one who learns of the passing of a close relative after the mourning period is over. Afterward, they... said *Kaddish* [prayer] together in a mighty, terrible voice that shook the walls."

Around the time that Kotsuji was seeking to move back to Japan from Harbin, the closed doors of the Shanghai settlement finally opened, and the Amshinover Rebbe and the Mirrer Yeshiva students were free to leave for New York. Subsequently, the Amshinover Rebbe opened a synagogue in Brooklyn, and the students rebuilt their yeshiva there. R. Moshe Shatkes, who accompanied the Amshinover Rebbe to the interrogation with the Navy, went to the US, and became the head, or *rosh yeshiva*, of a yeshiva in New York. The refugees who had come to Japan went on to live free lives in a new world. Nazi Germany was gone.

Around that time, Kotsuji and his family were traveling somewhere in mainland China. They still had a long way to go before they would reach freedom. They traveled the treacherous road to Huludao, on their way to the ship that would take them back to Japan.

Chapter Fifteen

Home to Japan

Many people went missing or died during the repatriation process from mainland China. Japanese parents were sometimes separated from their children. This journey for Kotsuji, with his wife and two daughters, was a matter of life or death. Just before leaving Harbin, he met a young man at a Japanese association meeting.

Ishizuka Kiichi was a twenty-year-old soldier who fled from the Kwantung Army just before the end of the war. Having deserted three times, if he were captured by the military again he could be executed by firing squad. Ishizuka was another person who had bet his life on escape.

Kotsuji hid him and looked after him. Ishizuka was born in Akita Prefecture to a farming family. He was short but sturdily built. "I was made to do everything in the military," he said. He took on household chores such as shopping, cooking, and laundry, and Kotsuji treated him like his own son. He decided to take Ishizuka back to Japan along with the Kotsuji family.

After about one month of traveling, they reached Huludao. With the ship now visible in front of them, they were sure at last they would be able to return to Japan. But the Chinese authorities had imposed severe conditions on repatriation. An official told Kotsuji, "One male from each family must stay behind and not board the ship." This was apparently intended to secure laborers, but it was not known what fate awaited those who remained behind. There was no guarantee of safety. Either Kotsuji or Ishizuka would have to stay. Ishizuka immediately volunteered.

"I will not let you do that," Kotsuji replied.

"I will be fine. Please allow me to stay." Ishizuka's resolve was firm. "You've done a lot for me." He bowed deeply to Kotsuji and Mineko. Kotsuji reluctantly decided to accept his offer.

"I believe that you will be able to return safely. May God bless you."

Kotsuji took off his shoes and gave them to Ishizuka. The ship with the Kotsuji family on board left Ishizuka behind and sailed for Hakata, Kyushu. Kotsuji and his family continued to wave to Ishizuka on the pier until they could no longer see him.

Their ship arrived at the Port of Hakata in October 1946. The port was crowded, bustling with people who were returning home. Parents shouting their children's names, others tearfully hugging loved ones. Kotsuji gently guided his exhausted and emaciated wife and daughters as they stepped onto Japanese soil.

The family walked on tired legs all over town in search of a place to stay. All the inns were full. There were no vacancies. Finally, as evening fell, they came upon one last option before resigning themselves to sleeping outside the train station. It was a facility called Kameiso, which cared for wounded and disabled soldiers. Kotsuji was relieved to finally be taken in, and when he signed the guest book, the innkeeper said, "Oh my goodness, could it be?" and brought something out.

It was a book, *Yudaya Minzoku no Sugata,* the book Kotsuji had written about the Jewish people to counter Nazi propaganda.

The innkeeper explained he had bought the book when Kotsuji lectured in Kyushu at the invitation of Ishibashi Tanzan. He said to the astonished Kotsuji, "You have endured so much." The innkeeper understood how dangerous it had been for Kotsuji to write such a book during the war. Kotsuji was overwhelmed by a whirlwind of thoughts and emotions, the memories of being summoned by the government's intelligence bureau, interrogation by the special police, and the torture he endured at the hands of the military police.

Japan was suffering from food shortages after the war, but the innkeeper managed to put together a Japanese meal to welcome the Kotsuji family. His first bath in a long time and the conversation with the innkeeper gave Kotsuji his first moments of peace and contentment since leaving Harbin.

On their way to his parents' home in Kyoto, Kotsuji stopped to visit his eldest brother in Nishinomiya. The whole family came out to greet him after his arduous journey back from Manchuria.

"If only you'd gotten here a little earlier," his brother said, his voice heavy with sadness. "Mother would have been so happy to see you again."

While Kotsuji was living in Harbin and being helped by Jewish friends, his beloved mother Fukuko had died. Fukuko had cherished Kotsuji, her youngest child, and had loved him deeply, always protecting him. His adoring mother, hearing rumors of mass killings of Japanese in Manchuria, fell ill from worry that her son had been caught up in the mayhem, and as she drew her last breath had called for "Setschan," her nickname for him. As Kotsuji listened to his brother, he remembered when he was in Harbin and suddenly had felt a stabbing pain in his chest, an intense longing to see his mother. He thought it must have been when his mother had been calling his name. He wept, feeling he was a terrible son to have missed being with his mother in her final days. It caused him immense grief.

Despite his anguish, Kotsuji had to find a way to support his family. The Kotsuji family headed for Tokyo. After spending a few days at a friend's house in the Jiyugaoka area, they returned to Kamakura. Being in the familiar seaside town again offered some comfort to Kotsuji's broken heart.

One day, a large wooden box was delivered to the Kotsujis' home. Inside they found a bounty of rice and vegetables. The sender was Ishizuka Kiichi, the young man they had left behind in Huludao, China. Somehow, he had been able to find his way onto a ship and return to his hometown in Akita, where he was now working on a farm. Kotsuji had been worried about Ishizuka ever since he had insisted on remaining in China. Kotsuji had always regretted leaving him and was relieved to learn that he was safe. Ishizuka loved Kotsuji like his own father, and Ishizuka and the Kotsujis continued their close relationship like a family.

Kotsuji began to work on rebuilding his life. Using his language skills, he worked hard to earn a living, finding work at the Red Cross Society and at a trading company. By nature, however, he was a scholar and not suited for business, so he did not last long working in the private sector. Kotsuji dearly wanted to return to teaching. But he was over fifty years old by this time and was unable to obtain a job at a university. Employment as a private tutor was nonexistent since there was no demand for Jewish or Hebrew studies in chaotic post-war Japanese society. Thanks to his language ability, Kotsuji was able to find work as an interpreter at a trading company, and he continued to write about Jewish studies, occasionally contributing articles to magazines. His daughter Teruko found employment and helped provide for the family while her frail sister Yuriko helped with the housekeeping. It was not a life of abundance, but the days were quiet and peaceful.

And yet, Kotsuji's heart was restless. Since being hired by Mantetsu in 1938 and moving to Manchuria, Kotsuji had grown accustomed to being with Jews. He spent eight years in the company of Jewish friends. He was able to extend the visas of six thousand Jews and helped them escape the evil hand of the Nazis. It might have started as sympathy for their persecution and suffering, or perhaps a scholar's sense of mission after being immersed in Jewish studies. In any case, ever since his experience during his interrogation by the military police, Kotsuji unmistakably felt the heart of Judaism dwelling inside him.

Kotsuji himself had to leave his homeland, hide his Japanese nationality, and live in fear of persecution, much as the Jews had throughout their history. Starting at around that time, he had begun seriously considering converting to Judaism. For Kotsuji, it seemed natural to decide to become a Jew. He wrote about these feelings in his autobiography: "From my suffering for the Jewish cause, my attachment to Judaism had grown and grown, and with it had grown my affection for the Jewish people."

Some of Kotsuji's Jewish friends did not support his conversion. They asked him why he would want to adopt a religion that was so likely to bring troubles and sorrow. But Kotsuji's resolve was firm: "I will come to Judaism with joy and pride."

Seeing his passion, eventually these friends came around to his way of thinking. One who had miraculously survived the Holocaust, Dr. Israel Ben-Zeev (at the time, he was director of the World Union for the Propagation of Judaism), enthusiastically encouraged Kotsuji's conversion. However, in order to convert to Judaism it was necessary to travel to Jerusalem. He would have to pass a rigorous oral examination before a religious council and then undergo circumcision. The cost of the trip and lodgings would be very high, prohibitively so given Kotsuji's need to support his family. Ten years passed while Kotsuji wrestled with his dilemma.

In February 1959, Kotsuji celebrated his sixtieth birthday, but still had not been able to convert. At this rate, he could die before converting. He was on the verge of giving up when Mineko spoke to him.

"Please go to Jerusalem. There's no need to worry about the money. We can just use the house as collateral, that's all."

"I couldn't do that."

Mineko told him, "Life is short. No matter what people say, please take the path that you believe in."

Chapter Sixteen

Mineko's Gift

It was not surprising that Mineko spoke these words to Kotsuji. She knew he had been on a spiritual journey, ever since he was born into a Shinto priest family in Kyoto and had turned to Christianity.

Kotsuji indeed described his life as a "spiritual journey." Religion had always been the foundation of his life. If God had not thrust him on this path, the six thousand Jewish refugees who came to Japan might have perished in the gas chambers. Mineko, the woman who accompanied him on this journey until the very end, continued to provide emotional support through her deep love and faith. She herself was a devout Christian. On two occasions when Kotsuji was at a crucial spiritual crossroads, Mineko showed him the way forward.

The first was in 1927 when Kotsuji had started questioning the New Testament and could not make up his mind whether to go to the US to intensively study the Old Testament and Hebrew. The second concerned his conversion to Judaism, as described above, in 1959. When telling the story of Kotsuji as a religious figure, Mineko cannot be overlooked.

The couple met in June 1923, the year of the Great Kanto Earthquake. Kotsuji was the senior pastor at the Asahikawa Church of Christ in

Kotsuji Setsuzo and Kotsuji Mineko

Hokkaido. Even though it was not even two months since his appointment, he had already hit a wall in his life as a pastor. His management of the church was going well. Church attendance had been on the decline, but people started coming back, perhaps because they were curious about Kotsuji, who had been sent there from Tokyo. Many of the congregants were young women. Kotsuji was well educated, fluent in foreign languages, handsome, and talented at the organ and violin. He attracted their attention. In his autobiography, Kotsuji wrote that he felt he was being treated more like a celebrity than a pastor. He was bewildered about what to do.

> ... [S]oon I was something of a minor celebrity in the city. My church began to fill up, especially with young, marriageable girls. A group of them circulated a photograph of me among themselves; it was obvious most of them were looking for husbands.

Additionally, Kotsuji felt that visiting people in their homes and drinking tea to add to the congregation or asking influential local residents for donations was a waste of time. As a scholar, he firmly believed that study and meditation were the duty of those who served God. It was at this time that he met Iwané Mineko at a party in Sapporo. Kotsuji was captivated by her at first sight. Mineko was well dressed and beautiful. She possessed good manners and refinement, as befitting the daughter of a respectable family.

Just looking at Mineko seemed to wash away the frustration and resentment he had been feeling. No matter how much praise and attention he attracted from other young women, he had never felt this way before. He believed that it was his destiny to meet Mineko, and he summoned his courage to write her a letter. To his surprise, he received a reply from her immediately. After exchanging several letters, the two met in Sapporo and eventually decided to get married.

In his autobiography, Kotsuji described his earnest feelings for Mineko. "What really swayed Mineko in my favor... was my scholarship. Everything about the situation fired me with new ambition to become a great scholar, so that I could justify my wife's faith in me."

From the beginning, their love was a little different from that of other young couples. It was based on absolute trust in God and mutual respect for one another. Kotsuji's intuition had been correct about Mineko. While frequently providing Kotsuji with religious inspiration, she partnered with Kotsuji throughout his tumultuous life and provided constant emotional support. Had he not had Mineko as his wife, his spiritual journey would likely have reached an impasse early on.

Mineko's father, Iwané Seiichi, was a major landowner in Sapporo. He ran a large ranch in nearby Hidaka. Seiichi had been born into the family of a senior vassal of the Tokushima clan and was known for his considerable contributions to Hokkaido's development. He was the author of *Hokkaido Iju Kaiko Roku* (Hokkaido Migration Memoir), the leading historical source on early Meiji Era Hokkaido. He also laid the foundation for Hidaka to become a horse-breeding region. It is said that Seiichi was the inspiration for the main character in the novel *Otose* by Funayama Kaoru, about a man who finds purpose in letting wild horses graze freely in Hokkaido pioneer times.

Their marriage became a reality only because Seiichi agreed. Having started with nothing and climbing his way to success, Seiichi may have appreciated Kotsuji's sense of adventure in leaving behind his Shinto family to dive wholeheartedly into Christianity based on nothing more than his own gut feeling. It might also be said that in choosing Kotsuji to be her husband Mineko showed she had inherited her father's pioneering spirit.

Kotsuji and Mineko married in autumn, on October 1, 1923, just four months after they met, at the Kitaichijo Church in Asahikawa. He was twenty-four years old and she was twenty-three. Their new home was the small parsonage next to the church. It was small, gloomy, and chilly. Kotsuji felt badly for his wife, who had grown up in affluent, comfortable surroundings, but instead of complaining Mineko expressed gratitude and delight in their life together.

While their married life was happy, Kotsuji was still dealing with troubles at work. Not only was he unable to fulfill his duties as pastor because he was busy proselytizing, but anti-American sentiment was rising in Japan, due to American policies aimed at Asian immigrants. These negative feelings were directed at Christian churches in Japan and caused Kotsuji grief. A censor from the military came to Kotsuji's house and interrogated him about his beliefs and activities, causing a commotion.

Kotsuji tended to be anxious and take problems to heart, and he had more and more worries about the future. Mineko embraced him with her big heart and cheerfulness. She would tell him, "Overthinking will only bring you sadness. Go to the bathhouse and wash away your worries."

Around this time, Kotsuji received a letter from a former teacher in Kyoto, saying they were looking for a pastor who was familiar with Christianity and Buddhism in Gifu, and that Kotsuji should put his hat in the ring.

In 1925, Kotsuji moved to Gifu with Mineko. Gifu was close to his hometown of Kyoto and was blessed with scenic natural places like the Nagara River and Mount Kinka. Kotsuji was pleased to be able to move his wife from a cold climate to a warm one, and he enjoyed the intellectual stimulation from the well-educated monks around them. He learned much and worked hard. The two years they spent in Gifu were happy times for the couple. It was here that their first daughter Aiko was born.

Kotsuji's interest in Judaism grew stronger during this period, after reading archaeological literature about the holy land of Jerusalem. This inevitably deepened his doubts about the New Testament. The transfer to Gifu gave rise to a new guideline for himself: "When one starts to question one's role as a clergyman and the heart is no longer fulfilled, immediately leave that position."

As his admiration of Judaism deepened, his satisfaction with his current work diminished. He wanted to study the Bible all over again from the beginning. To do this, he would need to study in the United States. These thoughts grew more intense in Kotsuji's mind every day. But the expense to make this a reality was not something Kotsuji could afford in those days.

One evening, Mineko, who had been observing her husband's struggle, spoke up. "It's about getting enough money. I know a good way to do it."

"A good way?"

"We're going to sell my kimonos." She said this cheerfully, but Kotsuji was bewildered. Kimonos were treasured assets for Japanese women at that time and were worn to show their worth.

"I really appreciate how you feel, but I can't let you do that."

Mineko looked directly into Kotsuji's eyes. "I have something to ask you. When Sarah, Abraham's wife, went to Ur, did she take a lot of clothing with her?"

Kotsuji looked at his wife in surprise. Abraham was the first prophet chosen and blessed by God in Genesis in the Old Testament. Mineko was asking if his wife Sarah had taken clothing with her when she and Abraham were led by God to the Promised Land.

"No...."

"Well then, I will follow the example set by Sarah."

A few days later, Mineko sold all but her favorite kimonos to a pawnshop. Kotsuji felt terrible about his wife's sacrifice, but thanks to her he was able to make his desire to study in the US a reality.

The Kotsujis set off for America from the Port of Yokohama with baby Aiko in July 1927. The year and a half they spent in Auburn, the upstate New York town where Kotsuji studied, was by no means an easy time for Mineko. Their living expenses had to be managed with the funds they had brought from Japan. As a result, the family had to live apart. Kotsuji stayed in the student dormitory while Mineko and Aiko rented a room in the home of a professor. Life was not easy for Mineko. In addition to not speaking English and living in a foreign country for the first time, she also had to care for a small child as she struggled to make ends meet. Nevertheless, she was happy to see her husband immerse himself in his academics. Mineko resolutely faced this and other hardships to come. Where did a young woman who grew up in carefree affluence find the strength to meet these challenges?

In the spring of 1929, when Kotsuji had gone as far as he could with his studies on Judaism and the Old Testament in Auburn, he decided to continue his studies at the Pacific School of Religion in Berkeley, California.

The Kotsuji family could not afford to take the train to Berkeley. So, Kotsuji came up with a plan to learn how to drive in one week (a friend would teach him), buy a used car for forty dollars, and then drive to Berkeley. This journey would take them across the Great Plains and the Rocky Mountains of the North American continent. Even today, a bus trip across the US can take about two weeks. The highway system was not well developed at that time, and it is questionable how good the roads were going through the Rockies.

Following his instincts and pushing forward through the unknown, one can get a sense of young Kotsuji's impulsive and single-minded personality. The seemingly reckless plan to cross the continent looked feasible to him. As for detailed plans to handle potential problems, the strategy was to deal with them as they came up. What could possibly go wrong? Many Jewish people will recognize this trait. Most Japanese will not.

Furthermore, Kotsuji was a complete novice when it came to cars, and the one he bought for forty dollars was an old clunker that would not go faster than twenty-nine miles per hour no matter how hard he stepped on the accelerator. In his autobiography, the story reads like a scene from a comedy.

> We had hardly left New York State when the car began to fall to pieces. As we wandered through the Midwest, we left behind us a trail of broken parts, along with small portions of our meager

> supply of money. Nearly every day a small repair had to be made. By the time we crossed Kansas and Colorado, we had only a few dollars left. As we entered New Mexico we had only sixteen carefully hoarded pennies to our name.

When Kotsuji was forced to leave the broken-down car to find help, Mineko and Aiko were left to wait for hours in the car in the middle of a landscape that was straight out of a Hollywood western. It was very unsettling for Mineko.

Mineko watched her husband drive as she sat beside him with Aiko on her lap. The two had many hours to fill as they crossed the great expanse of America. I cannot help but wonder about the conversations they shared.

The car broke down once again in Gallup, New Mexico, but then things took a rather miraculous turn. Just ahead of where it ground to a halt was a Japanese restaurant! The Kotsuji family was able to stay at the restaurant until a friend sent them money for the car repair.

In the end, this amazing transcontinental adventure was successful and the three made it safely to Berkeley. Later, Mineko often told her daughters stories about this trip. Surprisingly, it seems Mineko had pleasant memories, rather than memories of the difficulties. Mineko found joy in everything. That was her great gift and her strength.

At the Pacific School of Religion, Kotsuji was granted a scholarship, and he also found work as a tutor. Even so, they still struggled financially. However, he had the support of Professor Badè, whom he respected, and his days were content as he worked purposefully in pursuit of his doctorate.

The birth of their second daughter Teruko in February 1931 during the couple's time in Berkeley was an unforgettable event. For Kotsuji, just finishing his thesis, "The Origin and Evolution of Semitic Alphabets," the joy was doubled because he was actually present for the birth. The obstetrician was concerned about communicating with Mineko with her limited English, and he requested that Kotsuji be in the room. This was unheard of for a Japanese couple of that era, but Kotsuji and Mineko once again joined forces and took part in this blessed event of welcoming a new life together.

The four years of Kotsuji's studies in America (from 1927 until 1931) were a happy and fulfilling time for Mineko despite the financial hardship. After graduation, Kotsuji was offered a position at the University of California as a professor of Japanese language and history. Mineko apparently had hoped he would take this job. Her English had improved, she had experienced almost no anti-Japanese racism. People had treated her and her family kindly. She was sociable and outgoing and had learned to sew and bake from neighbors. She would often give away her fresh-baked cookies to children. Mineko was a modern young woman who wore high heels and liked wearing Western clothes. She likely wanted to continue to live in the US.

Even after returning to Japan and being plunged into wartime, Mineko's flair for style did not waver. During the war, men had to wear gaiters as part of their "national uniform" and women were supposed to wear *monpe* (baggy work trousers). Kotsuji, however, thought gaiters looked terrible and refused to put them on, while Mineko refused to wear the *monpe*. Of course, *furisode* kimonos with long sleeves were out of the question, but times were such that even wearing an ordinary kimono was considered unpatriotic. Mineko would wear a smart suit with high heels when she visited her daughters' classrooms. In part because of their mother's behavior, her daughters were treated unfairly at school. Mineko even then refused to conform herself to those around her.

These choices were not just because she wanted to look stylish. It seems to have come from a deeper conviction. In the US, where many people of different ethnicities and races lived, the acceptance of diverse and conflicting values leads to respect for the individual, allowing people to coexist harmoniously. Mineko experienced this firsthand in the US. Would it be an overstatement to say she tried to resist wartime totalitarianism in a small and subtle way with her suit and high heels?

In any case, she had an adaptability and openness to accepting people and experiences, together with a knack for enjoying whatever came her way. Just as her father suspected, Mineko really had inherited his frontier spirit. Mineko weathered the rough seas of her life with Kotsuji with strength and generosity. This despite times in her long life when she endured despair and loss that seem unimaginable.

In July 1932, the year after returning to Japan from the United States, their third daughter Yuriko was born. The family was at the height of their happiness. But it would not last. In October of the following year, they were struck by their greatest sorrow. Aiko, their eldest child, suddenly was taken from them by illness.

In the middle of the night, Aiko woke her mother saying her finger hurt. The next morning, she had a high fever and was very weak. They called the doctor right away, and she was diagnosed with the most serious kind of children's dysentery, cholera infantum. It progressed rapidly, and that night she fell unconscious. The doctor injected her with camphor through the night but by dawn her heart stopped beating. She was just six years old.

"In any religion, we are powerless when facing a personal loss."

Just the day before, Aiko had been lively and jumping around, and now she was a cold and lifeless body before Kotsuji. He must have felt that all his efforts and lofty studies were meaningless. And Mineko's grief was beyond comprehension. Children are born from their mothers' bodies, and her child's passing brought the death of a part of Mineko.

Though she might not have articulated this feeling, she may have blamed their return to Japan for Aiko's death. If they had stayed in California, Aiko may still have been alive and well. She was stricken with agonizing regret. "If we had only done this... or maybe if we had done that."

The family's misfortunes did not end with this tragedy. About two weeks after losing Aiko, Kotsuji fell ill with typhoid fever. He was quarantined in a hospital, and Mineko could only look in a daze as public health workers came and went about disinfecting their entire house.

Having just lost Aiko, Mineko must have feared that Kotsuji's death was imminent. She shook off these dark thoughts and devoted herself to caring for her husband. Thanks to her efforts, his high fever subsided within a week, and after three to four months he had mostly regained his health.

Then it was Mineko's turn to be felled by illness. She came down with pleurisy. Even if she wanted to get up, she had no energy. Before she even had a chance to heal from her grief over losing Aiko, her husband had become very sick, leaving her with two young daughters amidst her sorrow. She diligently nursed Kotsuji back to health. Mineko had physically and emotionally reached her limits. Now it was Kotsuji's turn to care for her.

Kotsuji had lost his job due to his illness, but while working part-time, he took care of his wife and two daughters, cooking, doing the laundry, and cleaning. Kotsuji had been accustomed to spending most of his time at his desk studying. Now for the first time he exerted himself as a contributor to home life for the benefit of his family. Truth be told, Kotsuji was in fact suffering from appendicitis at this time, but he endured the pain and managed the household until Mineko's condition stabilized.

Before they knew it, one year had passed since Aiko's death. Mineko's condition had improved gradually, and the chain of misfortune would soon come to an end. Kotsuji looked back on this time in his autobiography.

> At times like these, when the foundation of a family is shaken by disaster, many couples move toward divorce, holding each other responsible for their trials. That is the time, however, when the marriage bonds – the oath to love in sickness as well as health – ought to be remembered. Mineko and I remembered.

For Kotsuji and Mineko it was a long year of suffering, but somehow the couple were able to overcome these trials. It was just the beginning. Kotsuji would catch the attention of Matsuoka Yosuke, becoming his adviser at Mantetsu and moving to Manchuria. Consequently, Kotsuji was gradually drawn into the middle of history in the making. For the next ten years until the end of World War II, Kotsuji would live through turbulent times, but no matter what hardships they faced Mineko remained steadfast by his side.

Had it not been for enduring Aiko's death and the year that followed, I wonder if they would have been able to remain committed to their marriage vows until the very end. I cannot help but feel that, if there was a God, these challenges were put before Kotsuji and Mineko as a test, for the man who would go on to save the lives of six thousand refugees. Together they managed to survive these trials and become stronger than ever.

Throughout her half-century marriage to Kotsuji, Mineko generously gave her husband everything she spiritually and materially had, from her soul to her kimonos to her house and any other possessions. In particular, when Kotsuji was at a crucial crossroads spiritually, on both occasions she came up with the solution to break the impasse. Mineko respected and loved Kotsuji with all her heart and was dedicated to him. For Mineko as a devout Christian supporting her husband was not just her duty as his wife but seemed to also have deep religious significance.

In 1973, Mineko and their daughters were at Kotsuji's side in his final moments at their home in Kamakura. She died nineteen years later at the age of ninety-two. Born into a wealthy family, she had been reared in the lap of luxury. Needless to say, Kotsuji was unable to provide her with the life to which she was accustomed. Quite to the contrary, the path she walked with Kotsuji was by no means a smooth one. Why did Mineko write a reply to that first letter from Kotsuji, a humble pastor whom she had just met at that party in Sapporo? Did she sense her life would change forever? Her feelings will remain her secret.

Chapter Seventeen

The Journey to Conversion

On August 8, 1959, Kotsuji said goodbye to his family and headed for Israel. As the jet started rolling down the runway, Kotsuji felt he was embarking on a brand-new life. He arrived in Israel the following day, finally setting foot on the land that he had envisioned for so long.

> Without sleep for thirty-six hours, I dozed off in the car. I dreamed I was climbing up a silver ladder; my friends awoke me and said, "Look, Jerusalem." There on the mountaintop across a valley were the lights of the city shining in the dark. I was in the land of Isaiah.

Blue sky, dazzling sunshine, the laughter of children, and then in the city he could hear the voices of people speaking in Hebrew. He was standing in the place where the Bible had been written. That thought thrilled Kotsuji's heart, and he saw everything through eyes of love, everything looked beautiful.

> Children are the flowers of the culture of the home, society, or state. By its flower the health of the tree can be judged. For this reason, I tried to have as much contact with the children as I could, and from those little teachers I learned much. From them, I felt the real pulse of the country and got the real sense of the language.

One day, several days after arriving in Jerusalem, Kotsuji received a visitor. The man had a familiar face.

"Professor Kotsuji, it's good to see you again."

It was David Goorevitch, the fur dealer who had helped him during his time in Harbin.

"It's so good of you to come to see me," Kotsuji said. It had been fifteen years since they last met, and he was delighted to reunite with him.

"I came because I wanted to give this to you." And Goorevitch handed him a large piece of cloth that he was carrying.

It was the tapestry that Kotsuji had given him when he had to flee Harbin. Goorevitch had kept it safe for Kotsuji for all those years.

The tapestry had been well taken care of and looked just as it had back then. Its condition reflected Goorevitch's conscientiousness. Kotsuji wept as he accepted the fabric. As a token of their friendship, Kotsuji purchased another tapestry and presented it to Goorevitch.

During the Kotsuji family's move, they had been assisted by Mr. Plotkin and Joseph Moiseeff, who flew the red Soviet flag while hauling Kotsuji's belongings through the streets of Harbin. These two also appeared to see Kotsuji. Back in Harbin, virtually under martial law, these two men had brazenly driven a carriage loaded with the belongings of a Japanese family through town. If they had been stopped by Soviet soldiers, they could have been sent to a Siberian prison camp. And yet Plotkin and Moiseeff had taken this risk for the Kotsujis. Kotsuji never forgot how grateful he was for what they did. He was overjoyed to see them again in Jerusalem.

In September, Kotsuji took the examination before the *beit din*, the rabbinate court. He was the first Japanese to undergo this examination. When he was asked why he had chosen Judaism, he answered, "My entire past answers that question." The questioning took about thirty minutes, and afterward the rabbis told him they would be happy to accept him into Judaism. Kotsuji was circumcised at the Shaare Zedek Hospital and adopted the name Abraham Kotsuji.

Kotsuji was already feeling blessed to have converted, and he was to have another happy event. R. Chaim Leib Shmulevitz, the *rosh yeshiva,* hosted a celebration party for Kotsuji. It had been twenty years since Kotsuji had seen the refugees who had been in Kobe. All had survived the turbulent times. The ones who had been children and youths at the time had grown into respectable adults. Kotsuji shook their hands and hugged each of them, rejoicing in their reunion. The Jews were thrilled to see him again and to celebrate his conversion. Though they had gathered together many times like this while they were in Kobe, there they were always meeting to solve problems and the mood was often heavy with anxiety. This time it was different. Now they gathered to celebrate their benefactor, whose conversion made him a fellow Jew.

The Jews repeated the old stories over and over again, expressing gratitude for having survived, and praised Kotsuji for his efforts to save them. The memories kept coming. It was a genial and lively gathering. The survivors had added to their families and there were many spirited children in attendance. The children were hearing these stories for the first time, and Kotsuji was the first Japanese person they had met.

"He's really Japanese. But he's also Jewish, right?" one child said, and everyone nodded.

If Kotsuji had not acted to save the refugees, these children sitting in front of them might not exist in this world. The host of the party, R. Shmulevitz, stood up and began to speak.

"We will never forget what this wonderful man did for us nor how you risked your life to save us and guide us." Kotsuji accepted the warm applause from his dear friends. At the end of the party, everyone surrounded Kotsuji to take a photo to commemorate the event. (See page 195.) This was the photograph that Teruko and Yuriko showed me the first time I met them.

During the war, most of the yeshivas in Europe were destroyed by the Nazis, but the the Mirrer was the one school whose students and faculty were able to escape from Poland to Japan. Kotsuji enabled them to continue their studies in Kobe and arranged for their passage to Shanghai.

Those students were now successful members of society and standing before him on this day. Kotsuji looked at each of their faces and spoke to them.

> Everyone, I feel deep emotions as I stand here on this sacred ground. It brings back the memory of when the yeshiva came to Kobe and the many times I went to Kobe. I kept praying that somehow everyone would be saved. Since then, we have had a very deep bond. All that time I had been yearning to come to this place. This is holy ground. And now with the help of friends, I have been able to journey to Jerusalem, and also make my long-desired conversion a reality. Now I am a Jew. My fate is your fate. Your lives are my life.

The applause for Kotsuji's speech seemed unending.

The good news of Kotsuji's conversion was communicated to Jewish communities around the world. *Time* magazine covered it with an accompanying photo of Kotsuji upon his conversion. The *Sunday News* of New York (August 21, 1966) headlined its article, "'Angel' to Refugee Jews in Japan Now Lives Here," and included the story of R. Samuel Walkin, one of the refugees Kotsuji helped.

According to the article, R. Walkin, who had lived in Lithuania, lost his brothers and sisters to the Nazis and fled with his wife and two children to Japan. He had visas issued by Sugihara, but they were good only for three days. It was Kotsuji who stepped in. There were Nazi officers in Japan at that time and they were "agitating for the immediate expulsion" of the Jews, but Kotsuji was able to enlist the assistance of the local police to allow them to stay. It explains that this eventually led to Kotsuji being interrogated by the military police. R. Walkin's wife is quoted as saying, "It was the best time of all – the war years – for us."

In a column called "Close Up," the *New York Post* ran a story about Kotsuji along with his photograph. It described how Kotsuji grew up in a Shinto family and converted to Judaism, and how he had spoken in very orthodox Hebrew to give a cultural lecture.

In the *Jewish Post and Opinion*, under a headline that read "Abraham Kotsuji is our hero," was an article contributed by one of the refugees who was in Kobe, R. Abraham Hershberg, the same man who years later would visit the Jewish hostages inside the American Embassy in Tehran, which read in part:

> During World War II, those of us who were faculty members of a yeshiva in Lublin, Poland, had to flee to Japan along with 350 others to escape the Holocaust. This is when Kotsuji worked to get us permission to stay in Japan. Then when it was time for us to leave Japan, Kotsuji arranged for us to obtain a special permit to travel to Shanghai, and we set sail from Hiroshima on a military vessel. Thanks to his efforts, we were able to safely cross to Shanghai.

The news even reached Kotsuji's family in Japan. The *Sankei Shimbun* featured him, along with his photograph, as "The First Birth of a Japanese Jew, the Story of Kotsuji Setsuzo's Conversion." It reported that a reception was held at Solomon's Temple, attended by many high-ranking officials, including then-Prime Minister David Ben Gurion.

The *Yomiuri Shimbun* and *Asahi Shimbun* also reported on Kotsuji: "Jews welcome Dr. Kotsuji, Hebrew culture researcher; bust to be placed in Israeli museum."

It was at this time that a well-known Jewish sculptor, Sir René Shapshak (1899–1985), made a bust of Kotsuji that was to be exhibited in the Jerusalem National Eliezer Ben-Yehuda Memorial Art Museum. The bronze sculpture, however, was destroyed in a fire, and only a photograph of the sculptor with the uncompleted work survived.

The *Asahi Shimbun* took up Kotsuji's story in a "People" column that introduced him as the person who extended visas for Jewish refugees. In addition, the *Shukan Yomiuri* ran a two-page feature entitled "Cherished as Loving Father of Jews" and described his life and achievements.

After his conversion, Kotsuji was invited by an American Jewish association to go on a lecture tour of the United States. His return to his family would be delayed. His lecture tour continued from the US to Mexico, and it was not until September of the following year that he returned to Japan. International newspapers covered the family welcoming Kotsuji back home after more than a year. The *United Israel Britain* ran an article headlined "Jewish Hero Returns to Japan," which included a photograph of Kotsuji with Mineko and their daughters. His family embraced him warmly. Mineko's words of "Welcome back, congratulations" expressed her deep affection for her husband as well her pride in his new life as a Jew.

Bust of Kotsuji as a work in progress, with the sculptor René Shapshak

Chapter Eighteen

Passing

In 1961, Kotsuji established the Institute of Hebrew Culture in Japan. He wished to disseminate knowledge of Judaism, not so much as a religion but for purely educational and cultural purposes. He established a Jewish library in Tokyo, with the objective being to lecture and publish as many books on Judaism and Jewish history as he could. He was not able to achieve the results he envisioned. Even the Japanese newspapers that covered Kotsuji prominently after his conversion ran only small articles when the Institute of Hebrew Culture was created.

The 1960s was an era of strong economic growth in Japan. A plan to double household income was announced, and the Tokyo Olympics generated additional demand. People were interested in the Security Treaty between the United States and Japan. Hebrew culture and Judaism seemed far removed and from a distant world.

At the time, the word "Jew" was directly associated with the horrors of the Holocaust. It served as reminder of the atrocities of Nazi Germany, and thus brought back memories of Japan's militarism and the suffering and sorrow of the war years. Japanese people were enjoying a renaissance and did not want to awaken those dark memories. Quite the opposite, they were trying to forget the war. Kotsuji's achievements were buried in history.

Kotsuji began to write about his own life as if swimming against this tide. He decided to leave behind a written record of events that he had never revealed before. He wrote his autobiography, *From Tokyo to Jerusalem*, in English, and it was published in the US in 1964. Kotsuji closed his autobiography this way: "I will simply give them truth; and perhaps in a century's time, that truth will spread itself."

Although Kotsuji taught Jewish studies purely as an academic subject, and despite his desire to become a bridge between Japan and Israel, most Japanese only saw him as "Japan's first Jew." Kotsuji traveled to the US in 1962 and 1963 to give lectures, and these trips served to open his eyes to the different levels of interest between the two countries. Many Americans listened intently to stories that did not seem to resonate with Japanese people. Kotsuji decided to relocate his life and his work to the United States. Although he wished to take his family with him, his daughter Yuriko was in poor health and could not make the trip. When her condition improved, Mineko fell ill from the exhaustion of caretaking, so his family was not able to leave Japan. Kotsuji decided he would bring his family to the States after he had set up a comfortable home for them.

According to R. Tokayer, Kotsuji's life in New York was not blessed by good fortune. He had hoped to teach in New York, but that did not come to pass. Life was difficult. He had no choice but to work part-time and found a job at a clothing company while lecturing, writing, and engaging with Jewish congregations. Even under these circumstances, Kotsuji's heart was at peace because he had many Jewish friends around him. One of them was Warren Cavior, a businessman in New York. Cavior was drawn by Kotsuji's personality and inspired by his ideas. He became a friend and kindred spirit.

Kotsuji lived in New York until shortly before his death, and Cavior and his family helped to support him. Cavior's wife was a renowned Japanese-born modern dancer, Mariko Sanjo, and she regarded Kotsuji as her New York father.

Mariko had to convert to Judaism to marry Cavior, so she needed to study Judaism. They hired Kotsuji to be her private tutor, and that was the beginning of their friendship. Mariko's autobiography, *Ikarusu no yoni* (Like Icarus), published in Japanese, mentions Kotsuji.

> Even though Dr. Kotsuji wasn't the sort of person that someone like myself could talk to casually, he was kind like a father, and once a week he taught me about the Bible and the lives of Jewish people, and he lent me his own books in Japanese to use as textbooks.

It seems clear that Kotsuji was respected by many in the Jewish community in New York.

One day, the telephone rang at the Kotsuji family home in Kamakura. Yuriko answered.

"It's your father." His voice sounded tired and somber. "When you get old, it's lonely to be by yourself."

Yuriko was alarmed at the way her father sounded. Worried for him, her sister Teruko went to New York to visit him and spent a year with her father there.

When Teruko told him she needed to go back to Japan for a time, his face could not hide his sadness. In the summer of 1973 urgent news was delivered to his family in Kamakura. "Kotsuji is not well. He requires surgery. We need consent from immediate family. Please come as soon as possible."

Teruko grabbed a few things and headed to the airport. She was in such a rush she forgot her passport. Kotsuji had been diagnosed with stomach cancer. Surgery began immediately after Teruko's arrival, but once they opened his abdomen it was clear that he was already in such a late stage of the disease that there was nothing the surgeon could do. Kotsuji was told that he had a tumor in his stomach and that it was removed. No one used the word "cancer." The doctors considered treating him with chemotherapy but decided he was too physically weak to tolerate it.

Over the next several weeks, his condition stabilized somewhat and Teruko and Kotsuji were able to return to Japan together. Cavior and Kotsuji's other Jewish friends in New York had made the arrangements, believing he should be with his family. Cavior encouraged Kotsuji by saying, "I'm sure you'll get better if you recuperate at a Japanese *onsen* (hot spring)." Kotsuji agreed that he should return to Japan. It was the last time Cavior would see him.

Kotsuji still did not know how serious his condition was. He returned to his house in Kamakura accompanied by Teruko. Mineko greeted him as she always had when he returned home from work. "Welcome home," she said with a smile. Kotsuji joked, "I thought there wouldn't be any place for me to sleep anymore," to which Mineko replied, "This is your home." Mineko was shaken by how thin Kotsuji had become, but she did not betray any sign of her shock.

After Kotsuji returned home, Cavior sent a letter to R. Tokayer, who at the time was working at a synagogue in the Shibuya area of Tokyo.

> With the help of friends who love Abraham and appreciate his efforts for our people, he and his daughter flew to Tokyo a few days ago.... He was hospitalized... in the spring of this year... and in August, he entered Long Island Jewish Hospital for exploratory surgery. The surgeon, Dr. Arthur Aufses, Jr., told me he had found the tumor had spread beyond the stomach wall already and that surgery would be pointless. Abraham is unaware that he is dying of stomach cancer.... All of us who love Abraham hope and pray that his final days in Japan may be as free as possible from the dreadful pain and suffering. We ask that you use your good offices as you deem fitting to cheer him up.... Dr. Kotsuji displays your photo with pride and speaks of your kindness to his family.... I sincerely would appreciate your help to this great friend of the Jewish people.
>
> For example, if it is possible to arrange transportation from Kamakura to Shibuya, Abraham would love to attend Rosh HaShana services with you.... I am taking care of all obligations in this country, as a gesture of love. If I may assist in any way with information or action, please let me know.

The letter reflected Cavior's devotion to his friend in seeking a peaceful end for Kotsuji. Thanks to the efforts of Cavior and other friends, Kotsuji was able to spend his last days surrounded by his family in Kamakura. Mineko and her daughters lovingly nursed him. Kotsuji loved taking baths, so the three of them made sure he took plenty of hot, therapeutic baths.

"Maybe in a hundred years, someone who truly understands me will appear." It was during this time that Kotsuji spoke to his daughters the words that had left such a deep impression on me.

On October 12, Kotsuji wrote a letter to R. Tokayer. The letter was filled with affection for his family. He also expressed joy at Yuriko's recovery after a long period of poor health, which he felt was miraculous. Even on the threshold of death, Kotsuji was praying first for the health of his beloved daughter. He added a final thought: "Please let there be one more miracle." He had not given up hope of his own life.

On Kotsuji's last day, Teruko was attending her company's celebration for employees with long years of service. She could not return home early because she was one of the honorees.

While Yuriko was looking after Kotsuji, he started to talk about his memories of when she was younger, and said quietly, "Yuriko, you're a lot like me, aren't you?" Yuriko's facial features as well as her love of books and sharp memory were very much like her father's.

Kotsuji loved Yuriko's cooking, and he ate everything she made for him. This was only the case for her cooking, no one else. With the cancer having ravaged his stomach, he could hardly have been expected to eat anything, but he would say, "This is exactly what I wanted," and eat with gusto. He particularly liked her special juice and asked to drink it that day. As he sipped the juice, Kotsuji asked, "Teruko isn't home yet?" and seemed to be a little worried that she was not back from work.

When Teruko returned home it was after eight o'clock. She immediately went to her father and began washing his face as she did every night. She also rubbed his swollen feet, and then Kotsuji said "It's all right, I'm going to sleep."

But Teruko kept massaging his feet. She wanted to ease her father's pain, even if it was just a little. Before she knew it, she herself had fallen asleep, perhaps a result of fatigue from daily caretaking.

That night, Mineko, Teruko, and Yuriko all slept deeply. At dawn, Kotsuji appeared in Yuriko's dream. "I'm leaving now," he said. Yuriko thought, "I have to go to Father, I have to go right now." In a panic she tried to hurry, but she could not move. Kotsuji smiled at her, and then he vanished. At that moment, she woke up. She went to check on him, but Kotsuji had already drawn his last breath. His face was serene and gentle.

Abraham Setsuzo died on October 31, 1973, at age seventy-four. The man who had risked his own life to save six thousand Jewish refugees was called home by his God. Kotsuji had left his will with R. Tokayer. His final wish was to be laid to rest in Jerusalem.

Mineko and his daughters followed his wishes, and R. Tokayer immediately began preparations. Kotsuji's body was transferred to St. Luke's Hospital, embalmed, and readied for transport out of the country.

Israel, however, was in the immediate aftermath of the Yom Kippur War in the fall of 1973. R. Tokayer was having difficulty reaching anyone, as the nation had been engulfed in the conflict. One day passed, two days passed, and he still was not able to get through, even when he tried going through the Israeli Embassy. He decided to wait one more day and if he was still unsuccessful, the family would have Kotsuji buried at the Yokohama Foreign General Cemetery. Then he realized that the current Minister of Religion, Zorach Warhaftig, had been a refugee in Kobe and was Kotsuji's close friend.

He would remember Kotsuji. R. Tokayer promptly contacted him and explained, "Your friend Kotsuji has passed. His will states his wish to be buried in Jerusalem. I would like to fulfill this wish for him as soon as possible, but the airport there is closed and therefore he cannot be transported."

Shortly thereafter, Minister Warhaftig responded that the airport would be opened. Warhaftig instructed him to first send Kotsuji's body to London, and then to Israel. Warhaftig told R. Tokayer that he would be waiting at the airport. A few days later, amidst heightened security measures following the war, former Mirrer Yeshiva students who had known Kotsuji stood vigil awaiting his plane. Soon thereafter, Kotsuji was buried at the Har HaMenuchot Cemetery in Jerusalem, his final wish fulfilled..

R. Tokayer recalls that newspapers in Israel and New York covered the story of Kotsuji's death. In Israel, many people who learned of Kotsuji's passing and arrival gathered at the cemetery. Warhaftig delivered a eulogy.

My first meeting with the brilliant professor Avraham ben Avraham Kotsuji, may he rest in peace, was during the Second World War, when I arrived with fellow Jewish refugees from Poland to Lithuania, and from there through Russia to faraway Japan. We were 4,000 Jews.

During that period, we found a small group of Japanese intellectuals who were interested in Judaism and the Jewish people. Among them were two significant individuals. The first one was Professor Kotsuji, and the second was Captain Fukamachi. They were very helpful to us in this strange and foreign land. We had many deep discussions together on various topics.

Professor Kotsuji was in his forties at that time and seemed to us a strong, intellectual person with a deep interest in religion. He wasn't satisfied with Shinto, the Japanese religion…he studied the Bible a great deal, and he could quote many chapters by heart. He also knew how to write Hebrew.

He first encountered Jews when he was a Japanese government representative in Manchuria. There he became close with them, and with the Bible. Not once but many times he said that Christianity did not appeal to him because he sought originality. His curiosity about Jewish history and the struggle of the Jewish people to exist led him to begin his study of Judaism and its secrets.

…Through long conversations we built a friendship and deep trust between us. He did not speak of conversion. We saw him more as a righteous among the nations in its deepest sense. He was always by our side as a translator and mediator between us and the Japanese government authorities. As such, he helped assemble the Jewish diaspora in the city of Kobe. The Jews in Kobe had to promise that we would not settle in Japan, and that when the time came, we would leave.

His close familiarity with Judaism brought him to step forward and convert fifteen years ago. He had discovered that the dream of converting had been with him since 1941 and spiritually he came to see himself as a Jew. He hoped to convince his wife and two daughters to follow him in this conversion, but he passed away before his dream came true.

The depth of our friendship had many manifestations, including in one of his books, when he mentioned his three visits to Israel. The first was to convert to Judaism, and the third was to participate in my daughter's wedding.

Thanks to Kotsuji, I had the opportunity to dive deeper into the history of the Japanese people and their spiritual aspirations. I learned that this great nation is constantly in conflict, seeking spiritual fulfillment beyond what the religions of Shinto and Buddhism provide. Christianity failed in its attempts to penetrate deeply into Japan, and we felt that if the Jewish people had a tradition of encouraging other people to convert, then it would be appealing to many Japanese who continued to struggle with doubt. But Judaism does not seek converts. It does not try to walk these paths.

Professor Kotsuji did not arrive at Judaism due to outside influence. No one sought to convince him to convert. This came from a deep spiritual acknowledgement and realization that this was the way for him. We in Japan saw him as a righteous among the nations, and this was enough for us. We did not seek for him to become a Jew. We merely sought and found friendship with him.

During his old age, he walked in sorrow that his dream of opening the gates of Judaism to the Japanese people had failed. He felt alone and secluded in his own land. His fourth visit to Israel was in accordance with his personal wishes, which we fulfilled after he passed away, that he would be laid to rest in the Holy Land with the people he loved.

After I became interested in Kotsuji and read his autobiography, I was able to get to know the real person by translating the book into Japanese and then through my own research. I always wondered what drove Kotsuji to be the human being he became. How did he save the Jewish refugees, and why was he laid to rest in Jerusalem? The answers to these questions and many more gradually revealed themselves.

Kotsuji Setsuzo had an abiding sympathy for the Jewish people and became one of them. As a consequence of his helping Jewish refugees, he himself experienced similar persecution. Perhaps surprisingly, it was Jews to whom he reached out to for help at that time. This only deepened his regard for them, and theirs for him. The guardian became the guarded. Kotsuji was a Japanese person with a Jewish soul.

Chapter Nineteen

Jerusalem

I tackled the mountain of materials I had gathered through my research and wrestled with the English text to translate Kotsuji's autobiography into Japanese, which I then hand-bound into a book to give to his two daughters. On the first page, I wrote, "To Teruko and Yuriko, thank you."

When I handed it to them, they held it tight in their hands and repeated their thanks to me over and over. At that moment, they picked up a large package they had brought with them and gave it to me. Inside were photos of Kotsuji, young Setschan, Kotsuji as a freshly minted pastor, the bride and groom at their wedding, young and beautiful Teruko and Yuriko, and finally a photo of his gravesite. All of them made me feel nostalgic, as if I were looking at photos of a beloved relative.

Teruko said, "We would like to give this to you," as she pulled out a book with a thick, elaborate binding like an art book. "This is Father's thesis."

This was his treasured thesis, "The Origin and Evolution of Semitic Alphabets," from his time in Berkeley, when Kotsuji was so engrossed in his work that he forgot to eat or sleep.

"You're giving this to me?"

"Yes, we want you to have it. We think that would be best."

Teruko's words resounded in my heart. The stress and strain from my work on the translation were swept away in a single instant. This made it all worthwhile.

The substance of Kotsuji's thesis was difficult for me, but I knew it was full of Kotsuji's love for the Hebrew language. And then I seemed to hear his words in my head, "I want you to know more about me."

I had come to know many things about Kotsuji through my translation and research, but I still did not know everything. "Maybe in a hundred years someone who truly understands me will appear." Kotsuji said these words before leaving this world, and yet, I felt I still could not say that I really knew the true Kotsuji. There were still questions that remained unanswered.

Previously, when I had met the Israeli Ambassador to Japan, Nissim Ben Shitrit, he told me, "During the war, six thousand Jewish refugees fled to Japan and were saved. But now, the actual number of lives saved is tens of thousands, because they later had families, and many new lives were brought into the world."

Now, nearly eighty years since the war, not many survivors are still alive who can remember those times. Their children and grandchildren, however, have grown in number and are living in Israel. I wanted to hear their stories. I could not say that I really knew Kotsuji without hearing directly from them.

I had to see them. I had to meet the living legacy of Kotsuji's actions. After all, I had pursued Kotsuji's life this far, and I needed to see it through to the end. This idea grew stronger day by day. And so I decided I would go to Israel, the place that Kotsuji loved and where he will rest for eternity. I began preparing for a fact-finding trip to Israel.

On September 29, 2012, I departed for Israel. I had traveled overseas many times, but this occasion felt different, and I was somewhat nervous. Israel would be my first time in a Middle Eastern country. There were no direct flights from Japan, so I had to change planes in Seoul, Korea. The flight to Seoul was filled with Japanese tourists, but the second flight had almost none. As I looked at the names and phone numbers of the people Teruko had researched for me in advance, I wondered what kind of trip this would be and what Israel would be like.

On September 29, at 9:00 p.m. local time, we began our approach to Tel Aviv. The total flight time had been nineteen hours. I could see flickering lights from the city below. My pulse quickened. I was looking at the Land of Israel, the country Kotsuji loved, and where he was laid to rest.

We landed. As soon as I stepped off the plane, I was engulfed by an entirely different culture and atmosphere than Japan. The signs in Hebrew caught my eye. Whether I looked left or right, I saw letters that looked like incomprehensible symbols. I did speak English, but all I heard around me was Hebrew and I could not understand a word. In any case, after getting through immigration control, I tried to take a train to my hotel in Tel Aviv. That's when the circumstances of living in a Jewish nation threw me off balance.

It was Shabbat, the Sabbath, the day of rest in Judaism, and trains were not in operation. Shabbat began at sunset on Friday evening and continued until sunset on Saturday. The day I arrived was right in the middle of Shabbat. I had heard that everything closes, from government offices to banks and shops during this time, but I did not expect public transportation to come to a halt. Now I was experiencing firsthand what it was like to be in a foreign place where lifestyle and customs are totally different from what I knew. I had no choice but to take a taxi. I didn't speak the language and I didn't know how the fare would be set. Would I be able to get to my hotel? As I stood there, an airport worker who sensed my befuddlement came to my aid and negotiated the destination and fare with a taxi driver on my behalf. Thanks to him, I was able to head to my hotel in central Tel Aviv.

My relief was short-lived. Before we could enter the hotel, a security guard stopped the taxi and told the driver to open the trunk. He also checked my passport. I had not experienced this before, but in Israel these kinds of security checks are apparently common when entering public places. After a brief inspection, the stern-looking security guard smiled and said, "Welcome to Israel." I was relieved and glad to finally be able to check in.

The next morning, I was eager to begin interviewing as many people as possible during my two-week stay, and I made calls to three people on the list I had received from Teruko and Yuriko. My first phone call was to the daughter of Zorach Warhaftig, Nili. Kotsuji had attended her wedding. Warhaftig had passed away, but I had expectations that Nili would be the person with whom I would have the most enlightening conversations. Unfortunately, I was not able to reach her.

Next, I called Rivka Ezrachi. Rivka's father was Chaim Shmulevitz, one of the Mirrer Yeshiva teachers who came to Kobe as a refugee and who later became head of the Mirrer Yeshiva. Like Warhaftig, Shmulevitz had also been a good friend of Kotsuji, and they shared an emotional reunion when Kotsuji visited Israel for his conversion. He hosted the party for Kotsuji attended by many of the Jewish refugees he helped. Rivka came to Kobe with her father as a refugee when she was just five years old. She might not remember much from that time, but I hoped that she had heard from her father about Kotsuji. I was able to reach her, but she asked that I call back the following evening, on October 2, when she would be able to talk.

The third person was Ruth Blitzer. Ruth's father was Alfred Regensburger, who was a close friend of Kotsuji before he went to Manchuria. I got through to Ruth, but she was not able to meet me until the evening of October 3. Now what do I do? How should I spend my first day here?

I decided to call R. Marvin Tokayer in New York to see if there was anyone he could refer me to meet. With his characteristic frankness he observed, "You picked the worst possible time to be there." That's when I learned that the day I arrived coincided with one of the major holidays of the Jewish calendar, Sukkot (*Ḥag HaSukkot,* the Festival of Booths). Along with Passover and Shavuot, it is one of the three major pilgrimage festivals.

Observant Jews generally spend time only with their family during this holiday. Sukkot falls on different dates each year, and in 2012 it spanned the first seven days of October. The holiday started at sunset of the evening before the first day of October, so it had just begun. This might explain why I hadn't been able to reach Nili. Perhaps Rivka was not able to talk to me just now for the same reason. How was I to get anything done on this trip? I was speechless.

R. Tokayer tried to reassure me, "Your real work can start after Sukkot is over."

The next day I tried to call Nili, but I was not able to reach her. I called Rivka as promised but she did not answer. It seemed I would not get anywhere until after Sukkot.

I would get nothing done by sitting here. Rivka lived in Jerusalem. I didn't know if she would see me, but I decided to head there anyway. It was approximately one hour by car to Jerusalem from my hotel in Tel Aviv. I learned that there was a tour bus departing soon so I jumped on it.

As the bus approached Jerusalem, an expansive cemetery caught my eye. It was the Har HaMenuchot Cemetery, where Kotsuji was buried! I wanted to get off the bus immediately and start looking for Kotsuji's grave, but it was a huge cemetery, and I knew it would be hard to find. I would not be able to read the Hebrew writing on the gravestones. It would be impossible to locate on my own. As I watched the cemetery fade behind me, I decided I would hire a professional guide.

The tour bus made its first stop at the Mount of Olives, which boasted a breathtaking view of ancient Jerusalem. Jerusalem! It is a sacred place for three religions, Judaism, Christianity, and Islam, and 3.2 billion people.

The next stop was the Wailing Wall. It is the only remnant of the Temple that was destroyed by the Roman Army, and for Jews it is a place that symbolizes their bond with God. As I walked to the Wailing Wall, I could see that it was crowded with many religious Jews, perhaps because it was Sukkot.

Judaism is not a monolith. It has many sects and branches. For example, there are ultra-Orthodox, who are the most strictly observant of rules and customs, Orthodox, Conservative, and the liberal Reform Jews. Jews may follow precepts in their daily lives to varying degrees. One such rule is to wear a head covering as a sign of a person's respect for God. This is the opposite of the custom in Japan of removing one's hat to show respect. This is the difference I described earlier which caused problems for some of the refugees in Kobe that Kotsuji had to resolve.

I put on a cap so as not to cause offense and walked over to the wall. I lightly touched the wall. Interestingly, it was warm. The wall was made of many stones stacked high, and it felt smooth and round, serene. I wondered how many people had prayed at this spot. A tremendous "*ki*," or energy, seemed to flow from my fingertips to my body. Although it was not mentioned anywhere in his autobiography, Kotsuji must have visited and touched this Wailing Wall, recalling many memories from his extraordinary life.

From the Wailing Wall I walked the cobblestone street called Via Dolorosa, which means "Way of Sorrow." It is the path Jesus walked with the crucifix on his back to his crucifixion. Everywhere I looked I saw the world of the Bible around me.

On October 3, I left the hotel to meet Ruth as we had agreed. Her late father, Alfred Regensburger, had become friends with Kotsuji in Japan before the war. I climbed into a taxi and gave the driver Ruth's address in Bnei Brak. He looked dubious and repeated my destination to confirm. Bnei Brak is an area that is home to many Orthodox Jews. The driver still seemed skeptical. He must have wondered what business an Asian person like me would have there.

After we drove from a bustling business district into Bnei Brak, I began to notice Orthodox Jews dressed in black suits on the street. It definitely did not seem like a place where one would find many Asian people. The driver stopped in front of a four-story apartment building and said, "This is it." I looked up to see a man who was apparently Ruth's husband waving at me. I must have been easy to spot! He knew immediately who I was. I climbed the stairs and was greeted by Ruth in her doorway. She welcomed me warmly into their home.

Ruth began talking as she offered me tea. Her father, Alfred Regensburger, was born in southern Germany in 1902, making him three years younger than Kotsuji. In 1929, Regensburger came to Japan from Germany with his wife and spent ten years teaching physics and chemistry at a high school in Yokohama.

Kotsuji had returned to Japan from his studies in the United States in 1931 and would have been teaching Hebrew at Aoyama Gakuin University and at his school in the Seishokan Building around the time he met Regensburger. Both being teachers, they must have found a lot to discuss. Their friendship continued until 1938, when Kotsuji went to

Manchuria at Matsuoka's request. Regensburger was the first Jewish friend with whom Kotsuji became close in Japan.

As expected of a devout Jew, Ruth's home was decorated for Sukkot. The Sukkot holiday is said to have originated when Moses led the Jews out of Egypt and they lived in huts as they wandered the desert. In order to remember their experience, Jews erect a small sukka (hut) in their homes or on their balconies, which they decorate, have meals in, and sometimes even sleep in.

As I looked at the decorations, I thought Kotsuji probably learned a great deal about Jewish holidays, customs, and language when he met Regensburger. The Regensburger family left Japan in 1939, around the time that Hitler invaded Poland. Knowing they would face persecution if they returned to Germany, the family went to England, where they stayed until the war ended. Subsequently, they settled in Israel. During the Six-Day War in 1967, Regensburger was killed when the factory where he was working was hit by a bomb. He was sixty-five.

Ruth's elder brother Natan and his wife, Oshra, also joined us. According to the siblings, Kotsuji and Regensburger lost contact with one another after Kotsuji went to work for Mantetsu in 1938. When Kotsuji converted in 1959, the two met again for the first time in twenty years. Ruth was in her teens then and met Kotsuji for the first time. It warmed my heart to think of how delighted they must have been to see each other after having both survived turbulent times. I asked Ruth if she remembered Kotsuji.

"I'm sorry, I don't remember much. But I still have the impression of him as a kind, friendly gentleman," she said.

Unfortunately, Ruth's siblings did not remember Kotsuji either. Ruth herself, however, had not completely forgotten Kotsuji. In 2001, she happened to be listening to the radio and heard the name "Kotsuji." Surprised, she listened closely. The radio was reporting that there would be a ceremony honoring him at his gravesite at Har HaMenuchot. They wanted anyone who knew him to participate and noted that Kotsuji's daughters would be present. Ruth, unable to contain her excitement, dashed to the ceremony. It was then that she first learned of Kotsuji's achievements.

Author with Ruth Blitzer, Oshra (center), and Natan (right)

The day after meeting with Ruth, I received a call from a woman named Noami Shteinmetz. "I'm Ruth's sister. I'm calling because I heard about you from her." Noami heard that I had come from Japan to gather information about Kotsuji and decided to call me.

"I live in a city called Haifa. If you have time, would you like to come to my house? I would love to talk with you."

I wanted to leave immediately but the trains to Haifa were out of service until the end of Sukkot at sunset on October 8.

"Why don't you come on the 7:03 train on the evening of the 8th," she said. I told her I would be there. I hoped perhaps Noami would remember a little more about Kotsuji and was impatient for the end of Sukkot. While I received good news from this phone call, I also had some bad news. Rivka, whom I had finally reached, was apparently unwell and unsure when we would be able to meet. And I still had not been able to reach Warhaftig's daughter Nili. I was counting down my days in Israel. How many more people would I be able to interview about their knowledge of Kotsuji? I tried to suppress my anxiety and told myself that I had to wait until the end of Sukkot to have these conversations, as R. Tokayer had said. And I had one objective above all others that I had to achieve during this trip: to pay my respects to Kotsuji at his grave.

I went to the hotel's front desk and asked how I could hire a guide to take me to the cemetery. They told me they could refer me to a guide named Moses, who also had a car service. Since I would have the car for a full day, I thought I might as well have Moses take me to Yad Vashem, the Holocaust history museum in Jerusalem, and Shaare Zedek Hospital, where Kotsuji was circumcised. I asked the front desk to make the arrangements.

As promised, Moses picked me up at my hotel on October 5 at 10:00 a.m. He was a good-natured man around my age. It was a smooth, one-hour drive to Jerusalem. Just as I had seen from the bus, the vast Har HaMenuchot Cemetery spread out before me. As we got closer, I could see rows of white tombstones as far as the eye could see. I had never seen such a large cemetery before. I went to the information kiosk, but no one was there.

"Because it's Sukkot. They're off," explained Moses.

I was a little worried about finding Kotsuji's grave. But I had to try. Moses and I decided to go in and look for the marker. Moses said, "Wait," and from the inside of the car brought out a *kippa*, a cloth skullcap worn by Jewish men, and handed it to me. It is required head gear when entering a cemetery in Israel. For the first time in my life, I put a *kippa* on my head.

Block 54, Section 1, Row 4, No. 1. This was Kotsuji's gravesite. I had a general idea of the location, and I knew the plot number. But the cemetery was so big, it was hard to get an idea of where it was. I thought we could ask someone, but because of Sukkot there was no one in sight. Using the numbers engraved on the stone we were able to figure out what section we were in, but I was unable to find the plot even after much circling around. I was getting impatient, because I wasn't making progress, and the time was ticking by. I searched for an hour and half, but the gravesite remained elusive.

"Do you know anyone who would know the exact location?" Moses asked me. I suddenly remembered Professor Ben-Ami Shillony, a professor emeritus at Hebrew University and an Israeli historian. He had authored many books about Japan and Israel, and I had heard his name from R. Tokayer as well as Kotsuji's daughters several times. I looked up his contact information right away and called him, but there was no answer. Moses was beginning to look tired, and I decided it was time to break for lunch.

As we left the cemetery, we stopped at the restrooms, and Moses said to me, "In Judaism, when you leave the cemetery, you have to wash your hands." In Japan, we wash and purify our hands before entering a shrine. There seemed to be a symmetry in these actions to me.

After lunch, I tried calling Professor Shillony again but to no avail.

"There are two more places you want to go besides the cemetery today, right?" Moses said. Because our time was limited, we decided to head to the Shaare Zedek Hospital now. According to Moses, it was a famous hospital in Jerusalem. We arrived at a large hospital building in about twenty minutes. This was the place where Kotsuji was circumcised and became a Jew, I thought. I felt emotional as I stood there and pondered his journey to this place.

After a little while, I called Professor Shillony again, but again no answer. There was nothing I could do, so we went to Yad Vashem, the Holocaust history museum. The name Yad Vashem is derived from a passage in the Book of Isaiah 56:5: "To these I am giving, in My house between My walls, a monument and name better than sons and than daughters; I give them a name everlasting that will not be severed." Yad Vashem means "a monument and a name."

This place was built to commemorate the six million Jews killed by the Nazis. I had always planned to visit this museum even before deciding to go to Israel. Everyone needs to know what happened, and Yad Vashem is where this history is preserved.

Stepping inside, one enters a world that makes one want to cover one's eyes. I felt almost overcome. Yad Vashem has records and artifacts of a tragic history that should never be forgotten: articles on the Holocaust, photos, belongings of the deceased, so many exhibits that show how people can treat other human beings with such cruelty and brutality. It was a deeply painful experience.

And when I stood in the Hall of Names, which was lined with the portraits of those who were murdered, my heart broke. The photos and other materials exhibited here represent about two-thirds, or four million, of the six million Jews who were killed.

> To my eyes, it looked like a scene from hell.... I had never seen anything like what I saw at the moment: they were human, but you could not tell if they were male or female. Heads shaved, malnourished, unclean, and wretched. However, this was not the only thing that shocked me. What struck me the most was the expression in their eyes. They had what I can only describe as "the eyes of a dead person."[1]

The portraits of the deceased on the walls of Yad Vashem are intended to remember and respect each person as an individual with dignity. The eyes of these people became like the eyes of the dead at concentration camps, where people were not treated as human beings and where they were killed, just for being Jewish.

In his autobiography, Kotsuji described being asked by Jewish friends why he would want to adopt a religion that brought troubles and sorrow. His reply at the time was, "I will come to Judaism with joy and pride."

I believe that Kotsuji, who had contemplated what God was his entire life, might have intended to say something like this: I have been connected with you, the Jewish people, I have formed friendships with you, and I have seen the tragic history that you have suffered. Understanding all this, when I look back on the life I have lived, I am prepared to share all the pain and joy with you no matter what happens.

After leaving Yad Vashem, I immediately headed back to the cemetery. Once there, I was finally able to reach Professor Shillony and handed my phone to Moses, who confirmed the exact location of the grave. I thought now I would finally be able to see the grave, but it was not so simple. When we went to spot as instructed by Professor Shillony, there was a row of identical white gravestones. They were marked in Hebrew and I could not tell which was Kotsuji's, and although Moses was looking at each one, he was not finding it. What to do? Soon it would be sundown. Just then, Moses shouted, "Here it is! This must be it!"

---

1. Testimony of a concentration camp survivor, excerpted from commentary in the Japanese edition of Frankl's book *Man's Search for Meaning* (*Yoru to Kiri*).

I rushed over, and Moses pointed and said the grave read "Kotsuji." I thought it was possible Moses was tired of searching and was saying this to mollify me. To be sure this was the right grave, I asked him, "What else does it say?"

"... Professor Abraham Kotsuji ...."

"It really says 'Professor'?"

Moses replied yes, and added that it was also inscribed, "The person who became a Jew."

There was no mistake, this was it. I was finally able to meet Kotsuji. In this cemetery of countless rows of graves, unknown to most people, Professor Kotsuji Setsuzo was in his final place of rest in Jerusalem.

I spoke to him: "Mr. Kotsuji, what did you say to the Jewish people who arrived in Kobe to encourage them? After helping them, you endured torture at the hands of the military police, what kind of fear did you feel? Have I misunderstood anything about you? Now you are here, resting alone ... are you not lonely?"

I lingered in front of the grave, reflecting on Kotsuji's turbulent life. People saving people ... an act that seems so natural and yet not easily done. Kotsuji took the initiative and did it. In this action he transcended

Author at Kotsuji's gravesite

religious boundaries. After a time, I said good-bye and left the cemetery. From the highway, I could see the cemetery bathed in the rays of the sinking sun in the rear-view mirror. I suddenly thought I heard a voice and glanced behind me. The cemetery, glowing a deep red, was fading in the distance. I felt as if I could see Kotsuji standing there, seeing me off.

I had achieved my primary objective for this trip in visiting the grave, but my desire to interview people who had known Kotsuji was even stronger. I was keen to meet with Nili, the daughter of the former Minister of Religion Warhaftig, but I was still unable to reach her. I tried looking for other people, but it was difficult during Sukkot, and I was not getting results. So I holed up in my hotel room, organized my materials and interview notes, and waited impatiently for Sukkot's end.

On the evening of October 8, I left the hotel to meet Regensburger's eldest daughter Noami, as we had agreed. When I arrived at HaShalom train station, I found that the trains started running at sunset, just as Noami had assured me on the phone. I boarded the 7:03 train bound for Haifa as instructed. According to a sightseeing guide, Haifa is the third-largest city in Israel, after Tel Aviv and Jerusalem. It is located on the Mediterranean Sea, and many boats from Greece and other places arrive at the Port of Haifa. It is Israel's gateway to the sea.

The train headed north for about an hour. At 8:11 p.m., it arrived at Haifa's Lev HaMifratz Station, where Noami's husband Aharon met me. When we got into the car, it started to rain but then stopped after a few minutes. Aharon said it was the first time it had rained all year. Now that he mentioned it, I realized that the cities of Israel were very dry. From the car window I could see the lights of houses lining the hills in a picturesque landscape.

In about fifteen minutes we arrived at their house.

"Welcome! Please come in," Noami said as she met me at the door. She had prepared dinner for us. Her homemade pizza was very tasty.

"It's so good!" I said to Noami, to which she replied, "My grandchildren say the same thing, that Grandma's cooking is better than the food their mom prepares. Maybe grandmothers' cooking is always better. Even when I buy bread at the same store as their mother, they say my bread tastes better than the bread at home! They insist it's different." She smiled warmly.

I felt at ease and enjoyed the lovely meal Noami had cooked. Then she said something that stopped me in my tracks.

"I don't have any grandparents myself. Most of our generation are the same, because they were all killed."

Aharon said quietly, "Yes, that's true."

I was shocked, I had no words. I realized this generation of Jews do not know what it's like to have grandparents. They had all been murdered a long time ago. The atrocities of the Holocaust cast a long shadow across generations. I didn't know how to respond.

Aharon saw my expression and said, "Our parents did not want to say anything about those times. They wanted to pass on their hopes to their children, not frighten them." Noami nodded at her husband's words. I thought that for Noami and Aharon watching their carefree grandchildren eat and enjoy their grandma's delicious cooking was priceless and a treasured time.

For most people, sitting around the table sharing meals with loved ones is one of the great pleasures of life. This must be even more so for Holocaust survivors and their families. To eat is to live. Then I thought, the flavors Noami learned from her late mother must be alive in her cooking. And these flavors were passed on from her mother, Noami's grandmother. Her cooking carries on the legacy of her ancestors.

As I was enjoying the meal and thinking these thoughts, Noami began to talk about Kotsuji. Unfortunately, like her sister Ruth, she did not remember much about him. But she told me that her father, Alfred Regensburger, and Kotsuji were very close, and their closeness was demonstrated by a certain treasured keepsake.

She was describing a photo of the two of them with their arms around each other's shoulders. It was taken in 1959 when Kotsuji converted. They had just reunited after twenty-one years. Kotsuji and Regensburger met in 1931 and over the next seven years their friendship deepened in Japan. This includes the year 1933, when Kotsuji's eldest daughter, Aiko, died, Kotsuji and then his wife fell ill, and he lost his job. Kotsuji wrote about this time in his autobiography:

> ... [T]he biggest solace were the people who came and wept with us. When one is lonesome, those who join us in sorrow are most

Author with Alfred Regensburger's daughter
Noami Shteinmetz and her husband Aharon

Kotsuji with Alfred Regensburger

precious. Judaism says that visitor [sic] to a sick person takes away one-sixtieth of his illness.

Kotsuji and Regensburger were both in their late thirties at that time. It seems certain that Regensburger was one of those who consoled Kotsuji during this painful time.

At their reunion the two men were in their sixties, and the lines on their faces betrayed the hardships they had endured in the intervening years. Unlike now, there was no internet or international phone calls to stay in contact. During the war, even sending letters was not possible. For twenty-one years, they could not comfort each other nor share anger or laughter or tears. Now, they could finally embrace as if to verify that they had survived, and they stood shoulder to shoulder for the photo.

As I studied the photo, Noami said to me, "This is Kotsuji, right?" as she took out a tiny picture frame, about the size of a matchbox and showed it to me.

"Yes, it is!"

In the frame was a sketch of Kotsuli that Regensburger had drawn. Kotsuji's features were clearly recognizable, and it was a delightful

Drawing of Kotsuji likeness by Alfred Regensburger

likeness of him. Noami had found it in her father's belongings and had kept it safe. It had been forty-five years since her father died. I was moved that she had kept this sketch for all this time. She treasured this memento of her father's friendship with Kotsuji.

I had to express my gratitude to Noami for showing me this. Regensburger was an educator, and not only artistically inclined but also well versed in several languages and cultures. I'm sure Kotsuji enjoyed his interactions with this cultured man.

It was time for me to head back to Tel Aviv. When I left their house, I thanked Noami for the meal and for showing me her father's precious mementos. She said to me in parting, "Next time you come, please stay with us for a few days. We will show you around Haifa. We can go to all kinds of places."

I was grateful to Noami and Aharon for their hospitality. I reluctantly left to catch the last train, which departed just before midnight.

On October 9, I decided to go to Jerusalem one more time to visit the Mirrer Yeshiva. A yeshiva is an institution of higher learning where students focus on Jewish law, philosophy, and the Torah. Jews can spend their entire lives learning different aspects of Judaism. Today, the Mirrer Yeshiva is the largest yeshiva in Israel. As I described earlier, during World War II almost all of the yeshivas in Europe were destroyed in the Holocaust. The only yeshiva whose entire student body and faculty survived the fearsome Nazi persecution was the Mirrer Yeshiva, which had been located in Poland. All 350 of its students and faculty made it to safety by fleeing to Japan just ahead of the Nazis. Kotsuji's efforts then made it possible for them to travel to Shanghai from Japan.

After the war, they went to Israel and rebuilt the the Mirrer Yeshiva that stands today. Kotsuji was able to meet with many people from the yeshiva again in Jerusalem at the time of his conversion. He gave a rousing speech at the party they hosted for him. I thought perhaps there might be someone at the Mirrer who would remember Kotsuji.

The Mirrer Yeshiva was located in an area called Me'a She'arim in the northeastern part of the city. Mea She'arim means "land that yields a hundred-fold harvest," as referenced in Genesis (26:12). It is said this area was built in 1874, and only Orthodox Jews lived there. When I walked into this section, I could feel an indescribable aura. It was much stricter than the Bnei Brak neighborhood where Ruth lived, even though that was also an Orthodox area.

The sightseeing guidebook said that sleeveless shirts and short pants were forbidden even for tourists, and indeed the atmosphere was such that it seemed clear this kind of clothing would not be tolerated. A sign was posted in English: "Do not walk in our district in immodest clothing." Some Ultra-Orthodox Jews live their lives with limited access to outside sources of information, including television, computers, and movies, in observance of their stringent rules. Perhaps because of these conditions, there is a sense of insularity here.

Just in case, I had worn a white, long-sleeved shirt instead of my usual T-shirt, but I regretted very much that I did not wear a hat. Passersby gave me hard stares as I walked by them. "What's a foreigner doing here?" "What are you doing here?" "Where are you going?" I felt a tremendous amount of unspoken pressure, as if my body was almost being pushed back. It was in no way a threatening place, but the directness of their stares was intimidating. Quite honestly, I felt completely out of place. But I could not turn back now.

Eventually I saw the building that housed the Mirrer Yeshiva. When I walked up to the front gate, I was stopped by a school official.

"What's your business here?" he asked.

"I'm doing research on someone," I answered. "That person was Japanese and then he became one of you."

The man looked at me suspiciously but let me through the gate, telling me to go to the reception area. While I was relieved to be allowed inside, the unfriendly stares inside the school were even more intense. "What's this guy doing here?" Everyone was peering at me.

A relatively young man caught my eye, but I figured that a young person was unlikely to be familiar with Kotsuji. I wondered if I might at least be permitted to look at pre-and post-war materials, so I approached the reception desk. Two men were sitting at the desk, both looked to be in their thirties. They were regarding me sternly. I was also aware of the hard looks I was getting from the students around me. I felt that any move I made would be noticed. Timidly, I spoke to the well-built man on the right. "I've come from Japan. Seventy years ago, the students of this school fled Nazi Germany and went to Kobe as refugees. I'm doing research on that subject. Are you familiar with the name Abraham Kotsuji?"

The man's face suddenly lit up and he covered his face with his hands as if he couldn't contain his surprise.

"Ah! I know him! I read his autobiography. And my wife's grandmother met him in Canada once!" He smiled at me.

"You know of him?" My voice suddenly went up a few octaves. I certainly did not expect to hear such a wonderful response here.

"Wait one moment," he said, and picked up his phone and called his wife. He told her there was someone here from Japan doing research on Kotsuji. "Just wait ten minutes. She said she's calling her grandmother."

This man at the reception desk said his name was Eisenthal. As I waited on pins and needles, the grandmother called right away.

"She's hard of hearing so rather than talking on the phone she would like to meet you in person. She says she wants you to come to her house," said Eisenthal.

What was happening? I could not have even imagined this! I had been quite tense in this unfamiliar place, but now my body began to relax and my face warmed into a smile. I could see that students around me and others at the reception desk had apparently been listening with interest.

"You came all the way to Israel just to research Kotsuji?" someone asked.

When I said yes, they all suddenly started to smile.

"I hope it goes well. I'll pray for your good luck," he replied.

Being told "Good luck" in this very strict environment felt like magic.

The woman that Eisenthal introduced me to was Mrs. Cissy Flegg. To my delight, we agreed to meet that day at 5:00 p.m., and I left the school in high spirits. I clutched the piece of paper with Mrs. Flegg's address on it. Unlike my walk to the yeshiva, I was relaxed enough on my way back to notice the sights around me. The stares from the passersby were still sharp, but my heart was warmed by the kind words and smiles of the yeshiva students wishing me luck.

They live in a world completely different from the one in which Japanese people and even most modern people live. It is an entirely different dimension. They have no television or comic books and live their entire lives under strict rules. That creates a very different atmosphere in the streets and the city from what I had experienced to that point. I was initially overwhelmed by this difference. But the manner in which the face of the receptionist transformed from suspicious to smiling was no different from mine. We are all just human beings experiencing the same honest emotions.

Naturally, I was thrilled to have received the introduction to Mrs. Flegg. I was also happy for another reason. It was a truly great experience to interact directly with people whose culture and lives were so different from mine. It is on a separate level from simply trying a new food or seeing a new work of art. For me, this kind of experience was rare and precious.

I still had quite a bit of time before I was to meet Mrs. Flegg, so I decided to go back to Yad Vashem. The first time I went, I was preoccupied by whether or not I would be able to find Kotsuji's grave. So I wanted to visit again, thinking I might be able to learn more about Kotsuji's life by inquiring with a staff person there.

When I told the person at Yad Vashem's reception my intention, Eva, from the public relations office, assisted me. She was from Poland and had moved to Israel in 1970.

"Of the six million Holocaust victims, about half of them were Polish Jews," she said.

She also told me the same thing that Noami's husband Aharon had said in Haifa.

"My parents lived through that era but did not want to share anything about that time. I think we must pass on the stories of the people who risked their lives to help us Jews, along with the tragic history."

Yad Vashem honors Jews who were persecuted by the Nazis and recognizes the humanitarian efforts of people who put their own lives on the line to save them. Most of these individuals were living in Europe, and Sugihara Chiune, who issued the "visas for life," was among those who were awarded the designation of "Righteous Among the Nations." I asked Eva if she knew of Kotsuji.

"I know he wrote an autobiography. I'm sorry, I haven't read it yet. I think most people don't know about him," she answered. Then after a moment's thought she said, "It's possible that in the case of Kotsuji, the reason he hasn't been formally recognized may be because he converted to Judaism." The awards bestowed by Yad Vashem must go to individuals who were not Jewish. Then she told me an interesting story.

A Polish woman named Irena Sendler protected 2,500 Jewish children and saved them by keeping them from being sent to Auschwitz. It was a huge accomplishment, and many years later she was finally recognized as a Righteous by Yad Vashem. Eva believed that there must be many similar humanitarian acts buried in history.

At the same time, there may be those who loudly proclaim their good deed of having given water to Jews during the Holocaust, for example. Although it was certainly an act of kindness, this is not the sort of action that met the criteria for recognition by Yad Vashem. This formal designation was only given to those who risked their own lives to help Jews. For this reason, fact-finding investigations were essential to corroborate reported actions.

I felt that Kotsuji certainly met the criteria, having been a Christian pastor during the war years and being subjected to torture by the military police for helping the Jewish refugees. Fortunately, Eva was interested in Kotsuji, saying she would read his autobiography and research him.

I wanted to spend hours with her, but it was time for me to leave to meet Mrs. Flegg. I thanked Eva and was about to depart Yad Vashem. Eva asked me to let her know if I learned of any further witnesses or discoveries, and she said she would contact me if she found out anything new as well. As I left, she gave me a smile and said, "Maybe Kotsuji will emerge from buried history just like Irena Sendler."

Eva too had not known her grandparents. How could something so abhorrent as the Holocaust happen? A single word from Hitler led to an unprecedented mass slaughter such as the world had never seen. The frightening group-think psychology, the weakness of human beings, and ignorance all contributed to deep, dark fear and hatred. Yad Vashem. A memorial and a name. It contains memories for Jews that should never be forgotten.

I hurried to Mrs. Cissy Flegg's home, which was in an apartment building near the King David Hotel. I was given her address in English, but the street signs were in Arabic and Hebrew. I did not know what was where. But I eventually located her apartment. Mrs. Flegg said to me, "You've come all the way from Japan."

Even though we were meeting for the first time, she welcomed me as if I were an old friend. She said she was eighty-eight years old. Mrs. Flegg was born in 1929 in Shanghai and moved to Britain after the war. She became a nurse. She then moved to Canada, married in 1953, was blessed with four children, and now grandchildren. In 1971, she emigrated to Israel. She had never been to Japan. She was living in Canada when she encountered Kotsuji, and I asked her about their meeting.

"I saw Mr. Kotsuji about twenty years after the war, at a synagogue in Montreal," she said. One Saturday morning when Mrs. Flegg went to synagogue Kotsuji was among the seven rabbis standing in a line there. "He was one hundred percent Japanese but he was one of us, one hundred percent Jewish. He knew all of the prayers – he completely, one hundred percent, blended in with us. It was very natural, truly natural." She kept repeating how natural it was. Kotsuji wore a *kippa* and a prayer shawl called a *tallit*. In Mrs. Flegg's eyes, Kotsuji, despite his Japanese face, looked like a perfect Jewish rabbi. At the time, he was likely visiting Canada to see Pinchas Hirschprung, whom he had helped in Kobe. Hirschprung was the head (*rosh yeshiva*) of a yeshiva in Montreal. *Rosh Yeshiva* Hirschprung was chief rabbi of Canada and dean of the Rabbinical College of Canada.

I told Mrs. Flegg that I had traveled to Israel to research Kotsuji. I also said that I had visited Yad Vashem before coming to see her and had learned about the indelible scars left by this tragic history.

"Oh," she sighed. "It is really unbelievable. It's unbelievable, isn't it? I am so grateful to the people who rescued Jews, and I'm so proud of them. There was even a story of a German schoolteacher who went in the gas chamber with Jewish students to try to protect them."

I was at a loss for words. She continued.

"At the time, Japan and Nazi Germany were allies, and Germany ordered Japan to kill the Jews. I'm sure that the Japanese were told to kill the Mirrer students. But there were children among those students, and the Japanese could not do it. Their parents had been killed, they been in the freezing cold, they were hungry, frightened, and the Japanese refused, saying they couldn't kill people in such a state."

Then she told me the story of what happened after the Mirrer students that Kotsuji saved in Kobe went to Shanghai. They had arrived in Shanghai safely, but the 350 students had nowhere to stay, let alone continue their studies. The person who offered them lodging and a place to study was none other than Mrs. Flegg's father, R. Abram. I was astonished by this coincidence.

"When he was in Shanghai, my father was very poor, but he helped many different people, including Chinese people." Her father used to say that if you wanted to feel rich, share what little you have with those less fortunate than yourself. When Abram was the rabbi at Shanghai's synagogue, the yeshiva students came to him for help. The synagogue he led was in a rough area, and not many people came to worship. So Abram decided to offer the main hall to the students for lodging and gave the faculty a key. This is where the 350 Mirrer students stayed.

Mrs. Flegg only met Kotsuji at the Montreal synagogue and did not have any personal conversations with him. I told her about Kotsuji, and she listened intently, nodding.

"The students who came to Shanghai from Kobe spoke of how well they were treated by the Japanese people. It was a wonderful thing. I'm also very grateful."

Sugihara Chiune's visas for life were extended by Kotsuji in Japan, and then Mrs. Flegg's father Abram was the next link in the chain in Shanghai. I was awed by the power of destiny and its unexpected turns. In the midst of the terror that the Holocaust wreaked upon the world, Jews were helped by people who were connected by invisible bonds. Abram and Kotsuji never met, but his daughter Mrs. Flegg met Kotsuji by chance in distant Montreal, not knowing anything about this crucial bond. I could not help but be amazed at the mystery of how fate brings people together.

I told Mrs. Flegg that Kotsuji was buried in Jerusalem. She let out of cry of surprise. She had not known.

"That is wonderful.... I am to be buried at the Mount of Olives." When I was getting ready to leave, she told me, "Please come again anytime. You are my Japanese friend. I look forward to seeing you again."

On my last day before departing Israel, I was finally able to meet with Rivka Ezrachi. She had been unwell but let me know that she could see me at midday. I had almost given up on interviewing her. Her late father was Chaim Shmulevitz, one of the Mirrer Yeshiva faculty who came to Kobe as a refugee. He later became the *rosh yeshiva*. Rivka had been in Kobe with her father. She would be the first actual refugee I would meet. I was looking forward to hearing her stories.

I arrived at her house at 11:00 a.m. Her home was located in an area with many Orthodox Jews. Rivka cheerfully greeted me at the door. She said she was five years old when they arrived in Kobe, and she was now in her late seventies. In her sleek living room was a large bookcase, and a grand portrait of her father hung on the wall. Seated in front of the portrait, Rivka looked at me and said, "I was in Japan when I was a child. What do you want to ask me?"

"Do you know who Kotsuji is?"

"Of course, I know him. Because I met him here in Israel."

"You didn't meet him in Japan?"

"I don't know. I was so young, and it might just be that I don't remember meeting him," she replied.

"Do you remember why you had to go to Japan?"

Author with Rivka Ezrachi

Rivka nodded and began to talk quietly. This was the first time that I would be hearing directly from a refugee giving testimony to her experience.

"This was in 1939. The war had started, and the Russian Army had reached just east of Poland. At that time Russia and Nazi Germany had signed a treaty and the Germans occupied western Poland. Stalin, the Communists, took the east and the Nazis took the west. We were in the small village of Mir, and there was a yeshiva there. When the Russians came, they started abducting and jailing our people. The Nazis and the Russians hated the rabbis, the religious leaders of the Jewish people. It was a terrible time."

Rivka brought out an album and showed me an old photo.

"These are my parents. That's my father. He was so young there, wasn't he? He was a dean at the yeshiva then. There were three of us siblings, my sister, me, and my brother. Our backs were against the wall, to the point where it was decided to close the yeshiva and all of us would flee together. I was young, so I don't remember much. But we as a family and the Mirrer Yeshiva students left Poland. I think there were 350 of us. All of us fled to Vilnius in Lithuania. We stayed there about a year."

Those associated with the Mirrer Yeshiva were persecuted not only by the Nazis but also the Soviets. Squeezed between the Nazis to the west and the Russians to the east, they were in a precarious position but managed to flee to Lithuania.

The escape to Vilnius is described in detail by Zorach Warhaftig in his book *Refugee and Survivor: Rescue Efforts During the Holocaust.* On October 10, 1939, just three weeks after the Soviet invasion of Poland, the Soviet-Lithuanian Mutual Assistance Treaty was signed and the Vilnius area was placed under Lithuanian control. This was why Jews fled to Vilnius. Lithuanian territory was neutral, and from there they could travel to Palestine or to other European cities. Warhaftig acted as a leader for the refugees. He believed this would be their best chance for survival and decided to seek refuge there. Vilnius, the present-day capital of Lithuania, was about an hour's train ride from then-capital Kaunas. Rivka's father Chaim Shmulevitz and the Mirrer Yeshiva students all followed Warhaftig's decision.

"Their plan was to somehow try to flee Europe. The Nazi invasion was getting very close. If we were captured by the Nazis, what kind of horrible things would have happened? There are no words to describe the atrocities that happened. I'm sure you understand.

"That's when the vice-consul in Kaunas, Sugihara, saved us. He gave the Jews many visas, and those of us from Mir were among them. I was about five and a half years old, so I don't know the details, but I do remember being there. We got on the Siberian Railway train and eventually reached Japan.

"We were in Japan about half a year, from March to August 1941. There were many refugees besides the Mirrer students. Most of them had visas from Sugihara and arrived by the same route. Is this what you were interested in hearing about?"

"Yes."

"You're really interested? Really?"

She kept asking me as if to make absolutely certain, and I kept saying, "Yes, I am."

Her face expressed surprise, and then she seemed to be impressed as she said, "It's great that young people like you are interested in this."

Rivka said she heard about Kotsuji from her parents when she was older. She asked me, "Have you seen a 'visa for life'?"

"No." I had seen a photograph of one but never the actual visa.

"Our visa was only good for ten days. We couldn't stay in Japan long. But we were able to get it extended several times. And that was because of Kotsuji."

"Do you remember other things your father told you?"

"Yes, I do. My father said that Kotsuji was the person who acted as a liaison between us and the Japanese government. He conveyed our requests to the government and the instructions from the government back to us."

Now I had heard this stated clearly by a refugee who was present in Japan. Negotiations between the Jewish refugees and the government were conducted through Kotsuji. I remembered what R. Tokayer had said about Kotsuji being the only person who understood Jews and could solve problems for the Jewish refugees.

Rivka pulled out a single photograph. It was from the occasion when the Jewish representatives were called to the Navy Headquarters in Tokyo, and it shows the representatives and Kotsuji, who had accompanied them as their interpreter. It was published in newspapers and is quite a famous photo. She pointed to the white-haired Amshinover Rebbe.

"The Amishnover Rebbe was a truly great rabbi." He was the one who told the interrogators that after the Nazis had finished killing the Jews, the Japanese would be next.

Rivka informed me that the Rebbe's granddaughter was in excellent health. "Her name is Mrs. [Chaya] Milikowski, and she is still doing very well. I think she was about fifteen years old when we were in Kobe."

That would mean she was in her eighties now. I would have liked to meet her, but I had no time left during this trip. Rivka called Mrs. Milikowski for me. I was thrilled when she answered right away. I asked her if she remembered Kotsuji, but unfortunately, she did not remember much from that time. So I asked if she remembered where she lived in Kobe. And she answered the question in Japanese: "*Nozaki-dori yonchome*" [No. 4 Nozaki Street]. I was stunned. Nozaki-dori is in Sannomiya, just east of central Kobe in what is presently known as Chuo Ward in Kobe City.

Despite the passage of over seventy years, she still remembered her address in Japanese. Kobe is situated between Mount Rokko and the tranquil Seto inland sea. The memory of this place still remained in Mrs. Milikowski's mind. I told her I would love to meet her on my next visit to Israel.

Rivka's husband, who had been quietly listening to our conversation, apparently had mistakenly thought that I was Kotsuji's grandson.

"So you're Kotsuji's grandson. You came here to research your roots?" he asked.

When I told him I was not his grandson, he looked puzzled as to why I would come all the way from Japan. Rivka seemed to wonder as well. "Why do you want to do all this research?"

"I think it's important history that Japanese people need to know," I responded. "I want to learn as much as I can about what really happened. That's why I came."

Rivka seemed pleased. "That is wonderful."

Rivka, who used to be a teacher, said that she used to talk to her students about the Holocaust in school. She also told them about Kotsuji as someone who saved the lives of Jews.

"Yes, I would like for you to know too. And even though it was during the war, for us the time we spent in Japan was a very good experience. And this is very important. Many people in Japan helped us."

Rivka's words filled me with happiness, as if she were talking about me personally.

She continued, "And...there's one more thing I want you to know. The Japanese government wanted to expel us even before the visas expired. The visas were for a short time, and there was quite a lot of pressure from the Nazis, and strong pressure not to take in any more Jewish refugees. But still, while we were in Japan, nothing bad happened to us. I'm sure they didn't want us to settle down permanently, but they allowed us to live there, and the people were kind to us."

"Besides the Mirrer, were there other schools that went to Kobe?"

"Yes. But the Mirrer was the only one where the entire school came. There were just a few from other schools. To have 350 was very many, even among the yeshivas."

I asked Rivka, "Do you know anyone else who remembers being in Kobe?"

"There was someone in Bnei Brak, but he passed away about six months ago. He was very close to my father. Another person who remembered that time very well also died recently. The Holocaust survivors are all quite old and more are dying. But if you want to hear from other people, I can ask around." She promised that she would do so.

Although she was too young to remember Kotsuji from her time in Kobe, Rivka did remember when Kotsuji came to Israel in 1959 for his conversion.

"Was it big news when Kotsuji came to Israel?"

"Yes, it was big news. It was in the news when he was circumcised and converted, but also, they reported how he had saved the yeshiva and the refugees, that he had done so much for the Jewish people."

The news of Kotsuji's conversion was indeed widely covered in Israel. I showed Rivka the photo of the thank-you party that Teruko and Yuriko had given me. The photo showed the refugees who were in Kobe and the newly converted Kotsuji meeting again after twenty years. I wanted to know if Rivka had been at this gathering, and if so, what her impressions had been.

She took one look and exclaimed fondly, "Oh, I remember that! I met Kotsuji at this party. This was at my father's house."

At the time, Rivka was twenty-three years old. It was shortly before her wedding, and she remembered the party vividly. She pointed at the photo and said, "This is my uncle, this is Kotsuji. And this is Mr. Warhaftig. He was the leader of everything for the refugees."

She asked if I had any more photographs, and when I handed her another, she exclaimed as she pointed, "Oh, that's my father! This is lovely. Please let me make a copy of this."

"Of course, go ahead," I told her.

I wanted to confirm the speech that her father, R. Shmulevitz, had made at the party, and I pulled out the newspaper clipping that Teruko had given me.

"We will never forget what this wonderful man did for us nor how you risked your life to save us and guide us."

I asked her about it as I showed it to her. "Is this really what your father said?"

"Yes. It really is. This is what I wanted to tell you about! Yes, yes...." Rivka kept repeating "yes" as she read the article. "'We will never forget what this wonderful man did for us nor how you risked your life to save us and guide us.' Yes, that's exactly it."

"Your father said these things?"

"Yes, he did. Can I make a copy of this too? Oh, how wonderful this is!" Rivka seemed to feel very nostalgic about that time.

"My father talked about Kotsuji all the time," she said. "My father always felt *hakarat hatov* (gratitude) toward Kotsuji, and also to the many other Japanese people who helped them. He always said he would never forget what they did for us."

Even after leaving Kobe for Shanghai, R. Shmulevitz would on occasion talk to large groups about the generosity they had enjoyed in Japan. Rivka told me that her father gave a speech at one meeting convened by a Japanese person in which he said, "We must be grateful to the Japanese.

They gave us safe refuge, and I pray that after the war God will bless Japan with prosperity."

When Rivka told this story, her husband began to speak in Hebrew, which Rivka interpreted for me. "*Hakarat hatov* means gratitude in English. This is a very precious word in our religion. When we wake up in the morning, we are thankful that we have been given another day to live. This is what gratitude means for us. It's very important."

Waking up in the morning. This is something most of us take for granted. But he said to be thankful for each morning. I wonder how many people really feel gratitude for just waking up in the morning?

Hearing her husband's words, Rivka said, "My father always said the same thing in Shanghai. He was jailed in Shanghai. He was treated much better in Japan. But still my father said we had to be grateful in Shanghai too. Jail in Shanghai was still better than being in Europe, because no one was killed. No one. Nobody killed us there."

No one was killed. She repeated it twice. It seemed like something that should be expected, to not be killed. It reflected the terror that the Jews endured in those times. I felt an indescribable pain in my heart when I thought about their lives in those days.

Rivka spoke again. "There were twenty thousand refugees in Shanghai at the time. Not all of them came from Poland; many were from Germany and other places. Because they knew this was a place that accepted anyone. And it was the Japanese who were in control. But eventually the Japanese closed our Shanghai school and started using the building. It wasn't until after the war that we were able to get our school back."[1]

She continued, "Even though no one was killed, life wasn't all good. Of course, my father was jailed for a few days too. They tortured him to try to get him to reveal his ties to the United States. Our house was searched constantly," she said casually. "Even so, we didn't forget our feelings of gratitude. After all, our lives had been spared, right?"

All I could say was "Yes."

1. In 1941, when World War II broke out, there were approximately thirty thousand Jews living in Shanghai. Of those, roughly four thousand were refugees who came from Poland via Japan. The others arrived from Russia, mainland China, and Europe.

To which Rivka asked politely, "More tea?"

I asked Rivka, "Do you remember when Kotsuji died in 1973?"

"Yes, of course. He is buried here."

"Yes. I went to visit his grave."

She responded, "That's wonderful. You went to see Kotsuji." She added, "The date he died, isn't it the end of this month?"

"You remember that?" I couldn't hide my surprise as she nodded.

"We call the day of death *yahrzeit* and we recite *Kaddish*. We say *Kaddish* for Kotsuji and pray for his soul," she said with a smile.

It warmed my heart that Rivka and her family prayed for Kotsuji.

I told her that it was a shame that Kotsuji was not known at Yad Vashem. She said with a sigh, "Yes, he is not known, even though he was a great person."

Although I thought Rivka might know, I told her about Kotsuji's activities during the war, that he published a book to explain the true nature of Jews to counter Nazi propaganda, and that he toured around Japan giving lectures.

"In Japan, during the war? Wouldn't he have been arrested?" She was frowning. "He really risked his life to save us, didn't he? I'm sure my father knew this, and that's why he was grateful to Kotsuji."

Rivka gazed at the photograph taken at the reunion.

"He is someone who should be known as a great man who helped us."

Hearing her words reminded me of the passage from Kotsuji's autobiography: "I trusted my life to the hands of the Jews."

I said to her, "Take a look at this. Kotsuji helped the Jews, but in Harbin it was Jews who helped him. It wasn't only Kotsuji who helped. His Jewish friends helped him. That was a beautiful thing I learned as I researched Kotsuji. This is why I wanted to keep researching him."

Rivka looked intently at the book Kotsuji had written in English. "So Kotsuji was helped too, by Jews. I think it's a really great story." She nodded approvingly. "Kotsuji certainly did intervene with the government for us. But I think his greater achievement may be that he changed how Japan saw Jews, even though it was an ally of Nazi Germany. If he had not been there, we probably would have been deported immediately. I believe that was because of Kotsuji."

Just as Rivka said, Kotsuji worked hard to explain Jewish customs and sensibilities to Japanese people, and to change their perception of Jews. This had another significance as well. Not only did Kotsuji explain Jews to Japanese people, but he also helped newly arrived Jewish refugees understand Japan. One of those refugees, R. Pinchas Hirschprung, described this in his book *The Vale of Tears*.

> When we arrived in Japan, a foreign country with a foreign language and foreign way of life, we met a friend of the Jews....
>
> [Kotsuji] treated us with love and respect and did everything he possibly could to assist us. Thanks to him, Japan was a much more welcoming place for us than we could ever have imagined.

Rivka said, "I was a child so I don't really remember, but there was no suffering in Japan. That I remember. It was a little more difficult when we were in Shanghai though."

Rivka looked with interest at the materials relating to Kotsuji that I had brought with me. The photograph taken in 1959 at the thank-you party was the one she examined most closely. Finally, she said, "That was a really moving and beautiful party. I really felt how the determination of a single person can accomplish so much. He took responsibility... no, he did what he wanted to do and did what his heart commanded of him as a human being. It was a party that was full of pride."

"There's a verse from the Bible: 'Cast your bread out onto the waters, for in the long passage of days you will find it again,'[2] but he didn't do what he did expecting something in return. He did it because he wanted to help. That was from his heart." She spoke as if she felt great pride in what he did, clearly feeling that Kotsuji's character propelled his actions.

When I was leaving, I asked Rivka, "May I write about you?"

"Of course, please do," she said with a smile. This is how my thirteen-day research trip in Israel ended.

It seems inevitable that Kotsuji would be buried in Jerusalem. I reflected on this while flying back to Japan. Amidst turbulent historic

---

2. Ecclesiastes 11:1.

events, Kotsuji gave everything to save Jewish refugees. As if to assure himself of their bright future, he wanted to be laid to rest in the holy land of Jerusalem.

It was his final act of hope. I suddenly remembered part of Kotsuji's speech at the Mirrer Yeshiva: "My fate is your fate. Your lives are my life." Kotsuji was home.

Afterword

My grandfather, who died at the age of one hundred, used to say, "War is truly terrible. War should never happen again."

My grandparents, aunt, and mother repatriated back to Japan from Manchuria, and from the time I was a child I had heard stories about the hardships and brutality of war. For an elementary-school student, however, war was just something that happened in other countries very far away. Eventually, when I was living in Hawaii during middle school, I gradually began to understand what my grandfather meant when he talked about the tragedy of war.

In Hawaiian schools, students often visit Pearl Harbor on field trips to see the USS Arizona Memorial. This is a pure white structure floating in the harbor above where the massive warship came to rest after Japanese bombers sank it on December 7, 1941, precipitating the Pacific War. The memorial is the final resting place for those who perished.

Each time we visited, my American friends would say things like, "My grandpa was killed by Japs here," "Japs started the war," "Japs killed people." "Jap" is a derogatory word for Japanese people. It's not as if they had particularly deep motives in making these comments to me. And yet being told it was the fault of the "Japs" made my chest tighten. Dark, negative feelings would creep up inside me. Whether I liked it or not, I could not help but think about war.

To be associated with the war simply because I was Japanese and to be criticized for it, this stuck in my heart like a thorn. Because of these experiences, when I learned about Sugihara's visas for life, I felt pride in his accomplishment. It made me happy. I could not stop wondering what happened after the refugees received these visas. The chain of hatred brought about by the war, the bigotry, and the racism, these led to my discovery of Kotsuji Setsuzo.

Human beings are complicated. We can be kind at times, as well as cruel. We also have a side to us where we can be deceived by others, or by ourselves. But one thing is certain. We must always look at the world with our own eyes and analyze and understand for ourselves what is happening in order not to be led astray. We must not abandon this responsibility.

It is easy to say this. But would I be able to take the kind of courageous actions that Kotsuji did for the Jewish refugees under extreme circumstances in wartime? Would I be willing to save others at the expense of my own life? That is a very difficult question to answer. However, my study of the life that Kotsuji led caused me to think deeply about the horrors of war. I felt the importance of human dignity in a more visceral, profound way. This was a precious experience for me. As someone who has not lived through war, I feel I am now able to understand my grandfather's words.

I cannot forget what Noami and Aharon said about not having grandparents.

And Rivka: "No one killed us." Her words still echo in my mind.

Wake up in the morning. Go to work. See friends. Have dinner with family. We often take for granted the small and ordinary things we do daily. We should realize just how lucky we are and be thankful for them. To be able to live this day, isn't that something to be grateful for? Thanks to the lessons of Kotsuji's life, I have resolved to live my own precious life in this moment. I intend to live my life in gratitude.

These last several years that I have spent in pursuit of Kotsuji have taught me a great deal. In writing this book, I conducted many interviews.

I have done my best to convey what I learned, but my understanding of historical facts and my writing skills may be lacking. My aim was to uncover the man that Kotsuji was, in my own way. I will feel satisfied if you, the reader, have learned even a little about Kotsuji because of this journey.

Finally, I was assisted by many people in the writing of this book. First, I want to express my deepest appreciation to Teruko and Yuriko, Kotsuji's daughters, who provided me with materials and photographs and answered my awkward questions. In addition, I would like to thank R. Marvin Tokayer, who first encouraged me to write a book and gave me a large quantity of materials; Hironaka Toru, my lawyer; my friend Naomi Kunimune; Ichii Hisashi of NHK Publishing, Inc.; and Shimizu Yuuki, Shimizu Michio, and Inoue Tokiko for their support in gathering information and writing. Any errors in research and writing are entirely my own, but all that is good in the text is thanks to you. Please accept my heartfelt gratitude for everything you have done.

Jundai Yamada

References

REFERENCES IN ENGLISH

Frankl, Viktor. *Man's Search for Meaning.* Beacon Press, 2006.

Hirschprung, Pinchas. *The Vale of Tears.* Translated by Vivian Felsen. Azrieli Foundation, 2016.

Kotsuji, Setsuzo. *From Tokyo to Jerusalem: The Autobiography of a Japanese Convert to Judaism.* Bernard Geis Associates, 1964.

Kotsuji, Setsuzo. *Yudaya Nanmin no Sugata* (The True Character of the Jewish Nation), Meguro Shoten.

Mandelbaum, David A. *From Lublin to Shanghai.* Mesorah Publications, 2012.

Tokayer, Marvin, and Mary Swartz, *The Fugu Plan.* Paddington Press, 1979.

Warhaftig, Zorach. *Refugee and Survivor: Rescue Efforts During the Holocaust.* Feldheim Publishers, 1996. (Published in Japan as *Nihon ni kita Yudaya Nanmin* by Hara Shobo.)

REFERENCES AND SOURCE MATERIALS

アブラハム小辻「[From Tokyo to Jerusalem] Bernard Geis Associates, 1964.

ヴイクトル・フランクル著、霜山徳爾訳「夜と霧」(みすず書房)

References

小辻誠祐「ユダヤ民族-その四千年の歩み」(誠信書房)

ベン・アミー・シドニー、河合一充「日本とユダヤ・その友好の歴史」(ミルトス)

河合一充「雑誌みるとすNo. 91(ミルトス)

金子マーティン「神戸・ユダヤ難民1940–1941」(みずのわ出版) (Martin Kaneko, *Kobe Yudayajin Nanmin 1940–1941* [Kobe Jewish Refugees 1940–1941]. Published by Mizunowa Publishing.)

ハインツ・E・マウル著、黒川剛訳「日本はなぜユダヤ人を迫害しなかったのか」(芙蓉書房出版) (Heinz E. Maul, *Nihon wa naze yudayajin wo hakugai shinakattaka* [Why Japan Did Not Persecute Jews]. Published by Fuyu Shobo in Japan, available in German and Japanese only. Japanese translation by Kurokawa Tsuyoshi.)

エリ-エリヤフ・コーヘン、藤井厳喜著「ユダヤ人に学ぶ日本の品格」(PHP研究所)

ゾラフ・バルハフテイク著、滝川義人訳「日本に来たユダヤ難民」(原書房)

マーヴイン・トケイヤー、メアリ・シュオーツ著、加藤明彦訳「河豚計画」(日本ブリタニカ)

「満州国の幻影1931–1936」(毎日新聞社)

豊田穣「松岡洋右-悲劇の外交官-上下」(新潮文庫)

三好徹「松岡洋右-夕陽と怒濤」(学陽書房人物文庫)

松岡洋右伝記刊行会編「松岡洋右―その人と生涯」(講談社)

秦郁彦「昭和史の謎を追う-上下」(文春文庫)

「国際秘密力の研究」(国際政経会)

デビッド・A・マンデルバウム「From Lublin to Shanghai」(Mesorah Publications, 2012).

「人道の港敦賀」(日本海地誌調査研究会敦賀上陸ユダヤ難民足跡調査プロジェクトチーム偏)(*Jindo no Minato Tsuruga* [The Humanitarian Port]. Kaichishi Chousa kenkyukai hen.)

山本尚志「日本を愛したユダヤ人ピアニスト-レオ・シロタ」(毎日新聞社) [Yamamoto Hisashi, *Nihon wo Aishita Leo Sirota (Leo Sirota: The Jewish Pianist Who Loved Japan)* 朝日新聞社]

ヒルシュプリング「The Vale of Tears」(Eagle Pub. Co. Ltd.), 1944.

相田洋ほか「マネー革命1〜3」(NHK出版)

松岡洋右「満鉄を語る」(慧文社)

東京新聞出版局「自由への逃走」

「雑誌観光文化別冊2006・JULY号」(日本交通公社)

三条万里子「イカルスのように」(21世紀BOX) [Mariko Sanjo. *As Icarus*]

Image Credits

All images are copyright of the author, Jundai Yamada, unless otherwise specified:

Page 195 top, middle and bottom – © Kotsuji Teruko
Page 223 – Public Domain; Von Autor/-in unbekannt - This image is available from the website of the National Diet Library, Gemeinfrei, via Wikimedia Commons
Page 257 – © Kotsuji Teruko and by permission of the Amshinover Rebbe
Page 308 – © Kotsuji Teruko and by permission of the estate of the artist
Page 333 bottom – © Noami Shtinmetz
Page 334 – © Noami Shtinmetz

The fonts used in this book are from the Arno family

Maggid Books
The best of contemporary Jewish thought
from Koren Jerusalem